THE CLASSICS OF WESTERN SPIRITUALITY
A Library of the Great Spiritual Masters

Other volumes in this series

Julian of Norwich • SHOWINGS

Jacob Boehme • THE WAY TO CHRIST

Nahman of Bratslav • THE TALES

Gregory of Nyssa • THE LIFE OF MOSES

Bonaventure • THE SOUL'S JOURNEY INTO GOD, THE TREE OF LIFE, and THE LIFE OF ST. FRANCIS

William Law • A SERIOUS CALL TO A DEVOUT AND HOLY LIFE, and THE SPIRIT OF LOVE

Abraham Isaac Kook • THE LIGHTS OF PENITENCE, LIGHTS OF HOLINESS, THE MORAL PRINCIPLES, ESSAYS, and POEMS

Ibn 'Ata' Illah • THE BOOK OF WISDOM *and* Kwaja Adullah Ansari • INTIMATE CONVERSATIONS

Johann Arndt • TRUE CHRISTIANITY

Richard of St. Victor • THE TWELVE PATRIARCHS, THE MYSTICAL ARK, BOOK THREE OF THE TRINITY

ORIGEN

AN EXHORTATION TO MARTYRDOM, PRAYER
FIRST PRINCIPLES: BOOK IV
PROLOGUE TO THE COMMENTARY ON
THE SONG OF SONGS
HOMILY XXVII ON NUMBERS

TRANSLATION AND INTRODUCTION
BY
ROWAN A. GREER

PREFACE
BY
HANS URS VON BALTHASAR

PAULIST PRESS
NEW YORK • RAMSEY • TORONTO

Cover art:
The artist BETSY ROOSEN SHEPPARD graduated with a Fine Arts degree from Moore
College in Philadelphia. A fellowship winner, she went on for further studies in Europe, at
the Arts Students League and The School of Visual Arts in New York. She lives with her
husband and their two children in Newton, New Jersey. Of her cover painting she says, "I
wanted to portray the presence of Origen in the midst of the crumbling Roman Empire, for it
was this strong, intelligent, religious thinker who envisioned a bright Christian transformation of the eternal city."

Acknowledgment
The Second Coming: Reprinted with the permission of the Macmillian Company and A. P. Watt
and Son, Ltd, from COLLECTED POEMS by William Butler Yeats. Copyright 1924 by the
Macmillan Company, renewed 1952 by Bertha Georgie Yeats.

Design: Barbini, Pesce & Noble, Inc.

Library of Congress
Catalog Card Number: 79-84886

ISBN: 0-8091-2198-0 (paper)
ISBN: 0-8091-0283-8 (cloth)

Published by Paulist Press
Editorial Office: 1865 Broadway, New York, N.Y. 10023
Business Office: 545 Island Road, Ramsey, N.J. 07446

Printed and bound in the United States of America

CONTENTS

The Editor of This Volume

ROWAN A. GREER is Associate Professor of Anglican Studies at
Yale Divinity School, a post established through the Berkeley
Divinity School in memory of the Rt. Rev. Walter H. Gray. He is
a graduate of Yale College (A.B., 1956), where he did his
undergraduate work in the classics. A graduate of the General
Seminary (S.T.B., 1959), he was ordained an Episcopal priest by
Bishop Gray in 1960. After three years as a curate in the Diocese of
Connecticut, at St. Paul's, Fairfield, and Christ Church, New
Haven, he returned to Yale for doctoral work in the New
Testament, receiving his Ph.D. in 1965. From 1964–66 he was
chaplain of the Theological College of the Scottish Episcopal
Church in Edinburgh. In 1966 he joined the faculty of the Yale
Divinity School. His publications include *Theodore of Mopsuestia*
(London: Faith Press, 1961), *The Captain of Our Salvation: A Study in
the Patristic Exegesis of Hebrews* (Tübingen: J.C.B. Mohr, 1973), and
an Introduction and Commentaries in the edition of *The Sermon on
the Mount* published by the Limited Editions Club (Oxford: 1977).

Author of the Preface

HANS URS VON BALTHASAR was born in Switzerland in 1905. He studied Germanic languages and philosophy in Zurich, earning a doctorate for his study of "The Eschatological Problem in German Literature." From 1929 to 1939, he studied philosophy and theology as a member of the Jesuit order. He then served as editor of *Stimmen der Zeit* and as a chaplain to students in Basel. He has, in recent years, devoted his time to writing, translation, editorial work and lecturing. Many of his works have been translated into English, including *St. Thérèse of Lisieux*, *Elizabeth of Dijon*, *Prayer*, *Theology of History* and *Martin Buber and Christianity*.

PREFACE

Origen was as towering a figure as Augustine and Aquinas.
Even after the builder of the Hagia Sophia destroyed most of his
works, his overt and hidden influence has proved no less far-
reaching than theirs. In the Eastern Church his mysticism of ascent
to God remained immensely powerful through medieval and
modern times, more powerful than the mysticism of "dazzling
darkness" of the Pseudo-Areopagite (whose dominant influence was
in the West); in the Western Church both Jerome and Ambrose
unhesitatingly copied his work and thus bequeathed it to posterity.
Bernard, Eckhart, and Cusanus read him in the original, and Eras-
mus admitted that one page of Origen meant more to him than ten
pages of Augustine. His work is aglow with the fire of a Christian
creativity that in the greatest of his successors burned merely with a
borrowed flame.

The excellent introduction to this volume demonstrates that as
a pure philosopher he was not original but rather he made use of the
Hellenistic thought of his day (a mélange of Platonism, Stoicism,
and popular philosophy) as a medium for conveying to his contemporaries the depth and breadth of biblical Revelation. But such a
statement needs nuance! If his earlier work *De Principiis* (c. 230) still
expressed a belief in the possibility of incorporating the Greek
world view into Revelation, a late apologetic work, *Contra Celsum*
(c. 249) shows how sharp his eye had become to basic distinctions
(cf. below C. Andresen). Origen did not wish to be a philosopher
but a theologian, though not in the modern, specialized sense of the
term. He wanted to be a Christian nourished solely by the Word of
God and living wholly within the Catholic Church. Let us allow
him to speak for himself: "I wish to be a man of the Church, not the
founder of heresy; I want to be named with Christ's name and bear
the name which is blessed on earth. It is also my desire to do this in

xi

deed as well as in Spirit" (*Hom. in Luc.* 16). In another passage he continues even more passionately: "O Church! If I who seem to be your right hand, bearing the name of priest and preaching the Word of God, should ever offend against your canon and your Rule of Faith, thus giving scandal: Let then the Universal Church in unanimous accord cut off me, her right hand, and cast me away from her" (*Hom. in Josua* 7.6).

If the battle for and against him lasted hundreds of years—the Origenist monks preserved the very sentences that showed the most bias, and those condemned by Justinian at the Fifth Council derive substantially from that source—and in the Middle Ages absurd stories of his apostasy kept circulating, we must remember that a mind as fastidious as Newman's praised him highly and to one's amazement take note that he is represented in the New Roman Breviary with some marvelous lessons. I know members of religious orders who are praying for the canonization of this martyr and spiritual father of so many saints. Thus we should first point to his Christian greatness and only in the end refer to those limits and dangers inherent in his thought.

The central feature of his spirituality is an absolute and passionate love for the Logos, which has taken on personal lineaments for us in Jesus Christ, suffusing the total cosmos of men and angels. It is precisely the Johannine Logos, which as the Incarnate, becomes light, life, truth, and resurrection to all creatures. Origen finds him everywhere, and the entire Old Testament speaks of him only (*Joh.* 5, 46f.). In his first great commentary on the Gospels he addresses himself to John (231–240, 32 books), and only later does he turn to Luke and Matthew. (According to Eusebius and Jerome, the bulk of his work consisted of about two thousand books, which he mostly dictated.) The Logos becomes intelligible to us in a threefold incarnation of God's Spirit, Reason, and Word: in His historical, resurrected, and eucharisted body, in His ecclesiological body (whose members we are), and in His body of Sacred Scripture whose letters are animated by His living Spirit. For Origen these three forms of incarnation are inseparable from one another: They constitute a vast and all-encompassing sacrament. Hence he can look upon converse with the Written Word as sacred, and as much deserving of reverence as converse with the consecrated elements.

He frequently emphasizes that he who arbitrarily singles out words of Scripture or dissects them (like Marcion) does violence to the body of Christ and prolongs his passion. It has been erroneously held that Origen spiritualized the Eucharist; on the contrary, he sacramentalized Scripture, stating that God's Spirit dwells in it with the same real presence as it does in the Church. Thus, in an age in which the Church had ceased to appear exclusively in her sacred aspect, Origen was able bitterly to deplore her shortcomings (especially among her ministers) and apply to her the Old Testament reference of Jerusalem as a whore.

Origen's sacramentalism (unfortunately overlooked in W. Völker's book), through which the body is made transparent to its underlying spirit, the literal to its inherent divine meaning, the sacrament to its encounter with the personal Logos of God, animates the immense opus of the Alexandrian and makes comprehensible why he used Hellenistic philosophers to express the biblical contents of the faith. It should be remembered, however, that this breakthrough from the exterior, apparent, and profane into the interior and hidden truth of the Logos always leads into the sphere of holiness and mystery. Whoever seeks access from merely dogmatic faith into that inward realm where we see with the inner eye of faith enters a world of mystery demanding not only intellectual reverence but personal holiness as well. Origen was keenly aware of the true and universally valid implications of the *disciplina arcani*, as it was then called. Hence his Christian gnosis is inseparable from the practice of ecclesial sanctity. The entire weight of his preaching points to that unity.

Perhaps it can be said that this simultaneous viewing of prayer and exegesis, of scriptural interpretation and attention to the ecclesiastical canon and the *regula fidei*, of exact philology (as in the *Hexapla*) and search for the spiritual sense, is the most important aspect of Origenistic spirituality for our present situation. As dated as some of his interpretations are, the underlying attitude remains exemplary for us, perhaps more than ever before.

This remains true even when, adhering to his spirit, we transcend his limits, and I am speaking here only of his Christian limits. That certain flaws in his Trinitarianism have been corrected by Nicaea is shown in the introduction and should not concern us here. Though it must be admitted that his doctrine of apokatastasis (the salvation of all) was not securely anchored (though he had recourse to numerous scriptural texts), this in no way implies that it was incorrect: The Christian may hope for the salvation of all men, but may not forestall the judgment of God.

What is of far graver consequence is the unrestricted tendency of Origenist spirituality to strain "upward," the interpretation of Christian life as an unequivocal "ascent." This has an inevitable effect on the evangelical theme of "descent"—that of God into flesh, even to the death on the cross, the descent into hell, the admonition to take the lowest place, the praise not of the clever and the worldly wise but of the humble, to whom God's secret shall be revealed—in short, what is implied by the *via crucis* is bound to be somewhat neglected.

Perhaps he followed in this respect the logic that his system required and not his inner inclination. Whoever has spent sufficient time in his company, and perhaps reads his books on prayer and martyrdom, will perceive that his last and purest passion was not directed to the cognition of Christian truth but to the simple Imitation of Christ.

Hans Urs Von Balthasar

FOREWORD

In the second half of the sixth century Cassiodorus, whose political career was a casualty of Justinian's reconquest of the West, turned his hand to the establishment of two monasteries on his family estate in southeastern Italy. His instructions for the monks concerning their studies includes the following assessment of Origen:

> Certain men have said, not without cause, that he ought to be compared to anise, for, though he seasons the food of sacred letters, he himself is, nevertheless, thrown away when he has been boiled down and the juice extracted. (Cassiodorus Senator, *An Introduction to Divine and Human Readings*, tr. Leslie W. Jones, New York: W.W. Norton and Co., 1969, copyright 1946 by Columbia University Press)

In a sense, the following selections from Origen's writings are Origen "boiled down." The major works in which he addresses the meaning of the Christian life have been included, together with his theory of Scriptural interpretation and examples of its practice. The reason for this emphasis upon the Bible is that Origen's piety is Scriptural more than it is sacramental. By meditating upon the word of God the Christian begins to contemplate the eternal mysteries that supply the motive, power, and goal of the Christian life.

At the same time Origen has not himself been "thrown away." As the Introduction argues, Origen's own emphasis is very much upon the shape of the Christian life rather than upon speculation for its own sake. His Platonizing theology, his allegorical interpretation of Scripture, and his service of the Church as preacher, apologist, and theological expert all converge in his insistence that the Christian's life is one of freedom and hope exercised under the loving providence of God and shaped by a dialectic between contemplation and the moral life. Indeed, one can argue that this is what explains why he continued to be read in the Church even after his supposed errors were rejected. Moreover, his influence upon the Cappadocian Fathers of the fourth century means that he is an important source for the theology that became the classical articulation of Christian spirituality. Basil the Great, Gregory Nazianzen, and Gregory of Nyssa preserved Origen's thought for the Church and adapted it to a theological explanation of monasticism understood as the perfect life meant to be lived by all. Through the Cappadocians Origen's influence extends to Evagrius Ponticus, the Pseudo-Dionysius, John Cassian, and so to all Christian monasticism, both Eastern and Western. Indirectly as well as directly he has remained an important influence upon Western spirituality.

The selections that follow begin with Origen's elaboration of the spiritual ideal attaching to martyrdom. This ideal, in its broad configuration, is identical with his understanding of the Christian life of prayer. And it is one that, in Origen's view, may be derived from Scripture. Thus, we move from the practice of the Christian life to the theory that informs it; and with Book IV of *On First Principles* we can examine how Origen approaches the Bible and uses it as the basis and focus of his spirituality. In the last two selections examples are provided that illustrate Origen's use of Scripture in his commentaries and homilies; and it will be apparent that he is concerned to apply theory to the practice of the Christian life. The selections are meant to come full circle, beginning and ending with what Origen wishes to say about the Christian life. A later volume in The Classics of Western Spirituality will place Origen's interpretation of Song of Songs in the context of other Christian and of Jewish interpretations, treating his commentary as part of a broader tradition and addressing the central importance of Song of Songs for both Jewish and Christian spirituality.

Rowan A. Greer

INTRODUCTION

Origen was born immediately after what Edward Gibbon once called "the period in the history of the world, during which the condition of the human race was most happy and prosperous" (*The Decline and Fall of the Roman Empire*, chap. III, p. 95 in vol. I of Milman's edition of 1850). Commodus, the unworthy son of Marcus Aurelius, succeeded his father as emperor in A.D. 180, five years before Origen's life began in Alexandria. What can be written of the history of the Roman Empire during Origen's lifetime is little more than a list of imperial murders, civil wars, and their disastrous consequences in social and economic life. Plague and famine, together with barbarian invasions, complete the picture. To be sure, some degree of stability was maintained during the rule of Septimius Severus, the general who took authority after the murder of Commodus in 193 and maintained it until his death at York in 211. Indeed, his dynasty remained in power until 235. But of his successors, Caracalla and Elagabalus were virtual embodiments of a wicked and ruthless tyranny, and only Alexander Severus (222–235) succeeded in checking the tide of chaos that had already begun at the end of Marcus Aurelius's principate. At the time of Origen's death, about 254, the Empire was a helpless giant; within a few years it was dismembered. Gaul was held by a local emperor, and much of the East was added to the Empire of Odenathus and Zenobia, the rulers of Palmyra. In 260, as a kind of symbol of the chaos, the Roman emperor Valerian was captured by the Persians.

The contrast between Origen's life and work and the times in which he lived cannot be exaggerated. Upon first reading Origen's literary work, one could scarcely guess that he was living in a world where

Things fall apart; the center cannot hold;
Mere anarchy is loosed upon the world,

1

INTRODUCTION

The blood-dimmed tide is loosed, and everywhere
The ceremony of innocence is drowned.
The best lack all conviction, while the worst
Are full of passionate intensity.

—W. B. Yeats

The contrast between the serenity of Origen's writings and the anarchy of his times is not merely a product of the simple fact that life goes on even when society collapses. Origen was not concerned to address the anarchy of his times in any direct fashion. His preoccupation was with articulating in his words and in his life the Christian vision. The moral, intellectual, and spiritual dimensions of this enterprise will concern us in what follows. At the same time, his visionary work was meant to have an impact upon the issues of his day. Specifically, he saw the Christian hope not as an alternative to the Roman world, but as the catalyst that could rescue and transform what was best in it. His theology was an attempt to translate the Gospel into a language intelligible to the pagan, especially the thoughtful and educated pagan. Side by side with the enterprise of translation went the martyr's conviction of the absolute and exclusive commitment demanded by the Christian religion. It can be argued that it was the success of Christianity in holding in tension such an absolute claim and the desire to become all things to all peoples that explains the rise of Christianity in the third century and its apparent triumph in the fourth. However problematic a figure Origen was, it is difficult to deny him an important and even a central role in this development. In studying Origen we are witnesses to the death of the old Roman world and the birth pangs of a Christian and transformed Rome.

ORIGEN'S LIFE

Our knowledge of Origen's life is largely derived from Book VI of Eusebius of Caesarea's *Ecclesiastical History*. Eusebius considered himself a follower of Origen and collaborated with Pamphilus in an Apology for their master. The first book of this work survives in a translation by Rufinus of Aquileia, but is concerned with theological issues rather than with biography. As well, we

INTRODUCTION

possess a farewell speech addressed to Origen by one of his pupils, Gregory the Wonderworker. The evidence may be expanded by adding the testimony of Origen's later opponents as well as of his disciples. But again, it is theology rather than biography that dominates the literature related to the controversies over Origen. Only Eusebius's evidence gives us a coherent account of Origen's life. While it is sympathetic in its point of view, it is based upon Eusebius's acquaintance with "certain letters and information derived from pupils of his, whose lives have been preserved even to our day" (*Hist. eccl.* VI.ii.1).

We first meet Origen in the pages of Eusebius's History at the age of seventeen. He had been born into a Christian family in Alexandria and had already demonstrated his gifts as a Christian thinker to his father, Leonides. Eusebius reports that "it is said that many a time he [Leonides] would stand over the sleeping boy and uncover his breast, as if a divine spirit were enshrined therein, and kissing it with reverence count himself happy in his goodly offspring" (*Hist. eccl.* VI.ii.11). When Christians were persecuted under Septimius Severus in 202, Origen encouraged his father to embrace martyrdom without troubling himself about his wife and children. And he was prevented from following his father's example only because his mother hid his clothes. Though these stories have a ring of the legendary about them, it seems clear that they point to the zeal of a young man for the Christian religion. Origen was spared martyrdom, but he embraced in that spirit an ascetic life with its usual disciplines of fasting and moderate sleep, "which he was careful to take, never on a couch, but on the floor" (*Hist. eccl.* VI.iii.9). The same abstentions were used with respect to clothing and possessions. And at some point during his teaching career Origen took Matthew 19:12 rather too seriously and castrated himself "both to fulfill the Savior's saying, and also that he might prevent all suspicion of shameful slander on the part of unbelievers (for, young as he was, he used to discourse on divine things with women as well as men)" (*Hist. eccl.* VI.viii.2).

In one other respect the youthful Origen was unusual. He was a brilliant scholar. His education had progressed sufficiently by the time of his father's death so that he could support the family by teaching. The Church also recognized his ability, and in a short time, probably in 204, Bishop Demetrius appointed Origen head of the catechetical school of the Alexandrian church. His catechetical instruction attracted many, and Origen grew in his vocation as a Christian teacher. Partly for this reason and partly because a wealthy woman undertook to support him and his family, he gave up his secular teaching and sold all his pagan books. As time went on, he conceived the idea of setting up an advanced school for Christians. The catechetical school was turned over to Heraclas, and Origen devoted his energies to Christian study, modeled upon the philosophical schools of his day. A renewed use of pagan learning accompanied Origen's investigation of the deeper truths of his religion. And together with conversation and instruction there went a literary enterprise, the fruits of which we possess at least in part to this day.

The success of Origen's work inevitably brought difficulties. He became known throughout the Church and traveled about the Empire. He visited Rome, preached in Caesarea, and was asked by Julia Mamaea, the mother of Alexander Severus, to expound Christianity at the imperial court. He became involved in theological disputes throughout the Church, which he was called upon to adjudicate as a theological expert. His activity in the wider Church took him again to Caesarea in 230 and resulted in his ordination in that city. Demetrius, the bishop of Alexandria, took offense. The full story is not known, but Demetrius expelled Origen on the grounds that his ordination in Caesarea flouted the authority of the Alexandrian church and that he was a eunuch and so could not be ordained. As a result, Origen took refuge in Caesarea, where he spent the rest of his life. The crisis was a serious one for him, but it meant no more than a momentary halt to his work. For almost another quarter century Origen continued his many-faceted enterprise in Palestine. A Christian philosopher, he was also a popular and powerful preacher. An ascetic who strove to free himself from all earthly ties, he also busied himself with the life of the Church and of Caesarea. He assisted in ecclesiastical disputes, and the impression cannot be resisted that he talked incessantly—with other Christians, with pagans, with the Jews in Caesarea. The end came with the persecution of the Christians begun by the emperor

Decius in 250. Origen was arrested and tortured. He was released, but died somewhat later deserving of the title martyr.

Even so summary a discussion of Origen's life and work as the above suggests the debate that has continued about Origen ever since the third century. To put the question as simply as possible, was he a philosopher or was he a churchman? The issue may be complicated by other considerations, including his asceticism and his relationship to a more gnostic form of Christianity indigenous to Alexandria. Nevertheless, it can best be addressed by recognizing that Origen is rightly called a Christian Platonist. Both terms may be illustrated from the selections of Origen's writings included in this volume. His discussions of incorporeality and of matter in Book IV of the *De principiis* (see below, pp. 204 and 210-13) are representative of his point of view both because they demonstrate his firm grasp of the philosophical issues of his day and because they show that he is committed to what is usually called Neoplatonism. Indeed, it is likely that he studied under the Platonist teacher Ammonius Saccas, who was also the teacher of Plotinus. And Origen, as well as Plotinus, must be regarded as one of the founders of Neoplatonism. He shares with Plotinus a concern to move beyond skeptical and dualistic forms of Platonism, as well as a speculative and open approach to philosophical issues worthy of Plato himself. Moreover, Origen's interest in and use of philosophy is not limited to his more scholarly works, such as the *De principiis*. In the treatise *On Prayer* he is led by the expression "daily bread" in the Lord's Prayer to discuss the meaning of "substance" and to espouse a Platonist position (see below, pp. 140f.).

It is, however, equally clear that Origen is committed to the Christian religion. Of course, this is especially evident in the *Exhortation to Martyrdom*. The Christian martyr must not allow "the disquiet" of his soul to appear to "strangers" (see below, p. 43). He "commends . . . Christianity and the Father of Christianity to those before whom he confesses" (see below, p. 67). Origen understands that the absolute loyalty of the Christian martyr holds a persuasive power to bring pagans to the vision of the truth. Although he does his best to articulate that vision in his theology, he keeps one eye on the more pragmatic aspects of Christianity. The opening sections of *De principiis* IV (see below, pp. 171ff.) suggest that Origen is not concerned with mere abstraction but with a truth embodied in a living community. "And it is all the more amazing that while their teachers are neither very capable nor very many, nevertheless, this word is preached throughout the whole world so that Greeks and barbarians, wise and foolish uphold the religion of Christ's teaching" (see below, p. 172). It is this conviction that explains Origen's willingness to be a preacher to ordinary Christians and to assist in the institutional life of the Church of his time.

If Origen is committed both to Platonism and to the Christian Church, we must ask how that double commitment is managed. It would be possible to argue that one commitment governs the other. That is, one might say that Origen is a philosopher at the expense of his Christianity or, on the contrary, a churchman despite his philosophical interest. The first alternative was the one adopted by his enemies in the ancient Church and was what led to his rejection by Methodius, Epiphanius, Jerome, and finally by Justinian and the Fifth General Council of 553. It remains the point of view of much modern discussion of Origen and has colored the editing and translation of the *De principiis*. The second alternative is sometimes adopted by modern scholars in order to rescue Origen's reputation. The trouble with both these approaches is that they fail to see that Origen would have refused to accept the dilemma from which they proceed. In principle, he argued, the truth discovered by Plato and the other philosophers is the same truth revealed in the Scriptures. To be sure, the philosophers have made mistakes, and the truth of the Scriptures is the treasure hidden in the field. But if one searches wisely and carefully, one begins to find the place where contradictions are resolved and obscurities disappear. Origen is a Christian Platonist not because he has turned Christianity into Platonism or vice versa, but because he has found the Platonic idiom of his day capable of expressing the truth of the Gospel. It is inevitable that tensions appear in his double commitment, but the same verdict may be given of any Christian thinker who takes seriously both the perennial meaning of the Gospel and the thought forms of his own time. It is, at any rate, from this confessedly sympathetic point of view that Origen's thought will be described and assessed in what follows.

INTRODUCTION

THE STAGE SETTING

It is probably less misleading to call Origen's theological view a story than to speak of it as a system. His speculative bent of mind prevented him not only from drawing easy conclusions, but also from committing himself to any conclusions irrevocably. "We maintain that that only is to be believed as the truth which in no way conflicts with the tradition of the Church and the apostles" (*De princ.* I. praef. 2). The traditional rule of faith supplies the foundation for speculation and the main line of Origen's theological "story." And Origen's thought soars from that basis in flights of imagination that represent his deep convictions, sometimes his puzzles, but never his absolute certainties. With this caution it is possible to proceed to a description of Origen's theological view. The protagonist of the drama is the rational mind or soul, and the story explains the pilgrimage of the soul from creation to salvation. But this story is set within a cosmology that supplies the context for Origen's understanding of the Christian life. It is with this stage setting that we must begin.

Even before the story Origen expounds, God is thought to exist absolutely apart from any notion of space or time. Biblical statements that might appear to argue to the contrary must be reinterpreted according to this fundamental insight. Thus, when we pray "Our Father in heaven," the phrase should not be understood to confine God to a place and so imply that He is corporeal (see below, pp. 127f.). He is equally removed from time (see below, pp. 205f.). The point of defining God in this fashion is to argue that there is "nothing uncreated except the nature of the Father, Son, and Holy Spirit" (see below, p. 213). Origen means to be insisting upon the Biblical witness that God is the Creator and Sovereign Lord of the created order. And he is able to expound the idea not only by using Scripture, but also by employing philosophical ideas. One line of argumentation lies behind the discussion in *De principiis* IV.iv.1–2 (see below, pp. 205ff.). God is not contained by the created order, but He informs it with His own presence and power. The theme is originally Jewish and may be found both in Philo and in the rabbinic writings. Its earliest explicit occurrence in Christian literature is in the first mandate of the

INTRODUCTION

Shepherd of Hermas (ca. 140), where God is described as "one, who made everything from nothing, and who is uncontained while containing all." In other words, God's transcendence implies His immanence; and the very fact that He is not limited by the creation enables Him to fill all things with His presence and power. A second but related theme concerns God's incorporeality. Origen's argument is that to regard God as the first principle of the universe requires that He be defined as a unity and incorporeal. As he points out, the very notion of matter or corporeality carries with it the implication of diversity. Material things are put together from different elements. Thus, if God is to be transcendent and the first principle of the universe, He must be one. And if He is one, then He is beyond the diversity characteristic of corporeality. The logic of the One and the many is employed so as to demonstrate that God is incorporeal and spiritual. The Creator is "He who is" (Ex. 3:14, see below, p. 129), and the Biblical and philosophical themes are united in a vision of God who is not limited by space or time and so is the Lord of creation.

Complications begin to appear in Origen's doctrine of God as soon as the Trinitarian question arises. In order to retain monotheism, the Christian heritage from the Jews, he must insist upon the unity of God; ". . . the Father and the Son are one and the same and differ in no respect" (see below, p. 225). At the same time, the distinct divinity of the Word or Son of God must be preserved so as to define Him as a "being and subject distinct from the Father" (see below, p. 112). Origen's solution to the dilemma that results from these two convictions is complicated and cannot be treated in detail. But the most persuasive way of describing his thought is to suggest that he defines the second person of the Trinity by describing a series of relations in which the Word of God is to be found. In His relation to God, the Word *is* God in precisely the same way that no real difference can be made between a thought and its thinker (cf. *Comm. in Johann.* I.32, 42; II.2, 5). But in relation to Himself the Word is a distinct being and is to be thought of in Platonic terms as what Plotinus called "Mind." That is, He is to be equated with the Demiurge of Plato's Timaeus, as well as with the Model by which the Demiurge fashioned the visible universe. The Platonic forms, which are the intelligible ar-

8

chetypes after which the perceptible world is made, comprise the Model and are thought of as ideas in the Demiurge's mind. Finally, the Word may be understood in His relation to rational beings. Like the World Soul of the Timaeus or "Soul" in Plotinus, the Word in this relation informs and gives life and knowledge to rational beings.

In general terms Origen's solution to the Trinitarian problem depends upon an elaboration of Platonizing themes that takes place along the lines of a "great chain of being" view of reality and is designed to supply a monistic understanding of the world. The Word of God occupies the crucial position in the view, since He mediates between God the Father and the rational creation. At one level He is identical with God; at another, with the souls who participate in God through Him. The eternal generation of the Son by the Father is compared to will proceeding from mind or to radiance issuing from light; and it is a doctrine meant to insist upon the paradox that the Word is both the same as and other than God. Most important of all, Origen's mediatorial view of the Word is functional in character. He is less concerned with pursuing the ontological implications of the view he has constructed than with insisting that the Word acts as Mediator, binding God and the creation together in unity. Here the Platonic themes are once more woven into the Biblical witness concerning Christ. The Mediator is the High Priest and the Advocate who represents humanity to God and God to humanity (see below, pp. 100f.). The perceptible and material world is bound together with the intelligible and spiritual world; the creation is united in perfect fellowship with the Creator. The Word serves this function both in general and in the Incarnation.

While Origen's focal concern is to define the Word as Mediator, his view sometimes implies a subordination of the Word to the Father. Twice in the selections included in this volume he cites Mark 10:18 in the form "No one is good but God the Father alone," adding the words "the Father" to the text (see below, p. 46 and p. 114). In his discussion of the Agony in the Garden Origen notes that the Father's will was "wiser than the Son's will, since He was ordering events by a way and an order beyond what the Savior saw" (see below, p. 61). And in the treatise On Prayer he rejects prayer to the Son (see below, pp. 112–14). These difficult passages, when examined in the light of Origen's work as a whole, conform to his mediatorial view of the Word. Subordination is related to Origen's view that the Word is other than God, but it must be balanced by his recognition that from another point of view the Word is the same as the Father. The paradox was not easy to maintain, and in the theological development after Origen it was abandoned. The orthodox, such as Athanasius and the Cappadocians, insisted upon the sameness of Father and Son, while the Arians developed the subordinationist implications of Origen's theology by detaching them from the paradox and by drawing the conclusion that the Son was a creature. A related problem attaches to Origen's understanding of the Holy Spirit. Sometimes the Spirit is defined as the same as God, but elsewhere He is made subordinate to the Father (see below, p. 85).

To complete the vision Origen has of the Beginning, before time begins and matter comes into existence, his understanding of the rational creation must be described. For Origen God is essential goodness, and consequently He wills to have beings to whom He may convey His goodness by giving them life and knowledge of Himself. To this end He creates, apparently without reference to time, the rational natures. They are minds, all incorporeal, equal, and eternal. We can imagine them as pupils in a heavenly school room, directing their attention to the Word, who reveals the Father to them. The same point of view is to be found in Origen's doctrine of the image of God. The Word is the image of God, while the rational natures are made *after* the image of God. The first conclusion is based upon New Testament passages such as Colossians 1:15 and 2 Corinthians 4:4 (see below, pp. 125, 215). The second derives from a careful reading of Genesis 1:26, where man is made *"after the image of God."* But woven into the Scriptural basis for the doctrine is the philosophical notion of the kinship between the soul and the World Soul, a kinship that enables us to know the truth. Our mind or soul is constituted by nature to participate in the intelligible world (see below, p. 76). Only God the Father is pure Being, pure Truth, pure Life, pure Good, pure Beauty. The Word, as His image, participates in all these aspects of God, and so is love, wisdom, power, righteousness, Word, and truth (see below, p. 226).

INTRODUCTION

The rational natures also participate in God, but do so through the Word. Thus, the Father is archetype with respect to the Word, while the Word is archetype with respect to the rational beings. In this way life and knowledge are radiated from the Father through the Son (and in the Holy Spirit) to the rational beings.

In summary, Origen's view of the Beginning is one of a rich spiritual unity. The distinctions between Father, Son, and Spirit are not meant to divide the Godhead. And the fact that the rational natures (or minds or souls) are created does not prevent them from participating fully in the life of the Creator. The emphasis in this vision is upon God's revelation of Himself; and if knowledge is the key word, it is a knowledge that includes not only what we should call intellectual understanding but also the moral and spiritual aspects of our nature. For this reason Origen is quite comfortable in speaking of the primordial unity in the Biblical metaphors designed to describe the fellowship between God and humanity intended by the Creator. Indeed, the real difficulty with Origen's view is that it tends to obscure the distinction between God and the rational natures. Both are invisible and incorporeal. At the same time, as we shall see, the rational natures are mutable and so are capable of being placed in bodies. And it is this that marks them as creatures and explains their fall from the perfection of the Beginning.

So long as the rational natures direct their motions toward God through His Word, the primordial unity is preserved. But this did not happen, and all of them except the soul of Jesus directed their attention away from God. Origen does not attempt to explain in any detail why this happened. The fall of the rational natures is compared to the loss of his skill by a doctor who fails to pay attention to his discipline (*De princ.* I.4.1). Neglect, forgetfulness, boredom, and satiety are the words Origen associates with the fall. In the light of his thought as a whole, the implication is that the Beginning is unstable because it is innocent. As we shall see, it is the experience acquired by the rational nature during its pilgrimage that furnishes it with a motive for being attentive to the divine teacher and in this way renders the End stable. In falling the rational natures move away from "the divine warmth" and become cool (*psychesthai*); hence, they become "souls" (*psychai*) (cf. *De princ.* II.8.3). The point is a minor one, since Origen uses rational nature,

11

mind, and soul virtually as synonyms. But his notion of souls as "cooled off" minds or as minds in a fallen condition explains why he can speak of gaining something better than a soul through martyrdom (see below, p. 46; cf. pp. 66, 99).

The fallen mind or soul is immediately given a body. This is because Origen sees a correlation between the diversity of the mind's motions when it turns away from God and the diversity characteristic of corporeality. It should be emphasized that he defines a human being as a mind or soul, and regards the body partly as an outward symbol of the state of the soul and partly as a function of God's providence. More must be said later about this. For the moment, however, the main point to make is that the fallen minds or souls are immediately placed in bodies (see below, p. 186). Furthermore, the kind of body given the soul is proportionate to the degree of its fall. Thus, there is constituted a hierarchy of embodied souls ranging from angels at the top through human beings and, finally, to demons at the bottom of the scale. The souls are now incorporated and unequal. They have the possibility, however, of moving up or down the hierarchy established by the original fall. At times this idea results in some of Origen's more esoteric speculations (see below, pp. 195ff.). And it involves the notion of successive world orders (see below, pp. 144ff.). There are certain passages in Origen that imply that the process is somewhat like moving from grade to grade in school. During the grade one has the opportunity of moving up or down in rank. And at the end of the session the rank one has achieved determines one's place at the beginning of the next grade. But these speculations must not be allowed to obscure the main point. The soul once fallen is on pilgrimage, and its destiny is to return to God.

The two forces that operate to drive the souls back toward God are the freedom each soul possesses and the providence of God. Origen feels obliged to insist upon the freedom of the rational creation (see below, pp. 93ff.). Part of the reason for this is that he accepts as axiomatic the assumption of Greek philosophy that the soul is capable of moving itself and is not limited to being moved by another or moved as a simple reflex of its nature. In other words, freedom is part of the definition of a rational being that makes choices. As well, Origen is concerned to refute the deterministic views held by Christian gnostics, certain pagan philosophers, and the man in the street and to offer an alternative to the fatalistic mood of his times. From this point of view it is the soul's freedom of choice that enabled it to fall in the first place, and it is the same capacity that allows it to choose God again and to move toward Him. The perfection of freedom derives from the right choice irrevocably made, and salvation consists in returning to the original perfection and then to that perfection "by which it remains therein" (*De princ*. II.11.7). It should be emphasized that the soul does not lose its freedom in the fall, even though the conditions in which it then finds itself make it more difficult for freedom to be exercised. Origen's emphasis is retained by his successors and ultimately becomes what can be called the Pelagian theme, namely, that a human being can still take the first steps toward God.

Nevertheless, Origen is equally insistent that the progress of the soul is dependent upon God's providence. Obviously, a contradiction seems at first implied. If the soul has freedom, then is not God's providence undermined? Contrariwise, if God is the providential Lord, foreseeing and foreordaining, how can we be said to retain our freedom? The puzzle had already been stated pretty much in this form ca. 150 B.C., when the Platonist Carneades attacked the contradictions of the Stoics and pointed out that they could not logically believe both in freedom (the *to eph'hēmīn*, that which is in our control) and in fate. Both Platonists and Stoics attempted to move beyond the contradiction, and there can be little doubt that Origen depends upon the treatment of the problem given by the Platonists. In pseudo-Plutarch's treatise *De fato* a solution is reached by denying that fate is an antecedent cause. Instead, fate is compared to the law, which is hypothetical and consequential. *If* I break the law, *then* I suffer its penalties. Thus, the first step is to equate fate with the causal framework of the world order. And while this places conditions upon the exercise of human freedom, it by no means eliminates it.

This first part of the solution implies a further step, namely, a distinction between fate and providence. If fate is what determines not our actions but their consequences, providence is a divine and mysterious power that weaves the consequences of all human actions together into harmony. By placing freedom and providence on two different levels Origen succeeds in removing the inevitability of their conflict. This solution is implied in the discussion in the treatise *On Prayer* (see below, pp. 90–97). God foreknows everything, even the activity of our freedom. Nevertheless, He does not foreordain our free choices, but only what "meets" them from providence. That is, the consequences of our choices inevitably depend upon the causal framework of the universe, and are woven into a higher pattern of harmony by God's providence. The pattern is clarified by Origen's discussion of "God gave them up" in Romans 1, which may be found later in the treatise *On Prayer* (see below, pp. 156ff.). The person who makes a wrong choice by his use of freedom brings punishment upon himself. But God uses that punishment as a way of satiating the sinner with his vice and so driving him back to Himself. In other words, in this mode providence is punitive; but while the punishment is initially retributive, in the long run it is remedial and aims at the reformation of the sinner. The metaphors of the divine physician and the divine teacher are repeatedly employed to make the point. Thus it is that our freedom and God's providence work together, and it is Origen's conviction that ultimately God's providence will be able to draw everyone to Him so that we may all exercise perfect freedom by choosing Him. Origen tends to understand the process as an education of souls. The pupil always retains his freedom, but God the Word is so powerful a teacher that His lessons will eventually be learned by all. And salvation in fact hinges less upon freedom than upon providence. Our freedom is itself the gift of God's providence; its exercise takes place in the context of providence; and it is God who elicits that exercise by calling us home to Himself. Although it remains flawed by importing the concept of time into our notion of God, it is better to think of God, in Origen's view, as standing at the end of time summoning us to Himself than as antecedent to history determining what will happen in the future.

It is at this point that Origen's understanding of the body may best be considered. At a number of places in the selections from his writings that follow the issue of corporeality is addressed (see below, pp. 140f., 204ff., 210ff., 212ff.). But his most extended treatment is in Book II of the *De principiis*. Here it becomes apparent that he is not concerned with an ontological definition of the body, but wishes to define it by its function. The body is not integral to the definition of a human being, who is a soul or incorporeal nature making use of a body (see below, p. 204). Rather, the body is a sign of the fallen state of the soul; the greater the fall, the grosser the body. At first the idea seems utterly foreign to us, but it may be that it depends not only upon philosophical assumptions but also on commonsense observations of the relationship between body and what we might call the personality. At any rate, if the body is a sign of the state of the soul, it is a punishment that the soul has brought upon itself. And since the punishment is also an operation of God's providence, the body functions in a remedial way to drive the soul back to God. From one point of view the body cuts the soul off from God and blocks its vision. From another point of view it is the vehicle whereby God reveals Himself and through which the soul moves toward God.

The providential use of the body is found in a different fashion in the Incarnation. Here the divine Word of God, without in any way being confined by the Incarnation or producing any division in the Godhead (see below, p. 207), uses a human soul and body as a means of revealing God to fallen humanity. For Origen the Incarnation is providential and revelatory. His fundamental notion is that revelation must be given in a manner capable of being received by those to whom it is given. Thus, the Word of God is, indeed, "Truth embodied in a tale" that all may read. Once the believer grasps "Christ crucified," he is led toward a deeper knowledge of the eternal Word. The problems that attach to Origen's Christology are secondary to this basic view. They include an ambiguity concerning the ontological character of the Christological union. Sometimes Origen's Christ appears so unified as to be virtually docetic—"veiled in flesh the Godhead see." Sometimes, however, Origen is concerned to distinguish the different elements in the Incarnate Lord—the Word of God, the soul of Jesus, and the human body (see below, pp. 208ff.). Indeed, in a number of passages he can speak of "the Man" in language that appears to foreshadow the much later divisive Christology of Antioch (see below, pp. 67, 135). As well, Origen is not clear as to whether the Incarnation is a necessary and permanent dispensation of God's providence. Once again, however, these difficulties should not be allowed to obscure the main lines of his thought and his insistence that the Incarnation is a focal revelation designed to bring all rational natures back to the Father.

The Apocatastasis or Restoration of all things marks the end of Origen's theological "story." What is certain is that Origen believes that this End will involve not only a return to the perfection of the Beginning, but the winning of a greater perfection from which the rational beings can never fall. It is less clear whether the Apocatastasis will be reached after a succession of ages or after the mounting of heavenly spheres. Another problem attaches to the final vision. The pure contemplation "bare of words, symbols, and types" is sometimes described as the face-to-face vision Paul hopes for in 1 Corinthians 13:12 (see below, pp. 50f., 102, 133). But sometimes we see a dynamic at work, where God will always be teaching and the rational natures always learning. The major problem with Origen's view of the Apocatastasis, however, concerns the charge often made against him that he denies the resurrection and has no way of keeping the End stable, running the risk of eternal cycles of fall and return. These charges, at any rate, can be confidently refuted. They represent false deductions from Origen's principle "the End is like the Beginning" and unfairly impose what is thought to be a philosophical logic upon his thought. Origen does not say that the End is the same as the Beginning. It is *like* the Beginning because the original harmony is restored. But the Restoration is upon a higher level. It is the perfection from which the rational natures can never fall. The stability of the End presumably depends upon the points at which it differs from the Beginning. First, the souls have resurrection bodies. While it is not this body that is raised, the soul has a characteristic form that generates the new body of the resurrection. Second, the souls are no longer equal, but are ordered in a hierarchy according to their worth. Origen does not put it this way, but it would appear that the corporeality and inequality of the souls at the End stand for the experience they have had on their pilgrimage. And it is that experience which enables them to ply the Word with endless questions and to maintain their interest in His teaching.

Much of the "stage setting" that has been described appears unique to Origen and somewhat foreign to early Christian theology. And, of course, his speculations led to attacks upon him even during his lifetime and have provoked misunderstanding ever since. It has been impossible to argue for the conclusions reached here, and it would be unfair to suppose that they are persuasive to all. Nevertheless, if one looks at Origen's theological story as a whole, it begins to become clear that it is the same story—somewhat dressed up—told by an Irenaeus or a Gregory of Nyssa. The fundamental pattern is a movement from innocence to experience. The creative purpose of God extends from the Beginning to the End, and is only achieved when the process encompassing fall and Incarnation is completed. We must not be deceived by the philosophical and cosmological elaborations. Beneath them and expressed through them is the authentic vision of the early Church. That vision united all of human history in a single movement from the childhood of our first creation to the perfect humanity of the new creation revealed in Christ and to be consummated at the End of time.

The Drama

The cosmological framework that has been described in its general outlines supplies the broad story of Origen's theological view. But even a brief acquaintance with his writings reveals that his primary interest lies in the drama of the soul's struggle to return to God. His understanding of the Beginning and of the Apocatastasis is meant to furnish a context for giving meaning to the Christian life, which is for the most part the preoccupation of the selections that follow. Origen's views of martyrdom, prayer, and Scripture merge into one vision of the Christian life as a movement toward perfect knowledge of God and perfect fellowship with Him through Christ. That vision is rich and complicated. It cannot be expounded in any fully systematic fashion, since Origen does not attempt to forge his insights into any systematic view. Nonetheless, all that he says is coherent; and the different metaphors he uses, together with the different aspects he analyzes, reinforce one another. The many facets contribute to a single picture of the soul's progress toward its destiny. The drama may be initially discussed by underlining three different metaphors Origen uses to articulate it: the journey, the growth to maturity, and the warfare against sin and evil.

It would not be far from the mark to suggest that the journey is a fundamental metaphor for human life in all cultures. The experience of change and constant movement is an elemental one for human beings. And whether we think of the Odyssey, the wandering of Israel in the wilderness, or the migration of the soul to its destiny, the paradigm of human life becomes a pilgrim's progress. Origen, of course, derives his metaphor of the journey in large part from the Scriptures. One theme is that there are different roads by which we may travel. According to Matthew 7:13f. one is broad and easy, but leads to destruction. The Christian pilgrim must choose the narrow and straitened road that leads to his destiny. That road is a difficult one. It must be traveled in the winter of hardship and persecution (see below, pp. 62, 121). In *Homily XXVII on Numbers* Origen uses the wandering of Israel in the wilderness as a basis for meditating upon the different stages along the way. The remarkable feature of his treatment is that the journey does not proceed in a straight line. As for the children of Israel, the Christian's journey to the promised land is not by the easiest or the shortest route (cf. Ex. 13:17). The long and convoluted journey has its own logic and is meant to train and prepare the soul for its destiny.

In addition to complicating the metaphor of the journey in this fashion Origen introduces two other themes. First, however much the journey depends upon the soul's own powers of endurance and courage, it is accompanied by God's grace and Christ's presence to strengthen the pilgrim. The forty-two stages of Numbers 33 correspond to the forty-two generations through which the Word of God descended in order to be born of the Virgin (see below, p. 249). The Savior descended so that He might accompany and assist the soul in its journey of ascent to the true promised land. He is the "door" of every stage, and the coherence of freedom and providence finds specific expression in this dimension of Origen's understanding of the soul's journey (see below, pp. 248f.). Second, there are really "two journeys," one in this life by which we progress "from virtue to virtue" and one after our death by which we ascend to heaven (see below, p. 248). As the reader will quickly see, it is not so much that these are two different journeys as that they are two aspects of the soul's pilgrimage, one moral and the other spiritual. To be sure, the moral aspect of the journey is more properly located in this life, while its spiritual dimension finds its fulness only in the life to come. But Origen never breaks the continuity of the journey. The moral dimension remains even at the Apocatastasis, and the spiritual dimension sheds its light even upon our present darkened world.

This pilgrim's progress can also be thought of as a growth toward maturity. Using Genesis and passages from Saint Paul, Origen distinguishes in each human being between the inner and the outer man (see below, pp. 220ff.). The inner man is the soul or mind made after God's image, while the outer man is the corporeal man of dust. The two "men" correspond to one another, and every expression that can be used of the corporeal man can be taken metaphorically to refer in a spiritual sense to the inner man. Thus, vision, which is corporeal, corresponds to knowledge, which is a kind of spiritual "vision." Origen's notion of spiritual senses is correlative with his view that there are spiritual foods corresponding to the stage of development of the inner man. Using 1 Corinthians 3:2f., Hebrews 5:12–14, and Romans 14:2ff., Origen arranges these foods in a hierarchical order. "Milk" is for "babes in Christ"; "vegetables," for the weak; "solid food," only for the mature or perfect. In principle, the soul is meant to grow from childhood to maturity, and all are destined to receive the solid food (see below, p. 218). All the different foods are to be equated with the Word of God, who accommodates His nourishing revelation to the condition of the one receiving it. Once again revelation descends through a series of stages, while our response ascends through the same series. This is how we receive our "daily" bread, which strengthens our "being" and enables us to grow to maturity (see below, pp. 138ff.). As well, the Word of God nourishes us through the Scriptures, and different passages and books are thought to correspond to the different foods. Our responsibility for seeking the right food is never forgotten, but Origen's emphasis is upon God's gift and His providential guidance of our growth toward perfection.

In Origen's view even the different ages of the inner man

imply that a distinction must be made in the Church between the simple and the perfect. From one point of view the notion merely reflects Origen's assessment of the realities of his time. He is fully aware that there are, indeed, many simple Christians, who have only a crude and immature understanding of their religion. And he recognizes that even amongst the martyrs some deserve greater rewards than others (see below, pp. 44, 51f., 180). Origen even attributes the same distinction between the simple and the perfect to John the Baptist's followers. John's disciples are those who have not only been baptized, but have also been taken into the narrower circle of his "disciples" (see below, p. 86). It must be emphasized that Origen does not mean to distinguish different natures of Christians, as the gnostics did. On the contrary, all are destined for perfection and maturity. But Origen realizes that this growth to perfection cannot be accomplished for most Christians within the confines of this present life. Periods of growth remain after this life and before the Apocatastasis during which the simple will be enabled to grow until they can receive solid food. Of course, Origen does posit a hierarchy in the Apocatastasis, and it may be that there is something illogical about degrees of perfection. But what he wishes to suggest is that we shall all be perfect in a way that preserves our individuality and the character of the experience we have had in our pilgrimage and during our growth to maturity.

A third metaphor Origen uses to describe the Christian life is that of warfare. The martyrs led in procession to execution are really celebrating the triumph of their victory against the forces of wickedness and evil (see below, p. 73). The pilgrim soul on its journey encounters war and must be ready for it (see below, pp. 258, 264). Shifting the metaphor slightly, Origen often thinks of the warfare as an athletic contest. The martyrs, in particular, are athletes contesting before a cosmic audience consisting not only of human beings but of good and evil angels. When they behave with courage, they are cheered by the good angels and by the whole created order (see below, pp. 53f., 41, 57). Needless to say, Origen draws upon the Scriptures for his use of the related metaphors of warfare and of the games. The same metaphors are commonly employed in the popular philosophical sermons of the time. The struggle that is described in this way is one both against sin and against the spiritual powers of evil. On the one hand, it is a moral struggle that aims to assert the control of the mind over the body and its passions. Here Origen employs Stoic themes attaching to the body-soul relationship. Virtue, by definition, is the activity by which the soul governs the body and its motions; vice, an activity in which the motions or passions of the body wrongfully gain control of the governing mind and the servant becomes master. Even though Origen's discussions are colored by ancient philosophical themes, the main point he wishes to make is that the moral life is a struggle, and virtue is acquired only by discipline. There is, as well, a dimension of the struggle that goes beyond morality. Origen believes the world is filled with spiritual forces of evil. And he explains this by speaking of Satan (the devil, the Enemy, the Adversary, the Evil One) and his armies of evil angels or demons. These hosts of wickedness war against the Christian, tempt him with their food, and seek to destroy his "house" built upon the rock (see below, pp. 48, 63, 74f., 77, 134f., 143, 162f, 256f.).

Integral to Origen's metaphor of the warfare or the athletic contest is his understanding of temptation. Indeed, temptation is really just another way of speaking of the struggle. And Satan and his demons are the chief tempters. In the selections that follow, particularly in *Homily XXVII on Numbers* and in his discussion of temptation in the treatise *On Prayer*, Origen develops an understanding of the significance of temptation that derives from Scripture and becomes an integral part of discussions of Christian spirituality in the early Church. He uses Job 7:1 (LXX) to demonstrate that from one point of view the whole of human life is temptation (see below, pp. 152ff.). The idea includes not only what we would usually call temptation, the attempt to make us sin, but also the idea of testing or affliction. In both senses temptation is meant to show us what we are (see below, p. 161 and cf. Deut. 8:2). Using the stock metaphor, Origen thinks of temptation as a testing of gold in the fire. But he tends to go further. Temptation not only tests what we are, it is also a providential process by which we are fashioned into what we should be. God is a divine goldsmith who hammers us into an object of beauty suitable for His grandeur (see below, p. 266). From one point of view temptation is a "protection and defense" (see below, pp. 263, 265). It necessarily accompanies the winning of virtues, and like salt it preserves those virtues once acquired. From another point of view temptation is creative. The pattern is unfolded in Origen's discussion of the progress from the Bitter Waters to Halus by way of Helim, the Red Sea, Sin, and Raphaca. The struggle with bitterness is followed by the refreshment of Helim, strengthening the soul for its further temptation at Sin. The result is the healing of the soul at Raphaca, and that healing prepares the soul for the toils of Halus. What Origen is observing is that growth is a painful process, and that temptation and struggle never leave us until we have attained the maturity of perfection. The struggle with temptation is one not only against sin and evil in our outer life; it is also intellectual in character. In particular, it is a struggle with the Scriptures, where intellectual and spiritual temptations abound (see below, p. 267).

The journey, the growth to maturity, and the warfare or contest are all dependent upon the freedom of the Christian. But as has been suggested, they are also placed within the context of God's providence, which continually trains our freedom. Christ accompanies the Christian on his journey, feeds him with true bread, and assists him in his struggle. Moreover, providence assists the Christian through the saints, both departed and present, and through the angels. The Christian life is thereby given a wider setting. The moral example of the saints, particularly figures from the Old Testament, is a source of strength for the Christian. He finds himself in the place of Ananias, Azarias, and Misael, of Daniel, of Mordecai and Esther, of Judith, and of Jonah (see below, pp. 63, 105f., 115f.). It is remarkable that these stories, which are used homiletically by Origen, also appear in early Christian art. The catacomb frescoes tend to focus upon these Old Testament stories of deliverance. The literary and iconographical evidence belongs together and enables us to say that the central emphasis in early Christianity was upon deliverance. The Christian life, then, marks a deliverance both from this world and for this world. The Old Testament examples become not just models to follow, but assurances of God's power to rescue His saints. Origen also thinks of that power as mediated through the guardian angels (see below, pp. 53, 101f., 103f.). If our warfare is against Satan and his hosts, we have spiritual powers for good on our side so that the conflict is not unequal.

INTRODUCTION

The progress of the Christian is placed within the cosmic struggle between good and evil.

In the preface to his *Commentary on the Song of Songs* Origen approaches the Christian life he has described by the different metaphors just examined from a slightly different point of view (see below, pp. 231f.). The three books of Solomon are related to the traditional divisions of Greek philosophy: moral, natural, and contemplative. Origen's fundamental move is what lies behind a long and fruitful development in the history of Christian spirituality. It results in a definition of the Christian life as comprising purgative, contemplative, and unitive stages. It would be wrong, however, to understand Origen in a fully systematic fashion. To be sure, he regards the three as arranged in a progressive order. One passes from ethics to physics or the contemplation of the natural order, and finally to the contemplation and love of God. But the three are mutually involved with one another, and there is a sense in which the higher stages comprehend the lower ones. It is probably better to speak of the three as different aspects of the Christian life arranged in hierarchical order. The preliminary aspect is the moral life (Proverbs), by which the Christian prepares himself for growth in his religion. The next aspect involves the intellectual contemplation of the created order and the consequent realization that it is "vanity" and contingent upon God (Eccles.). The highest aspect is represented by Song of Songs and is referred to the contemplation of God Himself. Not only must we not suppose that Origen is speaking of definite and separated stages, we must also beware of relating his idea too systematically to other themes in his thought. For example, it is tempting to suppose that the three aspects should be equated with his division of Scripture into body, soul, and spirit. Even though some correlation seems to exist between the "spirit" of Scripture and the contemplation symbolized by Song of Songs, the other details of the two patterns do not admit of being fused together. Origen's themes are united by the fact that they are all different ways of looking at the same thing and not by any clear linking of the themes into a system.

Nevertheless, the idea of the three aspects of the Christian life helps clarify Origen's discussions of it. His emphasis in the selections that follow is very much upon the moral aspect, and this is only what we should expect from material that is largely homiletical in character. Moreover, we occasionally find him suggesting that the moral life is a preliminary to the deeper dimensions of being a Christian. For example, in discussing prayer he makes it clear that a moral preparation is necessary before one can approach God (see below, p. 164). Furthermore, his understanding of the second aspect brings into focus a theme that repeatedly occurs throughout his writings, namely, the emphasis upon separating the soul from what is earthly and corporeal (see below, pp. 42, 74, 115, 263). In *An Exhortation to Martyrdom* this has concrete reference to the death of the martyr and his rejection not only of life but also of his family (see below, p. 69). At first the theme appears dualistic and seems to stand in contrast to Origen's monistic approach. And it may be that we cannot purge his thought completely of a moral dualism, though he certainly disavows a cosmological dualism. Nevertheless, we should remember that in the second aspect of the Christian life one learns that the created order is contingent. And this knowledge is designed to allow us to distinguish what is earthly and lowly from what is great and heavenly (see below, p. 263). Discernment is the key to Origen's idea. The Christian must learn to look beyond corporeal and visible things to the Creator. If sometimes Origen expresses his idea as a rejection of the world, we must keep in mind that it is the world as a fallen order and as a place of torment for the soul that is rejected. It may be that we shall end by being dissatisfied with his understanding of matter and corporeality as epiphenomena and shall insist that the body be defined as integral to a human being and matter as integral to the created order. But we should not misread Origen so as to suppose he takes an ultimately pejorative view of the body.

The final aspect of the Christian life, which is represented by Song of Songs, raises the question of whether Origen is a mystic. The answer depends very much on how we define *mystic*, and there is even a sense in which the issue is at best unimportant and at worst misleading. Nevertheless, three points can be made. First, Origen believes that in the highest aspect of the Christian life we shall know God, see Him face to face, and be joined with Him in a union of love. Second, this destiny represents the completion of our nature; we were created after God's image in order to have perfected knowledge of and fellowship with Him. Third, our natural destiny is merely potential until God rouses our minds and empowers them to become what in principle they are. Therefore, if one defines *mysticism* as a state in which we are somehow enabled to transcend ourselves, Origen is a mystic only in a qualified sense. From one point of view, the highest aspect of the Christian life simply completes our nature. But from another point of view, since only God can give us this power, Origen may properly be regarded as a mystic. At the very least it can be confidently said that Origen prepares the way for Gregory of Nyssa's mysticism. Not only does Origen regard the highest attainment of the Christian life as a gift of God enabling us to go beyond what would otherwise be possible, he also can describe our contemplation of God as endless and dynamic (see below, pp. 203f., 99). In such passages his emphasis is not upon the face-to-face vision that marks our destiny but upon the inexhaustible character of the quest for wisdom and the inability of thinking ever to find a final resting point. These themes are present in germ in Origen, but await Gregory of Nyssa for their full development.

The endlessness of the quest for truth and wisdom is, of course, a Platonic theme and is integral to the spirit not only of Plato but also of early Neoplatonism. In other respects, too, Origen's description of the highest aspect of the Christian life borrows themes from Plato. The goal of the Christian life is to be made divine (see below, pp. 58, 144). Here Origen depends upon the earlier Christian tradition and in particular upon Clement of Alexandria's use of the phrase from Plato's *Theaetetus* that defines human destiny as "likeness to God so far as possible." The theme is integrated with Origen's image theology. Plato also understands this destiny as the flight of the soul to God. In the *Phaedrus* the soul gains wings for its return to heaven, and Origen alludes to the idea when he speaks of the soul returning like an eagle to God (see below, p. 52). The myth of Diotima from Plato's *Symposium* may also be seen to influence Origen's thought. The soul must mount the scale of beauty in order to arrive at Beauty itself (see below, p. 117). And the love that distinguishes the highest aspect of the Christian life was dimly seen by the Greek philosophers (see below, p. 219). That love is a spell given the believer by God, and it enables him to give birth to visions (see below, pp. 59, 106). These themes derive from a development of Plato's theory of love that took place in Platonism. God's creative love is given priority and is what bestows on the soul its natural yearning for God. The believer's love is still appetitive, and so Plato's emphasis is retained. But more importance is attached to the reciprocal character of human love for God and to the unity between God and the soul it produces.

Moreover, the love of which Origen speaks is described not only by the use of philosophical themes, but also by drawing upon Scripture. The longing of the soul for God is like the longing of Israel for the promised land. It is a yearning for paradise and when purified allows the soul to pass the flaming swords of the cherubim and gain access to the tree of life (see below, pp. 67f.). Or it is the pilgrim's desire for his true city, the heavenly Jerusalem (see below, pp. 194ff.). The promised land, paradise, and the heavenly Jerusalem are, of course, different aspects of the new creation of the Apocatastasis. While Origen certainly colors his descriptions with themes that derive from his speculation, he in fact preserves the Christian tradition expounded in Scripture, developed in the theology of the early Church, and expressed in the Christian liturgy. Baptism, for example, is consistently presented in the patristic Church as the Exodus and entrance to the true promised land, as the restoration of paradise, and as entrance into the heavenly Jerusalem. The stock themes are associated by Origen with the contemplative aspect of the Christian life in which the union of the soul with God is effected.

One final dimension of Origen's understanding of the contemplative aspect of the Christian life must be mentioned. His emphasis, of course, is upon the individual's pilgrimage to God. But he does not forget the communal character of the Christian life. In the selections that follow we are occasionally reminded of Origen's commitment to the Church as a community. The point is especially clear in *An Exhortation to Martyrdom*, where the martyrs not only come from the Church but serve it by their baptism of blood, cleansing and purifying it (see below, p. 62). Occasional asides in which he alludes to the Church's catechetical and penitential systems and to the sacraments of baptism and the eucharist demon-

INTRODUCTION

strate that the Christian life he describes always has its setting in the life of the Church (see below, pp. 53, 90f.). Even though his treatment of prayer tends to underline its personal and individual aspects, he remembers that prayer in the community is more powerful and must be the Christian's joy as well as his duty (see below, pp. 166ff., 103). One may fault Origen's emphasis upon the individual and his comparative neglect of the community and its sacramental and institutional life. But one cannot say he has rejected these elements of the Christian life and can even argue that he constantly assumes them.

The pattern of the journey, growth, and warfare of the Christian life, analyzed in its three aspects, suggests that the Christian aim is the pure contemplation of God. To be sure, this is the end of the journey, the term of the growth, and the consequence of victory; and it represents the Christian destiny of the Apocatastasis. But we must beware of supposing that this means that Origen gives priority to the contemplative over the active life. Indeed, he argues for a dialectic between contemplation and action that must be maintained until the Apocatastasis, when action will no longer be required. Even the contemplation of prayer includes "deeds of virtue," and one can say "Our Father" or "Jesus is Lord" only if actions as well as words make the affirmations (see below, pp. 104, 124). Moses and Aaron symbolize the one "hand," which includes faith and knowledge of the Law together with works (see below, p. 251). From one point of view the active life is purgative and prepares the soul for the contemplation of God. But from another point of view contemplation bestows upon the soul the vision that enables it to act. Like Plato's philosopher, the soul that has glimpsed God must return to the cave and work. A circular pattern is thereby established, and the Christian life is not thought of as exclusively spiritual or contemplative. In this respect Origen is followed by the Cappadocians. It is only in the fifth century with Evagrius Ponticus and the pseudo-Dionysius that the notion arises that the contemplative life is higher than the active.

Origen's thought is highly complex, especially at the level of what has been called "the stage setting." He is a sophisticated and learned thinker, fully acquainted with the traditions of Jews and Christians and fully educated in ancient rhetoric and philosophy.

27

INTRODUCTION

He is a complicated thinker, as well, because of the inquiring spirit of his mind and his tendency to complicate and then chew upon rather subtle problems. The point attaches particularly to his cosmology, his Trinitarian thought, his view of the preexistence of souls and of the functional character of the body, and his understanding of providence and freedom. And yet his cosmology is nothing but an elaborate setting for the drama of the soul's pilgrimage from innocence to experience and to the perfection that represents its destiny. This is his real concern. He does not accord our life in this world a primary reality. But by showing that it points toward an eternal destiny, he gives it a significance it could not otherwise have. Like Plato he wishes to show how our Heraclitean experience is informed and made meaningful by its participation in the Parmenidean world of ultimate reality. And as a Christian he is persuaded that our destiny has been revealed in Christ.

Origen starts with the fundamental problem of human life. He insists that we are free and responsible and yet must recognize that we are involved in a world of evil, where outward disaster and our very corporeality impede our freedom and keep us from knowledge of God. His theological story is a kind of theodicy and has the function of explaining why evil has arisen; the precosmic minds misused their freedom and brought into existence this fallen order. The body and the material world imprison us in a bestial or even an insensate life, but these chains are not made so by nature and do not inevitably function this way. God's providence uses our prison house to make us long for a better state, and He uses corporeality as a means of revealing Himself. What was opaque gradually becomes translucent, and Christ's light shines into the prison house. The Christian life, then, is a response to revelation. We begin to know God and to move toward the face-to-face vision that perfects our fellowship with Him. The dimensions of this life are ethical, intellectual, and spiritual or mystical; and they involve us in the life of the Church and in action in our world.

ASSESSMENT

Origen was a controversial figure in the ancient Church, and any assessment of his work must reckon with the fact that much of his thought was rejected. The disputes over his teaching may conveniently if somewhat artificially be divided into three periods. The first is rather obscure, since we do not have a great deal of evidence for it. But it is clear that Methodius of Olympus, who died about 311, became the leader of opponents to Origenism. The central issue was Origen's peculiar view of the resurrection and his denial that *this* body will be raised. As well, Methodius rejected Origen's belief in the preexistence of souls and attacked his interpretation of Scripture. At the same time, Origen was not without his defenders at the turn of the fourth century. In Caesarea Eusebius was an avowed Origenist, and his account of Origen's life in Book VI of the *Ecclesiastical History* is in part designed as a defense of Origen. Pamphilus wrote an Apology for Origen that attempted to vindicate Origenism; the treatise is unfortunately only partially preserved in Rufinus's Latin translation. Finally, the fact that Origen's thought continued to attract thoughtful Christians more than a century after his death is demonstrated by the *Philocalia*, an anthology drawn from Origen's writings in 358–359 by the Cappadocians, Basil the Great and Gregory Nazianzen. We may presume that if Origenism remained a powerful current of thought in the Church, opposition to Origenism also continued.

The next period of controversy is well documented by those who participated in it. Epiphanius of Salamis, the heresiologist, about 375 attacked Origenism as a heresy. In addition to the doctrines of the resurrection and of the soul, Origen's Trinitarian thought came under fire. Included were the charges that Origen had taught the transmigration of souls, and his allegorical method of Scriptural interpretation and his Christology were also attacked. Epiphanius succeeded in persuading Jerome, who had been an admirer of Origen, to join in the attack. In 395 Jerome failed to persuade John, the patriarch of Jerusalem, to condemn Origen. But in 398 Rufinus's Latin translation of the *De principiis* appeared, adding fuel to the fire. In 400 Theophilus, the patriarch of Alexandria, condemned Origen and the Origenist views held by some of the monastic communities in Egypt. These monks were vigorously opposed by others, the so-called anthropomorphites; and Theophilus expelled their leaders, the "Tall Brothers." They attempted unsuccessfully to gain John of Jerusalem's assistance, and ended by taking refuge with John Chrysostom in Constantinople. The controversy did not, however, result in any universal condemnation of Origen.

In the sixth century such a condemnation was finally issued. Origenism began to stir up trouble in the monasteries of Palestine, and the opponents of Origenism persuaded the Emperor Justinian to write a letter condemning Origen to Mennas, the patriarch of Constantinople. Shortly afterwards, in 543, a synod in Constantinople condemned Origen and his views, and the condemnation was ratified by the Fifth General Council of 553. As the reader will be able to see by examining the footnotes to Book IV of the *De principiis* included in this volume, a central difficulty in interpreting Origen is that we must approach his writings through the controversies about them. The charges against Origen boil down to the accusation that his theology was adulterated by his philosophy. Themes in his thought were treated as though they could be understood by their philosophical logic more than by their function in Origen's thought as a whole. The distinction between what Origen had actually said and the opinions thought to be implied by what he said began to be lost. And no real attempt was made to distinguish Origen's own thought from what his later followers had made of it.

While it is impossible to treat the problem fully in a general introduction to Origen's thought, a sympathetic approach demands that we reject a reading of Origen that proceeds from the point of view of his enemies. It is true that Origen left himself open to the charge of being more a philosopher than a Christian. But there can be little doubt that this is not how he saw himself. As has been suggested, Origen believed he was a seeker of Christian truth, and his enterprise was one of articulating the rich and complex vision he had of the Gospel. In embarking upon this task his authorities lay not in philosophical concepts but in the canonical Scriptures of the Church and in the rule of faith that established their basic meaning. He regarded these authorities as a basis for further speculation and not as a boundary of thought. But he consistently argued that the rule of faith and the Scriptures must be used to test his speculations. If they can be demonstrated contrary to these authorities, they must be rejected. Origen's commitment was to the Christian faith; and however much his vision of that faith proceeds from conviction, he did not confuse his convinced opinions with his fundamental loyalty to the Church.

Book IV of the *De principiis* expounds the approach to Scripture Origen advocates. He employs all the technical literary tools of his day in approaching the text. This involves establishing the proper text, comparing different manuscripts and translations, and collating words and passages throughout Scripture as we should do by using lexicons and concordances. The chief product of his scholarly work at this level was the *Hexapla*, a work that put in parallel columns the Hebrew Old Testament, its Greek transliteration, and the different Greek translations available. The major point to make is that Origen uses all these methods in order to read the text as carefully as possible. It is impossible to exaggerate the care with which Origen notes details in Scripture. As well, he makes full use of the exegetical traditions available to him. He is aware of Philo's work and the results of Hellenistic Jewish interpretation of the Old Testament. He is fully acquainted with the rhetorical methods of pagan scholars and with their allegorical approach to Homer and Hesiod. He takes seriously the work of Christian gnostic interpreters like Heracleon. And he repeatedly tells us that he consults the Jewish rabbis. The impact of all this upon Origen's writings is immense. There are passages like the etymological interpretations of *Homily XXVII on Numbers* that closely resemble Philo. And discussions in *The Prologue to the Commentary on the Song of Songs* show his acquaintance with rabbinic literature and can be paralleled by the Talmud and the tannaitic Jewish literature.

All these influences and approaches are bound together by Origen in a theoretical framework that supplies his approach to Scripture. First, following the rules of Greek literary analysis, Origen argues that the narratives of Scripture are filled with impossibilities and incongruities. These stumbling blocks mean that the letter of the text cannot be followed and that a deeper meaning must be sought. Second, the deeper meaning is to be equated with Origen's theological view. Sometimes the deeper meaning is subdivided into the "soul" and the "spirit" of Scripture, but Origen's fundamental distinction is between the letter and the spirit, between the narrative and obvious meaning and the theological meaning toward which it points. At one level, this theological meaning involves the fulfillment of the Old Testament by the New and the resulting typological relationships. The shadow of the Old Testament yields to the image of the New, which in turn will yield to the reality of the Apocatastasis. But at another level, this typological framework is drawn into a wider pattern, which Origen can also call typological (see below, pp. 109, 180f., 184f.). That is, the earthly realities of the two testaments point to the heavenly realities of the Beginning and the End. For example, the tabernacle of the Old Testament finds its typological fulfillment in the Church and its consummation in the Apocatastasis. But in a broader sense both the tabernacle and the Church are earthly shadows cast by the heavenly reality of Origen's vision of universal destiny. Thus, Origen's allegorical interpretation does not so much dissolve temporal sequence as catch it up into eternity. And the pattern that emerges parallels the theological story that has been examined above. Origen's approach to Scripture or his hermeneutical principle is really nothing more than his theological view.

We are left in a circle. On the one hand, Origen begins with Scripture, and his careful reading of it yields the theological conclusions that comprise his view as a whole. From this point of view he is certainly a Christian and, indeed, a Biblical theologian. And the charges made against him in the early Church will be seen to be unfounded. On the other hand, Origen approaches Scripture with preconceptions that are in great part determined by his philosophical training and bent of mind. At this level it is possible to charge him with simply importing Greek philosophy into his interpretation of Scripture. The resulting puzzle is not easily solved, but it can be argued that all interpreters approach Scripture with presuppositions. Moreover, the presuppositions, while they do determine the questions the exegete asks of the text, do not determine the interpretation provided the exegete respects the autonomy of the text and reads it carefully. They do, however, shape and color the resulting interpretation. If we can reason this way, then perhaps the basic issue in assessing Origen's work is whether his Platonizing presuppositions are congruent in general terms with the Biblical message. There is certainly room for disagreement with respect to this question. But if we allow Origen his basic premise that there need be no contradiction between Greek and Biblical thought, then our assessment of Origen may be a positive one.

Origen must be granted one other premise if we are to maintain a positive judgement about his work. He assumes the fundamental unity of mind, will, and spirit. It is the mind that wills and that preserves the spiritual kinship between the individual and God. Part of our difficulty in reading Origen is that we no longer make his assumption. We think of will as a separate and different faculty from the intellect. As a result, we tend to hear words like *knowledge*, *understanding*, *mind*, and *reason* in a narrowly intellectual sense. Nothing could be more misleading in reading Origen. For him mind includes not only the intellectual activities of a human being, but also his moral and spiritual powers. Indeed, the point is fundamental to Origen's thought and explains why the three aspects of the Christian life, moral, intellectual, and contemplative or spiritual, must be held together in unity.

As will be apparent, this introduction adopts a sympathetic view of Origen and grants the two basic premises just outlined. They, in turn, suggest a way of defining Origen's contribution to his own time. In the first instance Origen's importance lies in bridging the gap between Christianity and the Graeco-Roman world. He was able to expound the Gospel in terms meaningful to his pagan contemporaries and, perhaps more important, to Christians who retained that culture even upon conversion. It may be that conversion sometimes entails a radical break with a person's past, a substitution of the new for the old. But this is not the only way to understand conversion, and such a radical break involves dangers for the convert. Another view would see conversion as a transformation, where the old life is not abandoned but is transformed and renewed. This was Origen's point of view, and his conviction was that Christianity had the power to transform the old culture and make it fruitful. He, therefore, represents in miniature what in fact happened to the Roman world in the centuries following his death.

Yet perhaps more important than Origen's translation of the Gospel and his correlation of Christian and philosophical truth is a contribution that derives from his assumption of the unity of mind, will, and spirit. Implied by this view of a human being is the notion of freedom. A person can think and will; he can know and have fellowship with God. Origen's emphasis upon freedom and the responsibility carried with it is unmistakable. But it is when we remember what his world was like that the true significance of this emphasis emerges. He strenuously attacked determinists, whether they were philosophers or Christian gnostics. And his message of freedom was designed to proclaim hope in a world where hope was almost buried beneath chaos. His ringing optimism does not fail to take seriously the tragedy of human life, but it points to something deeper than tragedy, to the joy that comes from sorrow, to the victory from defeat, and to life that comes from death. In this respect Origen's writings are at root tracts for his time. It is tempting to go further and to suggest that his message of freedom and hope is a perennial one.

Origen's contribution is, of course, not limited to his own time. While the theological edifice he had constructed fell to ruins after his death, it supplied the stones from which new theological structures were built. It was not only the Arians who mined his writings; the orthodoxy of the fourth century articulated by Athanasius and the Cappadocians was deeply dependent upon Origen. In this way Origen's theology represents one of the foundations of all traditional Christian doctrine. The ecclesiastical dogmas of the Trinity and of Christ's person cannot rightly be understood without some knowledge of Origen's thought. In another way Origen's legacy has become a perennial part of the Christian tradition. As developed by the Cappadocians his thought became in the fourth century an ideology for monasticism. The story would have to be carried forward so as to include Evagrius Ponticus, the pseudo-Dionysius, John Cassian, Gregory the Great, Maximus the Confessor, and others. Suffice it to say that the themes Origen uses in giving definition to the Christian life persist to this day in the classical expositions of Christian spirituality.

BIBLIOGRAPHICAL NOTE

General introductions to Origen's thought may be found in the standard histories of doctrine. But Jean Daniélou, *Origen* (London & New York: Sheed & Ward, 1955, Eng. transl. of *Origène*, Paris: La Table Ronde, 1948) is to be recommended to the beginner. C.

INTRODUCTION

Bigg, *The Christian Platonists of Alexandria* (2nd ed., Oxford: Clarendon Press, 1913) remains an excellent introduction to Clement and Origen in English. As well, the essays on Origen in R. A. Norris, *God and World in Early Christian Theology* (New York: Seabury Press, 1965) and H. Chadwick, *Christianity and the Classical Tradition*, (Oxford: Clarendon Press, 1966) are extremely helpful. L. Bouyer's volume in the History of Christian Spirituality, *The Spirituality of the New Testament and the Fathers* (New York: Desclée & Co., 1963, Eng. transl. of *La Spiritualité du Nouveau Testament et des Pères*, Paris: Aubier, 1960) includes a chapter dealing with Origen's spirituality. The following list includes major books on Origen:

Origen and Greek philosophy:
   C. Andresen, *Logos und Nomos. Die Polemik des Kelsos wider das Christentum* (Berlin: Walter de Gruyter & Co., 1955)
   H. Koch, *Pronoia und Paideusis. Studien über Origenes und sein Verhältnis zum Platonismus* (Berlin & Leipzig: Walter de Gruyter & Co., 1932)
   J. M. Rist, *Eros and Psyche: Studies in Plato, Plotinus, and Origen* (Toronto: University of Toronto Press, 1964)

Origen and Scripture:
   R. M. Grant, *The Earliest Lives of Jesus* (New York: Harper & Bros., 1961)
   R. P. C. Hanson, *Origen's Doctrine of Tradition* (London: SPCK, 1954)
   R. P. C. Hanson, *Allegory and Event* (Richmond: John Knox Press, 1959)
   H. de Lubac, *Histoire et esprit. L'intelligence de l'Écriture d'après Origène* (Paris: Aubier, 1950)

Origen's theology:
   H. Crouzel, *Théologie de l'image de Dieu chez Origène* (Paris: Aubier, 1956)
   B. Drewery, *Origen on the Doctrine of Grace* (London: Epworth Press, 1960)
   M. Harl, *Origène et la fonction révélatrice du Verbe Incarné* (Paris:

Patristica Sorbonensia, Editions du Seuil, 1958)

Origen's spirituality:
A. Lieske, *Die Theologie der Logosmystik bei Origenes* (Münsterische Beiträge zur Theologie 22, Münster, 1938)
W. Völker, *Das Vollkommenheitsideal des Origenes* (Tübingen: Mohr, 1931)

Further study of Origen should make use of H. Crouzel's *Bibliographie critique d'Origène* (The Hague: M. Nijhoff, 1971). The introduction to the present volume has been influenced by the unpublished work of James Armantage, to whom it is greatly indebted. Mr. Armantage's titles are: *"And on the Third Day . . .": A Descriptive Essay Concerning Origen's Views on the Resurrection* (1973), *What the Apostles Didn't Tell Us: A Proposal for Reconstructing the Order and Plan of Origen's Peri Archōn* (1976), and *The Delicate Balance: A Speculative Essay on the Originality and Unity of Origen's Thought* (1977).

NOTE ON THE TRANSLATIONS

The translations that follow have been made from the texts prepared for the Berlin Corpus *(Die Griechischen Christlichen Schriftsteller der ersten drei Jahrhunderte*, Berlin: Akademie Verlag). The following list includes the specific reference to the critical editions and the available English translations:

An Exhortation to Martyrdom (written in 235 at Caesarea), *ed.* P. Koetschau, GCS 2 (1899).
Translated in The Library of Christian Classics, *Alexandrian Christianity* (Philadelphia: Westminster Press, 1954) by H. Chadwick, and in Ancient Christian Writers 19 (Westminster, Maryland: Newman Press, 1954) by J. J. O'Meara.
On Prayer (written *ca.* 233 at Caesarea), *ed.* P. Koetschau, GCS 3 (1899).
Translated in The Library of Christian Classics, *Alexandrian Christianity* (Philadelphia: Westminster Press, 1954) by

J. E. L. Oulton, and in Ancient Christian Writers 19 (Westminster, Maryland: Newman Press, 1954) by J. J. O'Meara, and in a separate volume by E. G. Jay (London: SPCK, 1954).

On First Principles (written between 220 and 230 at Alexandria), *ed.* P. Koetschau, GCS 22 (1913). The only complete text is Rufinus's Latin translation.

Translated by G. W. Butterworth (London: SPCK, 1936, Harper Torchbook edition, 1966) and by F. Crombie in vol. 4 of the Ante-Nicene Fathers.

Commentary on Song of Songs (written *ca.* 240 at Caesarea), *ed.* W. A. Baehrens, GCS 33 (1925). The only text is Rufinus's Latin translation.

Translated by R. P. Lawson, Ancient Christian Writers 26 (Westminster, Maryland: Newman Press, 1957).

Homilies on Numbers (written between 244 and 249 at Caesarea), *ed.* W. A. Baehrens, GCS 30 (1921). The only text is Rufinus's Latin translation.

The only translation into a modern language is by A. Méhat into French, *Sources chrétiennes* 29, (Paris: Éditions du Cerf, 1951).

It should be noted that Origen's Biblical citations have been conformed to the Revised Standard Version so far as possible. Sometimes changes have been required because of Origen's interpretation. More important, since Origen was citing from the Septuagint, the Old Testament citations often differ widely from the Hebrew text and the Revised Standard Version translation of it. When the differences are extreme, the citation includes the notation LXX to indicate the Septuagint. The numbering of the Psalms follows the Hebrew and the Revised Standard Version unless otherwise noted.

ORIGEN

AN EXHORTATION TO MARTYRDOM, PRAYER
FIRST PRINCIPLES: BOOK IV
PROLOGUE TO THE COMMENTARY ON
THE SONG OF SONGS
HOMILY XXVII ON NUMBERS

THE CLASSICS OF WESTERN SPIRITUALITY

AN EXHORTATION TO
MARTYRDOM

I. "You who are weaned from milk, you who are taken from the breast, each of you expect affliction upon affliction, expect hope upon hope, yet a little while, yet a little while, by the contempt of lips, through another tongue" (Is. 28:9–11, LXX).

So, most God-fearing Ambrose and most pious Protoctetus, you are no longer of the flesh or babes in Christ (cf. 1 Cor. 3:1), but have grown in your spiritual stature (cf. Lk. 2:52). You no longer need milk but solid food (cf. Heb. 5:12). As those called by Isaiah "weaned from milk" and "taken from the breast" listen how not simply one but "affliction upon affliction" is prophesied for athletes who have been weaned. The person who does not refuse the "affliction upon affliction" but welcomes it like a noble athlete as well immediately welcomes "hope upon hope," which he will enjoy shortly after the "affliction upon affliction." For that is what "yet a little while, yet a little while" means.

II. Furthermore, if strangers to the language of the holy Scriptures should hold us in contempt or disparage us as either impious or fools, let us remember that the "hope upon hope" to be given us in "yet a little while" will be given "by the contempt of lips, through another tongue." And who would not welcome "affliction upon affliction" that he might immediately also welcome "hope upon hope"? He will consider with Paul "that the sufferings of this present time" with which, as it were, we purchase blessedness "are not worth comparing with the glory that is to be revealed to us" from God (Rom. 8:18). The truth of this judgment is apparent because "this light momentary affliction" (2 Cor. 4:17) both is and is said to be "light" for those not burdened by present hardships, since it is quite outweighed by the greater and heavier "weight of eternal glory" it is "preparing for us" (2 Cor. 4:17). This will happen if, when our persecutors wish to weigh down our souls, as it were, we turn our governing mind from our sufferings and look not at the present sufferings but at the prizes kept for athletes who by their endurance of these tests compete according to the rules in Christ by the grace of God (cf. 2 Tim. 2:5). He multiplies His benefits and gives as much beyond what the toils of the contestant deserve as it is right for Him to give as the God who does not quibble about trifles and who in His munificence knows how to increase His gifts to those who have demonstrated they love Him with all their soul by despising so far as they are able their earthen vessel (cf. 2 Cor. 4:7).

III. And I think that God is loved with the whole soul by those who through their great longing for fellowship with God draw their soul away and separate it not only from their earthly body but also from every corporeal thing. For them no pulling or dragging takes place even in putting off their lowly body (cf. Phil. 3:21), when the time allows them to take off the body of death through what is supposed to be death. Then they will hear the apostolic prayer and statement "Wretched man that I am! Who will deliver me from this body of death?" (Rom. 7:24). For which one of those who groan in this tent (cf. 2 Cor. 5:4) because they are weighed down by a corruptible body (cf. Wis. 9:15) would not also give thanks, first saying, "Who will deliver me from this body of death"? And when he sees that he has been delivered from the body of death by his confession,[1] he will make the holy proclamation "Thanks be to God through Jesus Christ our Lord!" (Rom. 7:25). If such a view seems hard to any one, then he has not thirsted for God, the Mighty One, the living God; nor has he longed for God "as the hart longs for fountains of waters"; nor has he said, "When shall I come and behold the face of God?" (Ps. 42:1–2). And he has not considered in himself what the prophet considered when someone said to him, "Where is your God?" "Daily" he poured out his "soul" by himself, rebuking it again and again for becoming sorrowful and disquieted in its weakness, and saying, "I will enter the place of the marvelous tabernacle up to the house of God, with the voice of rejoicing and of

---

1. Reading *homologia* instead of the manuscript reading, *homilia*.

the thanksgiving of a festal sound" (Ps. 42:3–4).

IV. Therefore, I beseech you to remember in all your present contest the great reward laid up in heaven for those who are persecuted and reviled for righteousness' sake, and to be glad and leap for joy on account of the Son of Man (cf. Mt. 5:10–12; Lk. 6:23), just as the apostles once rejoiced when they were counted worthy to suffer dishonor for His name (cf. Acts 5:41). And if you should ever perceive your soul drawing back, let the mind of Christ, which is in us (cf. Phil. 2:5), say to it, when it wishes to trouble that mind as much as it can, "Why are you sorrowful, my soul, and why do you disquiet me? Hope in God, for I shall yet give Him thanks" (Ps. 42:11). I pray that our souls may never be disquieted, and even more that in the presence of the tribunals and of the naked swords drawn against our necks they may be guarded by the peace of God, which passes all understanding (cf. Phil. 4:7), and may be quieted when they consider that those who are foreigners from the body are at home with the Lord of all (cf. 2 Cor. 5:8). But if we are not so strong as always to preserve calm, at least let not the disquiet of the soul be poured forth or appear to strangers, so that we may have the opportunity of giving an apology to God, when we say to Him, "My God, my soul is disquieted within me" (Ps. 42:5, 11). The Word exhorts us to remember also what is said in Isaiah as follows, "Fear not the reproach of men, and be not dismayed at their contempt" (Is. 51:7). For since God clearly rules over the motion of heaven and what is in it and over what is accomplished on earth and sea by His divine skill—the births, origins, foods, and growths of all the different animals and plants—it is foolish to close our eyes and not look to God (cf. Is. 6:10; Mt. 13:15; Acts 28:27), but instead turn our eyes toward the fear of those who will soon die and be handed over to judgment according to their deserts.

V. Of old it was said by God to Abraham, "Come out of your land" (Gen. 12:1). But to us in a short while it will perhaps be said, "Come out from the whole earth." It is good to obey Him, so that He may presently show us the heavens in which exists what is called the kingdom of heaven. Now we can see that life is filled with contests for many virtues, and we can see the contestants. Many who do not belong to God's portion (cf. Deut. 32:9; Col. 1:12) will appear to have contested for self-control, and some will seem to have died courageously in keeping the purpose of the Lord of all. Those who are skillful in searching out arguments will seem to have been concerned with wisdom, and those who have purposed to live a righteous life will seem to have given themselves over to righteousness. Even the mind of the flesh (cf. Rom. 8:6) and many other capacities of those outside our faith go to war for each of the virtues. But the only people to join the contest for true religion is the chosen race, the royal priesthood, the holy nation, the people for His possession (cf. 1 Pet. 2:9; Ex. 19:6; Is. 43:20–21). Other men do not even pretend that if there are contests waged against religious people, they will offer to die for their religion, preferring death for their religion to life without it. But every one of those who wish to belong to the chosen race is convinced at every time, even when those who pretend to worship many gods but are really atheists plot against him, that he must hear God, who says, "You shall have no other gods before me" (Ex. 20:3) and "you shall make no mention of the names of other gods in your hearts, nor shall it be named by your mouth" (Ex. 23:13). That is why such people believe in God with their heart for justification and confess Him with their mouth for salvation (cf. Rom. 10:10). They understand that they will not be justified unless they believe in God with their heart so disposed and that they will not be saved unless their speech corresponds to their disposition. For they deceive themselves who suppose that it is sufficient for gaining the goal in Christ to believe with the heart for justification, even if the confession with the mouth for salvation is not added. It is even possible to say that it is better for the one whose heart is far from God (cf. Is. 29:13; Mt. 15:8) to honor Him with his lips than to honor Him with the heart, if the mouth does not make the confession for salvation.

VI. Suppose, however, that the One who says, "You shall not make for yourself a graven image or any likeness, and the rest" (Ex. 20:4) implies that there is a difference between "You shall not bow down to them" and "You shall not worship them."[2] Then perhaps the person who really believes in idols worships them; but the one

---

2. Here Origen seems to be examining the view, held by some gnostics, that martyrdom is a matter of indifference. He does not deny the importance of the inner disposition, but chapters 5 and 7 demonstrate that he believes the argument does not go far enough. Cf. *Contra Celsum* VII.66 and Chadwick's note.

who does not believe but pretends to worship them through coward-ice, which he calls an accommodating temper, so that he may seem to be religious like most other people, does not worship idols but only bows down to them. Then I might say that those who deny Christianity on oath at the tribunals or before they have been put on trial do not worship but only bow down to idols when they take "God" from the name of the Lord God and apply it to vain and lifeless wood. Thus, the people who were defiled with the daughters of Moab (cf. Num. 25:1) bowed down to idols but did not worship them. Indeed, it is written in the text itself, "They invited them to the sacrifices of their idols, and the people ate of their sacrifices, and they bowed down to their idols, and performed the rites to Baalpeor" (Num. 25:2–3). Observe that it does not say "and they worshiped their idols"; for it was not possible after such great signs and wonders in one moment of time to be persuaded by the women with whom they committed fornication to consider the idols gods. Perhaps it was also in this way that in the story of the Golden Calf in Exodus they bowed down but did not worship the calf they had seen made (cf. Ex. 32:8).

At least we must suppose that the present temptation has come about as a testing and trying of our love for God.[3] "For the Lord is tempting you," as it is written in Deuteronomy, "to know whether you love the Lord your God with all your heart and with all your soul" (Deut. 13:3; cf. Mt. 22:37; Deut. 6:5). But when you are tempted, "you shall walk after the Lord your God, and fear Him, and keep His commandments," especially "you shall have no other gods but me." And you shall hear His voice and cleave to Him, when He takes you from the regions here and associates you with Himself for what the Apostle calls "the increase of God" in Him (Col. 2:19).

VII. But if every evil word is an abomination to the Lord your God (cf. Mt. 12:36; Prov. 15:26), how great an abomination must be supposed the evil word of denial and the evil word of publicly proclaiming another god and the evil oath by the Fortune of men, something that has no existence.[4] When this is proposed to us, we

---

3. In this respect Origen is willing to accept the argument he is considering.
4. Here Origen rejects the negative implication of the argument he has just considered in chapter 6.

must remember the One who taught, "But I say to you, Do not swear at all" (Mt. 5:34). For if the person who swears by heaven transgresses against the throne of God, and if the one who swears by earth commits sacrilege by making what is called "the stool of God's feet" a god (cf. Is. 66:1; Mt. 5:35), and if the one who swears by Jerusalem sins though it is the city of a great king, and if the one who swears by his own head offends—how great a sin must we suppose it is to swear by someone's Fortune? We must then remember the saying, "For every careless word you will render account on the day of judgment" (Mt. 12:36). For what other word is as careless as the oath in denial?

And it is likely that the Enemy will wish to trick us by his powers to bow down to the sun or the moon or all the host of heaven (cf. Deut. 17:3, 4:19). But we shall say that the Word of God has not commanded this. For we must never bow down to the creatures when the Creator is present, sustains us, and anticipates the prayers of all (cf. Rom. 1:25). Nor would the sun himself wish to be worshiped by those of God's portion (cf. Deut. 32:9; Col. 1:12), or, it is likely, by anyone else. Rather, he imitates the One who said "Why do you call me good? No one is good but God the Father alone" (cf. Mk. 10:18; Lk. 18:19; Mt. 19:17; Origen adds "the Father"). It is just as though the sun were to say to someone wishing to bow down to him:

> Why do you call me god? There is one true God. And why do you bow down to me? For you shall bow down to the Lord your God and worship Him alone (cf. Mt. 4:10; Deut. 6:13, 10:20). And I am a creature. Why do you wish to worship someone who worships? For I, too, bow down to God the Father and worship Him. And in obedience to His commands I am subjected to vanity because of the One who subjected me in hope. And though I am now clothed with a corruptible body, I shall be set free from the bondage of corruption for the glorious liberty of the children of God (cf. Rom. 8:20–21; Wis. 9:15; 1 Sam. 25:29).

VIII. We should also expect a prophet of impiety, or perhaps not one but many, who will speak to us, as though it were the Lord's, a word that the Lord has not commanded (cf. Deut. 18:20, 22) and a word of wisdom foreign to wisdom (cf. 1 Cor. 12:8), so that he may slay us with the word of his mouth. But as for us, even when the sinner conspires against us, let us say, "But I am like a deaf man, I do not hear, like a dumb man who does not open his mouth. I have become like a man who does not hear" (Ps. 38:13–14). For deafness toward impious words is noble when we despair of correcting those who speak of baser things.

IX. And in times when we are called upon to meet adversity it is useful for us to understand what God wishes to teach by saying "I the Lord your God am jealous" (Ex. 20:5). I think that it is like a bridegroom who gives all his attention to the bride so that she will bring all she is to live devotedly with the bridegroom and keep herself in every way from mingling with anyone other than the bridegroom. And if he is wise, such a bridegroom displays jealousy, employing such an attitude toward the bride as a kind of medicine. So also the One who gives the commandments, especially if He appears as the First Born of all creation (cf. Col. 1:15), says to His bride, the soul, that God is jealous, thus keeping those who hear Him from fornication with demons and so-called gods. It is as a God jealous in this way that He says of those who have in any way ever gone fornicating after other gods, "They have stirred me to jealousy with what is no god; they have provoked me to anger with their idols. So I will stir them to jealousy with those who are no people; I will provoke them to anger with a foolish nation. For a fire is kindled by my anger, and it will burn to the depths of Hades" (Deut. 32:21–22).

X. Even though it is not for Himself that the bridegroom turns His betrothed away from all defilement, since He is wise and without passion, nevertheless, for her sake, when He sees her defilement and filth, He will do everything He can to heal her and to turn her back, addressing her as a free agent with words exhorting her away from fornication. And what worse pollution could you think of happening to the soul than that she should ever proclaim another god and fail to confess Him who is truly the one and only Lord? At any rate, I think that just as he who joins himself to a prostitute becomes one body with her (1 Cor. 6:16), so the one who confesses some god, especially in the time when faith is being tried and tested, is mingled and united with the god he confesses. And when he is denied by his own denial, which like a sword cuts him off from the One he denies, he suffers amputation by being separated from the One he denies. Know, therefore, that it is probably because it is a matter of course and of necessity that the one who confesses is confessed, and the one who denies is denied, that it is said, "So every one who confesses me before men, I also will confess before my Father who is in heaven" (Mt. 10:32; what follows should be added). The Word Himself and the Truth Himself might be saying to the confessor and to the denier:

> "The measure you give will be the measure you get back (cf. Lk. 6:38, Mt. 7:2, Mk. 4:24). You, therefore, who have given the measure of confessing me and have filled up the measure of your confession (cf. Mt. 23:32), will get back from me the measure of my confession shaken together, pressed down, running over; and it will be given into your lap (cf. Lk. 6:38). But you, who have given the measure of denial by denying me, will get back in proportion to your denial the measure of my denial of you."

XI. We may consider in the following way how the measure of confession is either filled up or not filled up and found lacking. Suppose that during the whole time of our testing and temptation we do not give place in our hearts to the devil (cf. Eph. 4:27), who wishes to defile us with evil thoughts of denial or of doubt or of any plausible argument urging us to conduct hostile to our martyrdom and our perfection. Suppose, in addition, that we do not defile ourselves by any word foreign to our confession, and suppose that we bear from our opponents every reproach, mockery, laughter, slander, and the pity they think they have for us because they suppose we are in error and are fools and so call us mistaken. Suppose, as well, that we are not diverted from our purpose when we are drawn by our affection for our children or for their mother or for any of those we hold dearest in life to hold onto them and to stay alive, but suppose that we turn away from all of them and belong totally to God and to life with Him and near Him, as those who will join in communion with His Only Begotten Son and His fellows (cf. Heb. 3:14). If all these conditions are met, we should say that we have filled up the measure of our confession. But if we are lacking even one of them, we have not filled up but have defiled the measure of our confession; and we have mixed into it something foreign. Then we shall be lacking as those lacked who built on the foundation wood or hay or straw (cf. 1 Cor. 3:12).

XII. We must also understand that we have accepted what are called the covenants of God as agreements we have made with Him when we undertook to live the Christian life. And among our agreements with God was the entire citizenship of the Gospel, which says, "If any one would come after me, let him deny himself and take up his cross and follow me. For whoever would save his soul would lose it, and whoever loses his soul for my sake will save it" (Mt. 16:24–25). And we have often come more alive when we hear, "For what will it profit a man if he gains the whole world and forfeits his soul? Or what ransom shall a man give in return for his soul? For the Son of Man is to come with His angels in the glory of His Father, and then He will repay every one for what he has done" (Mt. 16:26–27).

That one must deny himself and take up his cross and follow Jesus is not only written in Matthew, the text of which we cited, but also in Luke and Mark. Hear Luke, when he says, "And He said to all, 'If any one would come after me, let him deny himself and take up his cross[5] and follow me. For whoever would save his soul will lose it; and whoever loses his soul for my sake, he will save it. For what does it profit a man if he gains the whole world and loses or forfeits himself?' " (Lk. 9:23–25). And Mark says, "And He called to Him the multitude with His disciples, and said to them, 'If any one would come after me, let him deny himself and take up his cross and follow me. For whoever would save his soul will lose it; and whoever loses his soul[6] for the sake of the Gospel will save it. For what does it profit a man, to gain the whole world and forfeit his soul? For what ransom can a man give in return for his soul?' " (Mk. 8:34–37).

Long ago, therefore, we ought to have denied ourselves and said, "It is no longer I who live" (Gal. 2:20). Now let it be seen whether we have taken up our own crosses and followed Jesus; this happens if Christ lives in us. If we wish to save our soul in order to get it back better than a soul, let us lose it by our martyrdom.[7] For if we lose it for Christ's sake, casting it at His feet in a death for

---

5. Origen omits "daily" from the text.
6. Origen omits "for my sake and" from the text.
7. Origen regards souls (*psychai*) as "cooled off" (*psychesthai*) or fallen minds. Cf. *De principiis* II.8.3.

Him, we shall gain possession of true salvation for it. But if we do the contrary, we shall hear that it profits in no way the one who has gained the entire perceptible world by losing or forfeiting himself. And once a person has lost or forfeited his own soul, even if he should gain the whole world, he will be unable to give any ransom in return for the soul he has lost. For the soul that was created in the image of God (cf. Gen. 1:27) is more precious than any body. The only One who has been able to give a ransom in return for our soul once it has been lost is the One who bought us by His own precious blood (cf. 1 Pet. 1:19).

XIII. And according to some deeper insights Isaiah says, "I gave Egypt as your ransom, Ethiopia and Syene in exchange for you, because you were precious in my sight" (Is. 43:3–4). You will know the accurate interpretation of this passage and others if you desire in Christ to learn and to go beyond instruction in an enigma and so hasten to Him who calls you. Then you will know as friends of the Father and Teacher in heaven, since you have never before known face to face (cf. 1 Cor. 13:12). For friends learn not by enigmas, but by a form that is seen or by wisdom bare of words, symbols, and types; this will be possible when they attain to the nature of intelligible things and to the beauty of truth. If, then, you believe that Paul was caught up to the third heaven and was caught up into Paradise and heard things that cannot be told, which man may not utter (2 Cor. 12:2, 4), you will consequently realize that you will presently know more and greater things than the unspeakable words then revealed to Paul, after which he came down from the third heaven. But you will not come down if you take up the cross and follow Jesus, whom we have as a great High Priest who has passed through the heavens (cf. Heb. 4:14). And if you do not shrink from what following Him means, you will pass through the heavens, climbing above not only earth and earth's mysteries but also above the heavens and their mysteries. For in God there are treasured up much greater visions than these, which no bodily nature can comprehend, if it is not first delivered from everything corporeal. And I am convinced that God stores up and keeps by Himself much greater visions than the sun, the moon, and the chorus of the stars have seen, indeed than the holy angels have seen, whom God made wind and a flame of fire (cf. Ps. 104:4; Heb. 1:7).

His purpose is to reveal them when the whole creation is set free from its bondage to the Enemy for the glorious liberty of the children of God (cf. Rom. 8:21).

XIV. Therefore, one of those already martyred and who possessed something more than many of the martyrs in their Christian love of learning will ascend quite swiftly to those heights. And you, holy Ambrose, by examining the saying of the Gospel with great care, are able to see that perhaps none or only a few will attain some special and greater flood of blessings. May such a lot be yours, if you get safely through the contest without flinching. Words put it this way; once Peter said to the Savior, "Lo, we have left everything and followed you. What then shall we have?" Jesus said to them (that is, the apostles), "Truly I say to you, in the new world, when God[8] shall sit on His glorious throne, you who have followed me will also sit on twelve thrones, judging the twelve tribes of Israel. And every one who has left brothers or sisters or parents or children or lands or houses, for my name's sake, will receive a manifold reward and inherit eternal life" (Mt. 19:27–29). Because of these words, if I possessed on earth as much as you have or even more, I should pray that I might become a martyr to God in Christ so that I might receive "manifold," or, as Mark says, "a hundred-fold," which is much more than the few things we leave behind if we are called to martyrdom, since they are multiplied by one hundred.

For this reason, if I become a martyr, I should wish also to leave behind children with lands and houses, so that from the God and Father of our Lord Jesus Christ, from whom every family in heaven and on earth is named (Eph. 3:15), I might be called the father of manifold, or to use the exact figure, a hundred-fold and holier children. And if there are fathers about whom it was said to Abraham, "You shall go to your fathers in peace when you have been buried in a good old age" (Gen. 15:15), someone might say (though I do not know whether he would be speaking the truth) that perhaps those fathers are those who were once martyrs and left children behind, in return for whom they have become fathers of the fathers, the patriarch Abraham and the other patriarchs. For in all likelihood those who have left children behind and become mar-

---

8. This is Origen's reading of the text instead of "the Son of Man."

tyrs are fathers not of infants but of fathers.

XV. But there may be someone who is zealous of the better gifts and calls martyrs blessed who are rich or who are fathers, since they will beget children a hundred-fold or gain lands and houses a hundred-fold, but who asks whether they will rightly have a manifold possession in spiritual things above those martyrs who were poor in this life. He must be given the answer that just as those who endure tortures and sufferings demonstrate in martyrdom an excellence more illustrious than those not tested in this way, so also those who by using their great love for God have broken and torn apart such worldly bonds as these in addition to their love of the body and of life, and who have truly borne the Word of God, living and active, sharper than any two-edged sword (Heb. 4:12)—these have been able to return like an eagle to the house of their master (cf. Prov. 23:5 LXX) by breaking apart such bonds and by fashioning wings for themselves. Therefore, just as it is right for those who have not been tested with tortures and sufferings to yield the first places to those who have demonstrated their endurance in instruments of torture, in different sorts of racks, and in fire, so also the argument suggests that we poor, even if we also become martyrs, should get out of the first seats for you who because of your love for God in Christ trample upon the deceitful fame most people seek, upon such great possessions, and upon affection for your children.

XVI. In addition, observe the reverence of Scripture in promising manifold and a hundred-fold brothers and children and parents and lands and houses; a wife is not numbered with them (cf. Mt. 19:27–29; Mk. 10:28–30). For it does not say that everyone who leaves brothers or sisters or parents or children or lands or houses or a wife for my name's sake will receive manifold reward. For in the resurrection of the dead they neither marry nor are given in marriage, but are like the angels in heaven (Mt. 22:30; Mk. 12:25).

XVII. Therefore, what Joshua said to the people when he settled them in the holy land, the Scripture might also say now to us. The text reads as follows, "Now fear the Lord and worship Him in sincerity and righteousness" (Josh. 24:14). And it will tell us, if we are being misled to worship idols, what follows, "Destroy the foreign gods which your fathers worshiped beyond the River and in Egypt, and worship the Lord" (Josh. 24:14).

Then in the beginning when you were going to be instructed, it would have been rightly said to you, "And if you be unwilling to worship the Lord, choose this day whom you will worship, whether the gods your fathers worshiped in the region beyond the River, or the gods of the Amorites among whom you dwell on the land." And the catechist might have said to you, "But as for me and my house, we will worship the Lord because He is holy" (Josh. 24:15). He does not have any reason to say this to you now; for then you said, "Far be it from us that we should forsake the Lord, to serve other gods. For the Lord our God, He is God, who brought us and our fathers out of Egypt . . . and preserved us in all the way that we went" (Josh. 24:16–17). Moreover, in the agreements about religion long ago you gave your catechist this answer, "We also will worship the Lord, for He is our God" (Josh. 24:18). If, therefore, the one who breaks agreements with men is outside any truce and alien to safety, what must be said of those who by denying make null and void the agreements they made with God, and who run back to Satan, whom they renounced when they were baptized? Such a person must be told the words spoken by Eli to his sons, "If a man sins against a man, then they will pray for him; but if he sins against the Lord, who will pray for him?" (1 Sam. 2:25).

XVIII. A great theater is filled with spectators to watch your contests and your summons to martyrdom, just as if we were to speak of a great crowd gathered to watch the contests of athletes supposed to be champions.[9] And no less than Paul you will say when you enter the contest, "We have become a spectacle to the world, to angels, and to men" (1 Cor. 4:9). Thus, the whole world and all the angels of the right and the left,[10] and all men, those from God's portion (cf. Deut. 32:9; Col. 1:12) and those from the other portions, will attend to us when we contest for Christianity. Indeed, either the angels in heaven will cheer us on, and the floods will clap their hands together, and the mountains will leap for joy (Ps. 98:8), and all the trees of the field will clap their branches (Is. 55:12)—or, may it not happen, the powers from below, which

---

9. Reading *synathroizomenōn* instead of *synagōnizomenōn*, as Koetschau suggests.
10. I.e., good and evil. Cf. Chadwick's note on *Contra Celsum* VI.27.

rejoice in evil, will cheer. And it is in no way foolish to see by using Isaiah's words what will be said by those in hell to the ones who have been defeated and have fallen from their heavenly martyrdom. This will make us shudder all the more at the impiety of denying. For this is what I think will be said to the person who has denied, "Hell below is stirred up to meet you; all the giants who ruled the earth have been raised up for you; they raise all the kings of the nations from their thrones. They will all answer and speak to you" (Is. 14:9–10). What will the defeated powers say to those who have been defeated? And what will those taken captive by the devil say to those taken captive by denial but this, "You have been captured as we were, and you have been numbered among us"? (Is. 14:10). And if someone with a great and glorious hope in God is overcome by cowardice or by the sufferings inflicted upon him for his faith, he will hear, "Your glory has come down to hell, and your great delight. They spread decay beneath you for a bed, and the worm is your covering" (Is. 14:11). If anyone has often shone in the churches, illuminating them like the day star, with his good works shining before men (cf. Mt. 5:16), and if afterwards in the great contest he has lost the crown of such a throne, he will hear, "How have you fallen from heaven, O Day Star, who rise early in the morning? You have been trodden down to the ground!" (Is. 14:12). And this will be said to him when he has become like the devil by his denial, "He shall be thrown on the hills like a polluted corpse with many who have died pierced with swords and who come down to hell. Just as a garment stained with blood will not be clean, so neither will you be clean" (Is. 14:19–20 LXX). For how shall he be clean who is defiled with blood and slaughter, by the polluted lapse of denial, and who is stained by so great an evil?

But as it is, let us show that we have heard the saying "He who loves . . . son or daughter more than me is not worthy of me" (Mt. 10:37). Let us stand fast lest there arise in us any hesitation whether we should deny or confess, lest Elijah's word be also said to us, "How long will you go on limping on both your thighs? If the Lord is God, follow Him" (1 Kings 18:21).

XIX. It is likely that we shall both be reproached by our neighbors and scorned by those who surround us and shake their heads at us as fools. But in these circumstances let us say to God,

"You have made us a reproach of our neighbors, a scorn and a derision of those about us. You have made us a byword among the nations, a shaking of the head among the peoples. All day long my disgrace is before me, and the shame of my face has covered me, at the voice of the reproacher and reviler, at the face of the enemy and avenger" (Ps. 44:13–16). But when all this happens, it is blessed to speak to God the word uttered by the prophet in his boldness, "All this has come upon us, and we have not forgotten you, and we have not been false to your covenant, and our heart has not turned back" (Ps. 44:17–18).

XX. Let us remember that while we are in this life we should think of the paths outside life and say to God, "You have turned our steps by your path" (Ps. 43:19 LXX–44:18). Now is the time to remember that this region in which we have been humiliated is a place of distress for the soul, so that we may say in our prayers, "You have humiliated us in a place of distress, and the shadow of death has covered us" (Ps. 43:20 LXX–44:19). But taking courage let us also say, "If we had forgotten the name of our God and if we had spread forth our hands to a strange god, would not God discover this?" (Ps. 44:20–21).

XXI. Let us enter the contest to win perfectly not only outward martyrdom, but also the martyrdom that is in secret, so that we too may utter the apostolic cry "For this is our boast, the martyrdom of our conscience that we have believed in the world . . . with holiness and godly sincerity" (2 Cor. 1:12). And let us join to the apostolic cry the prophetic one, "He knows the secrets of our hearts," especially if we are led away to death. Then we shall say to God what can be said only by martyrs, "For your sake we are slain all the day long; we are accounted as sheep for the slaughter" (Ps. 44:21–22). And if fear of the judges who threaten us with death should ever try to undermine us with the mind of the flesh (cf. Rom. 8:6f.), let us then say to them the verse from Proverbs, "My son, honor the Lord, and you will prevail. Fear no one else but Him" (Prov. 7:1 LXX).

XXII. And what Solomon says in Ecclesiastes is also useful for the subject under discussion, "I praised all who have died more than the living, who are alive till now" (Eccles. 4:2). Who would so rightly be praised as the person who died of his own accord, welcoming death for his religion? This is what Eleazar was like, who welcoming death with honor rather than life with pollution went up to the rack of his own accord (2 Macc. 6:19). And this Eleazar made a high resolve worthy of his ninety years and the dignity of his old age and the grey hairs that he had reached with distinction and his excellent life even from childhood, and moreover according to the holy God-given Law. And he said, "Such pretense is not worthy of our time of life, lest many of the young should suppose that Eleazar in his ninetieth year has gone over to an alien religion, and through my pretense, for the sake of living a brief moment longer, they should be led astray because of me, while I defile and disgrace my old age. For even if for the present I should avoid the punishment of men, yet whether I live or die I shall not escape the hands of the Almighty. Therefore, by manfully giving up my life now, I will show myself worthy of my old age and leave to the young a noble example of how to die a good death willingly and nobly for the revered and holy laws" (2 Macc. 6:24–28).

I pray that when you are at the gates of death, or rather of freedom, especially if tortures are brought (for it is impossible to hope you will not suffer this from the will of the opposing powers), you will use such words as these, "It is clear to the Lord in His holy knowledge that though I might have been saved from death, I am enduring sufferings in my body, but in my soul I am glad to suffer these things because I fear Him" (2 Macc. 6:30). Such was the death of Eleazar, as it was said of him, "He left in his death an example of nobility and a memorial of courage, not only to the young but to the great body of his nation" (2 Macc. 6:31).

XXIII. As well, the seven brothers described in 2 Maccabees, whom Antiochus tortured with whips and cords when they remained steadfast in their religion, will be a powerful and noble example of robust martyrdom for everyone who considers whether he will prove to be less a man than boys who not only endured their own tortures, but also demonstrated how strong their religion was by watching their brothers' tortures. One of them became, as Scripture calls it, "spokesman" and said to the tyrant, "What do you intend to ask and learn from us? For we are ready to die rather than transgress the laws of our fathers" (2 Macc. 7:2). Why do I need to tell what pans and cauldrons, heated to torture them, they endured after each had undergone different sufferings? For the one called their spokesman first had his tongue cut out. Then he was scalped, and he bore the scalping as others bear circumcision, believing that even in this he was fulfilling the word of God's covenant. Not satisfied with this Antiochus cut off his hands and feet while the rest of the brothers and the mother looked on, thus punishing the other brothers and the mother by the sight and thinking he would shake their resolve by what he supposed fearful sights. And so, not satisfied with this Antiochus commanded that the brother, when he was utterly helpless so far as the condition of his body was concerned because of the previous tortures, should be taken still breathing to the fire in the pans and cauldrons and should be fried in a pan (2 Macc. 7:5). And when the smoke of that noblest athlete of piety's flesh, roasted by the cruelty of the tyrant, spread widely, the others encouraged one another with their mother to die nobly, consoling themselves by considering that God was watching over all these tortures. For the conviction that the eye of God is present with those who endure was enough to give them endurance. And the Judge of the athletes of piety encouraged them, being encouraged Himself and, so to speak, cheering for those who were struggling against such great sufferings. And it would be appropriate for us, as well, in such circumstances to use their words to those behaving this way and to say, "The Lord God is watching over us and in truth has compassion on us" (2 Macc. 7:6).

XXIV. When in this way the first brother had been tried as gold is tried in the furnace (cf. Wis. 3:6; Prov. 17:3), the second was brought forward for their sport. The servants of the cruel tyranny tore off the skin of his head with the hair and called on the one who had suffered to change his mind, asking him whether he would eat the idol meat rather than have his body punished limb by limb (2 Macc. 7:7). And when he refused to change his mind, he was brought forward for the next torture. He remained steadfast to the last breath, for he did not break down or yield to his sufferings. And he said to the impious tyrant, "You accursed wretch, you dismiss us from this present life, but the King of the universe will raise us up to an everlasting renewal of life, because we have died for His laws" (2 Macc. 7:8).

XXV. Then the third brother counted his offerings as nothing and trod them underfoot because of his love for God. When it was demanded, he quickly put out his tongue and courageously stretched forth his hands (2 Macc. 7:10) and said, "By leaving these behind for the laws of God, I hope to get them back from God the way He gives them to those who are athletes for His religion" (2 Macc. 7:11).

Likewise the fourth brother was tortured, bearing his torments and saying, "One cannot but choose to die at the hands of men and to cherish the hope that God gives of being raised again by Him in a resurrection that the tyrant will not have. For he will be raised not to life but to reproach and to shame" (2 Macc. 7:14).

Next the fifth brother was tortured. He looked at Antiochus and reproached him with failing to let his corruptibility cut short his arrogance, since he supposed that tyrannical authority for a few days was a great thing. And he said that even though it was so persecuted, the nation had not been forsaken by God, who would torture Antiochus and his descendants with such tortures as they had never seen (2 Macc. 7:15–17).

After him the sixth brother, when he was about to die, said, "Do not deceive yourself. Since we are paying these penalties for our sins so that we may be cleansed by our suffering, we suffer them willingly." And he said to him that he ought not to suppose he would be guiltless for trying to fight against God. For the one who fights against those who have been made divine by the Word fights against God (2 Macc. 7:18–19; cf. Acts 5:39).

XXVI. Antiochus then laid hold of the last and youngest brother; and since he was persuaded that he was a true brother of those who had counted such great sufferings as nothing and that he had the same resolve as theirs, he used other methods. Antiochus thought that he would be persuaded by appeals and by promises with oaths that he would make him rich and enviable, if he would turn away from the ways of his fathers, be enrolled among the tyrant's friends,[11] and be entrusted with royal affairs (2 Macc. 7:24). And when he got not even the first sign of a response, since the young man paid no attention to words so foreign to what he had freely chosen for himself, Antiochus called the mother to him and

---

11. An official title representing high rank.

urged her to advise the youth to save himself (2 Macc. 7:25). She pretended to persuade her son of what Antiochus wanted, but she mocked the tyrant and moved her son with many words about endurance. The result was that the young man did not wait for the torture to be brought, but took the initiative in summoning the officers ahead of time and said to them, "What are you waiting for, and why are you so slow? For we obey the Law given from God. It is not right to side with an ordinance contrary to the divine words." Moreover, like a king giving verdicts against those being judged by him, he pronounced judgment against the tyrant, judging him rather than being judged. And he said that since Antiochus had raised his hands against the children of heaven, he would not escape the judgment of the almighty, all-seeing God (2 Macc. 7:30–35).

XXVII. Then one could have seen the mother of such sons bearing their sufferings and deaths with good courage because of her hope in the Lord (2 Macc. 7:20). For the dews of true religion and the wind of holiness did not permit that fire of a mother's love which flames up in most women under such heavy evils to be kindled in her bowels. I think it extremely useful for what lies ahead to tell the story I have summarized from Scripture, so that we may see how much power against the harshest sufferings and the deepest tortures there is in religion and in the spell of love for God, which is immensely more powerful than any other love spell. Human weakness does not live in the same city with this spell of love for God, since it is driven abroad from the soul and has no power to act when a person can say, "The Lord is my strength and my song" (Ps. 118:14) and "I can do all things in Him who strengthens me, Christ Jesus our Lord" (Phil. 4:13; 1 Tim. 1:12).

XXVIII. We can also learn from this what martyrdom is like and how much confidence toward God it produces. Since a saint is generous and wishes to respond to the benefits that have overtaken him from God, he searches out what he can do for the Lord in return for everything he has obtained from Him. And he finds that nothing else can be given to God from a person of high purpose that will so balance His benefits as perfection in martyrdom. A reference to his perplexity may be found written in Psalm 116, "What shall I give back to the Lord for all His bounty to me?" (Ps. 116:12). And a reference to his solution of the perplexity about what he should give back to the Lord for everything he has received from Him may be found in the words, "I will take the cup of salvation and call on the name of the Lord" (Ps. 116:13). Martyrdom is customarily called "the cup of salvation," as we find in the Gospel. For when those who wish to sit on Jesus' right and left in His kingdom yearn for so great an honor, the Lord says to them, "Are you able to drink the cup that I am to drink?" (Mt. 20:22). He means by "cup" martyrdom; and the point is clear because of the verse, "Father, if it be possible, remove this cup from me; nevertheless, not as I will, but as you will" (Mk. 14:36; Mt. 26:39). We learn, moreover, that the person who drinks that cup which Jesus drank will sit with Him and rule and judge with the King of kings. Thus, this is "the cup of salvation"; and when someone takes it, he will "call on the name of the Lord." For whoever calls on the name of the Lord shall be saved (Joel 2:32; Acts 2:21; Rom. 10:13).

XXIX. But it is likely, because of the verse "Father, if it be possible, let this cup pass from me" (Mt. 26:39), that someone who does not accurately understand the intent of Scripture will suppose that the Savior proved a coward at the time of the Passion. And if He proved a coward, someone might say, who will ever prove to be noble? First, let us inquire of those who entertain such suppositions about the Savior whether He is inferior to the one who said, "The Lord is my light and my Savior; whom shall I fear? The Lord is the protector of my life; of whom shall I be afraid? When evildoers assail me to eat up my flesh, my persecutors and enemies grew weak and fell. Though a host encamp against me, my heart shall not fear; though war arise against me, yet I will be confident" (Ps. 27:1–3). But it may be that these words are spoken by the prophet of no one else but the Savior, who feared no one because of the light and salvation given from the Father, and who was afraid of no one because of the protection with which God shielded Him. And His heart was not at all fearful when the entire host of Satan encamped against Him. His heart, filled with sacred teachings, hoped in God when war rose up against Him. Therefore, it would be contradictory if it was from cowardice that He said, "Father, if it be possible, let this cup pass from me" (Mt. 26:39) and yet said with courage, "Though a host encamp against me, my heart shall not fear" (Ps. 27:3).

Perhaps, then, something in the passage has escaped our notice, and you will find it out by noting how the cup is mentioned in the three Gospels. Matthew writes that the Lord said, "Father, if it be possible, let *this* cup pass from me" (Mt. 26:39). Luke writes, "Father, if you are willing, remove *this* cup from me" (Lk. 22:42). Mark writes, "Abba, Father, all things are possible to you; remove *this* cup from me" (Mk. 14:36). Therefore, since every martyrdom completed by death for whatever motive is called a "cup," see whether you cannot say that when He says "let *this* cup pass from me," He does not refuse martyrdom in general, but only one kind. (Otherwise, He would have said, "let *the* cup pass from me.") Consider carefully whether it is not possible that the Savior saw, so to speak, what the different kinds of cups were and what would happen because of each of them, and that when He had considered their differences by some vast depth of wisdom, He refused one kind of martyr's death, while in secret He asked for another kind that was probably harder, so that some more general benefit that would overtake a greater number might be accomplished through that other cup. But this was not at all the Father's will, which was wiser than the Son's will, since He was ordering events by a way and an order beyond what the Savior saw. At any rate, clearly "the cup of salvation" in Psalms is the death of the martyrs. That is why the verse "I will take the cup of salvation and call on the name of the Lord" is followed by "Precious in the sight of the Lord is the death of His saints" (Ps. 116:13, 15). Therefore, death comes to us as "precious" if we are God's saints and worthy of dying not the common death, if I may call it that, but a special kind of death, Christian, religious, and holy.

XXX. Let us also remember the sins we have committed, and that it is impossible to receive forgiveness of sins apart from baptism, that it is impossible according to the laws of the Gospel to be baptized again with water and the Spirit for the forgiveness of sins, and that the baptism of martyrdom has been given to us. This is what it is called, as is evident from the fact that "Are you able to drink the cup that I drink?" is followed by "or to be baptized with the baptism with which I am baptized?" (Mk. 10:38). And in another place it is said, "I have a baptism to be baptized with, and how I am constrained until it is accomplished!" (Lk. 12:50). Consider, as well, whether baptism by martyrdom, just as the Savior's brought cleansing to the world, may not also serve to cleanse many. For just as those who served the altar according to the Law of Moses thought they were ministering forgiveness of sins to the people by the blood of goats and bulls (Heb. 9:13, 10:4; Ps. 50:13), so also the souls of those who have been beheaded for their witness to Jesus (Rev. 20:4, 6:9) do not serve the heavenly altar in vain and minister forgiveness of sins to those who pray. At the same time we also know that just as the High Priest Jesus the Christ offered Himself as a sacrifice (cf. Heb. 5:1, 7:27, 8:3, 10:12), so also the priests of whom He is High Priest offer themselves as a sacrifice. This is why they are seen near the altar as near their own place. Moreover, blameless priests served the Godhead by offering blameless sacrifices, while those who were blemished and offered blemished sacrifices and whom Moses described in Leviticus were separated from the altar (Lev. 21:17–21). And who else is the blameless priest offering a blameless sacrifice than the person who holds fast to his confession and fulfills every requirement the account of martyrdom demands? He is the one we have spoken of before.[12]

XXXI. But let us not be surprised if the martyrs' great blessedness, which will be theirs in deep peace, calm, and tranquillity, must take its beginning from such apparently gloomy and, so to speak, wintry conditions. For each one of the blessed will first be obliged to travel the narrow and hard way in winter (cf. Mt. 7:14) to show what knowledge he has acquired for guiding his life, so that afterwards there may take place what is said in Song of Songs to the bride when she has safely passed through the winter. For she says, "My beloved answers and says to me, 'Arise and come away, my love, my fair one, my dove; for lo, the winter is past, the rain is over and gone' " (Song 2:10–11). And you must keep in mind that you cannot hear "the winter is past" any other way than by entering the contest of this present winter with all your strength and might and main. And after the winter is past and the rain is over and gone, the flowers will appear that are planted in the house of the Lord and flourish in the courts of our God (Ps. 92:13).

---

12. Chapter 11.

XXXII. And we know that once we have been persuaded by Jesus to abandon idols and the atheism of worshiping many gods the Enemy cannot persuade us to commit idolatry, though he tries to force us. That is why he empowers those over whom he has authority to do such things, and he will make those who are tempted either martyrs or idolaters. And even now he says again and again, "All these I will give you, if you will fall down and worship me" (Mt. 4:9). Let us then take great care never to commit idolatry and subject ourselves to demons; for the idols of the Gentiles are demons (cf. Ps. 96:5, 1 Chron. 16:26). What a state the person is in who has deserted the easy yoke and the light burden of Christ (Mt. 11:30) to subject himself once again to the yoke of demons and to bear the burden of the heaviest sin! How can this be after we have known that the heart of those who worship idols is ashes (cf. Wis. 15:10) and their life more worthless than clay (cf. Jer. 16:19) and after we have said, "Our fathers possessed false idols, and none of them can bring rain"? (Jer. 14:22).

XXXIII. It was not just of old that Nebuchadnezzar's image of gold was set up, nor only then that he threatened Ananias, Azarias, and Misael that he would throw them into the burning fiery furnace unless they worshiped it (cf. Dan: 3). Even now Nebuchadnezzar says the same thing to us, the true Hebrews in exile from our homeland. But as for us, let us imitate those holy men so that we may experience the heavenly dew that quenches every fire that arises in us and cools our governing mind. Perhaps even now Haman wishes you Morecais to bow down to him. But you must say, "I will not set the glory of men above the glory of the God of Israel" (Esther 4:17 LXX; English Apocrypha 13:14). Let us overturn Bel by the Word of God, and let us slay the dragon with Daniel, so that when we come near the lions' mouths, we may be able to suffer nothing from them, while only those to blame for our present contest will be devoured by the lions that cannot eat us up (Bel and Dragon). Let us endure because among the noble deeds of Job it is said, "If I put my hand to my mouth and kissed it, this would be reckoned the greatest iniquity for me" (Job 31:27–28). And it is likely they will order us to put our hand to our mouth and kiss it.[13]

---

13. A gesture meaning worship of a pagan god.

XXXIV. Let us also observe that it is not in His addresses to the many that prophecies of martyrdom are made, but in those to the apostles. For first it is said, "These twelve Jesus sent out, charging them, 'Go nowhere among the Gentiles,' and the rest" (Mt. 10:5). Then there is added, "Beware of men; for they will deliver you up to councils, and flog you in their synagogues, and you will be dragged before governors and kings for my sake, to bear testimony before them and the Gentiles. When they deliver you up, do not be anxious how you are to speak or what you are to say; for what you are to say will be given to you in that hour; for it is not you who speak, but the Spirit of your Father speaking through you. Brother will deliver brother up to death, and the father his child, and children will rise against parents and have them put to death; and you will be hated by all for my name's sake. But he who endures to the end will be saved. When they persecute you in one town, flee to the next; for truly, I say to you, you will not have gone through all the towns of Israel, before the Son of Man comes" (Mt. 10:17–23).

And Luke writes as follows, "And when they bring you before the synagogues and the rulers and the authorities, do not be anxious how or what you are to answer or what you are to say; for the Holy Spirit will teach you in that very hour what you ought to say" (Lk. 12:11–12). And later on in his Gospel, "Settle it therefore in your minds not to meditate beforehand how to answer; for I will give you a mouth and wisdom, which none of your adversaries will be able to withstand or contradict. You will be delivered up even by parents and brothers and kinsmen and friends, and some of you they will put to death; you will be hated by all for my name's sake. But not a hair of your head will perish. By your endurance you will gain your lives" (Lk. 21:14–19).

Mark also has the following, "And when they bring you to trial and deliver you up, do not be anxious beforehand what you are to say; but say whatever is given you in that hour; for it is not you who speak, but the Holy Spirit. And brother will deliver up brother to death, and the father his child, and children will rise against parents and have them put to death; and you will be hated by all for my name's sake. But he who endures to the end will be saved" (Mk. 13:11–13).

AN EXHORTATION TO MARTYRDOM

Also the following exhortation to martyrdom, found in Matthew, was spoken to no others but the Twelve. We, too, should hear it, since by hearing it we shall be brothers of the apostles who heard it and shall be numbered with the apostles. This is the passage: "Do not fear those who kill the body but cannot kill the soul; rather fear Him who can destroy both soul and body in hell" (Mt. 10:28). And in the verses that follow the Lord teaches us that no one comes to the contest of martyrdom without providence. For it is said, "Are not two sparrows sold for a penny? And not one of them will fall to the ground without your Father in heaven. But even the hairs of your head are all numbered. Fear not, therefore; you are of more value than many sparrows. So every one who confesses me before men, I also will confess before my Father who is in heaven; but whoever denies me before men, I also will deny before my Father who is in heaven" (Mt. 10:29–33).

The following passage in Luke has the same meaning, "I tell you, my friends, do not fear those who kill the body, and after that have no more that they can do. But I will warn you whom to fear; fear Him who, after He has killed, has power to cast into hell; yes, I tell you, fear Him! Are not five sparrows sold for two pennies? And not one of them is forgotten before God. Why, even the hairs of your head are all numbered. Fear not; you are of more value than many sparrows. And I tell you, every one who confesses me before men, the Son of Man also will confess before the angels of God; but he who denies me before men will be denied before the angels of God" (Lk. 12:4–9). And in another place, "For whoever is ashamed of me and of my words, of him will the Son of Man be ashamed when He comes in His glory and the glory of the Father and of the holy angels" (Lk. 9:26). And Mark writes in a similar vein as follows, "For whoever is ashamed of me and of my words in this adulterous and sinful generation, of him will the Son of Man also be ashamed, when He comes in the glory of His Father with the holy angels" (Mk. 8:38).

Therefore, those who destroy us kill the life of the body; for such is the meaning of "fear not those who kill the body," found in the same words in both Matthew and Luke (Mt. 10:28; Lk. 12:4). And after killing the body, even if they wish, they cannot kill the soul; indeed, they have "no more than they can do" (Lk. 12:4). For how could the soul that has been made alive by the confession itself be destroyed? And in Isaiah the One who exhorts us to martyrdom joins in bearing witness to this with His Son. The passage reads, "You are my witnesses, and I am a witness, says the Lord God, and the Son whom I have chosen" (Is. 43:10 LXX).

And notice that this commandment is given not to Jesus' servants but to His friends (cf. Jn. 15:15), "Do not fear those who kill the body, and after that have no more that they can do" (Lk. 12:4). Therefore, the One to be feared is "Him who can destroy both soul and body in hell" (Mt. 10:28). For He alone "after He has killed" has "power to cast into hell" (Lk. 12:5). Those He casts into hell are they who fear those who kill the body and do not fear "Him who, after He has killed, has power to cast into hell." We may suppose that no matter who else has the hairs of his head numbered, the verse is obviously true of those who are cut off for Jesus. Therefore, we shall confess the Son of God before men and not before gods, that He who is confessed may confess us in turn before God and His Father, and confess the one who confessed Him on earth Himself in heaven.

XXXV. Who would ponder these considerations and not utter the apostolic cry "The sufferings of this present time are not worth comparing with the glory that is to be revealed to us!" (Rom. 8:18). For how can the confession before the Father fail to be much greater than the confession before men? And how can the confession made in heaven by the One who had been confessed fail to exceed in the highest degree the confession made by the martyrs on earth of the Son of God? But if anyone considers denying before men, let him remember the One who cannot lie and who said, "I also will deny him before my Father who is in heaven" (Mt. 10:33).

Now since Matthew wrote "I also will confess him before my Father who is in heaven," while Luke has "the Son of Man will also confess him before the angels of God" (Mt. 10:32; Lk. 12:8), I suggest that perhaps the First Born of all creation, the image of the invisible God (cf. Col. 1:15; 2 Cor. 4:4; Wis. 7:26) confesses the confessor before the Father in heaven; but the one born of the seed of David according to the flesh (Rom. 1:3), who is consequently the Son of Man, is the one who confesses the confessors before the angels of God. He is the one born of a woman (Gal. 4:4), who is herself human, and is therefore called the Son of Man, a term understood to refer to the Man in relation to Jesus.[14] And the corresponding view should also be taken concerning those who deny.

Furthermore, we must recognize that the person who confesses the Son before men commends, as far as it is his to do so, Christianity and the Father of Christianity to those before whom he confesses. But the one who is confessed by the First Born of all creation and by the Son of Man is commended through the confession of the Son of God and the Son of Man to the Father in heaven and to the angels of God. And if it is not the one who commends himself that is tried and true, but the one whom the Lord commends (2 Cor. 10:18), must we not suppose that the one tried and true is the one judged worthy of commendation to the Father in heaven and to the angels of God? And if the tried and true are this person and those like him, whom the Lord tried with tortures and tests like gold in the furnace and accepted like a sacrificial burnt offering (Wis. 3:6), what must we say about those who were tried in the furnace of temptation and denied? He who denies the person deserving denial denies them as tried but not true before the Father in heaven and before the angels of God.

XXXVI. And the contest must be waged not only to escape denial, but also to escape feeling the first inclination to shame when we are thought by those alien to God to be suffering what deserves shame. This is especially true of you, holy Ambrose, who have been honored and welcomed by a great many cities, if now, as it were, you go in procession bearing the cross of Jesus and following Him when He brings you before governors and kings (cf. Mt. 16:24; Mk. 8:34; Lk. 9:23). His purpose is to go with you and to give you speech and wisdom—and to you, Protoctetus, his fellow contestant, and to you others who suffer martyrdom with them and complete what is lacking in Christ's afflictions (Col. 1:24). And He is with you to show you the way to the paradise of God and how you may pass through the cherubim and the flaming sword that turns every way and guards the way to the tree of life (Gen. 3:24).

---

14. In Greek *ho kata ton Iēsoun anthrōpos*, an expression often found in Origen's writings for the human aspect of Christ.

For both, even if they guard the way to the tree of life, guard it so that no one unworthy may turn that way to pass through to the tree of life. The flaming sword will hold fast those who have built upon the foundation that is laid, Jesus Christ, with wood, hay, or straw (1 Cor. 3:11–12), and the wood, if I may call it that, of denial, which catches fire very easily and burns all the more. But the cherubim will receive those who by nature cannot be held by the flaming sword, because they have built with nothing that can catch fire; and they will escort them to the tree of life and to all the trees God planted in the east and made to grow out of the ground (Gen. 2:8–9). So, since Jesus is your guide to paradise, despise the serpent that has been conquered and crushed beneath Jesus' feet—and beneath yours through Him who gave you authority to tread upon serpents and scorpions and over all the power of the Enemy, so that none of them may hurt you (cf. Lk. 10:19; Rom. 16:20).

XXXVII. Thus, we must neither deny the Son of God nor be ashamed of Him or His own or His words; but we must listen to this, "Whoever denies me before men, I also will deny before my Father who is in heaven" (Mt. 10:33); and this, "Whoever is ashamed of me and of my words, of him will the Son of Man be ashamed when He comes in His glory and the glory of the Father and of the holy angels" (Lk. 9:26); and this, "For whoever is ashamed of me and of my words in this adulterous and sinful generation, of him will the Son of Man also be ashamed, when He comes in the glory of His Father with the holy angels" (Mk. 8:38).

Jesus once endured the cross, despising the shame, and therefore is seated at the right hand of God (Heb. 12:2, 8:1). And those who imitate Him by despising the shame will be seated with Him and will rule in heaven (cf. 2 Tim. 2:12) with Him who came not to bring peace on earth but to the souls of His disciples and to bring a sword on earth (Mt. 10:34). For since the Word of God is living and active, sharper than any two-edged sword, piercing to the division of soul and spirit, of joints and marrow, and discerning the thoughts and intentions of the heart (Heb. 4:12), this Word especially now awards our souls the prize of the peace that passes all understanding, which He left to His apostles (cf. Phil. 4:7; Jn. 14:27). And He draws a sword between the image of the man of dust and the image of the Man of heaven (cf. 1 Cor. 15:49), so that by taking our heavenly part at this time He may later make us entirely heavenly, if we are worthy of not remaining cut in two.

And He came to bring on earth not only a sword, but also fire, concerning which He says, "Would that it were already kindled!" (Lk. 12:49; cf. Mt. 10:34). Therefore, let this fire be kindled also in you to destroy every one of your thoughts that is earthly and drawn toward the body. And with great eagerness be baptized now with the baptism about which Jesus was constrained until it was accomplished (Lk. 12:50). And you, Ambrose, who have a wife and children, brothers and sisters, remember the saying, "If anyone comes to me and does not hate his own father and mother and wife and children and fathers and sisters . . . he cannot be my disciple." And both of you, Ambrose and Protoctetus, remember that "if any one comes to me and does not hate in addition to the former things even his own soul, he cannot be my disciple" (Lk. 14:26). So hate your own souls that by hating them you may keep them for eternal life. For He says, "He who hates his soul in this world will keep it for eternal life" (Jn. 12:25). Therefore, hate your souls because of eternal life, persuaded that the hatred Jesus teaches is noble and useful. And just as we must hate our souls so that they may be kept for eternal life, so you, Ambrose, who have them, must hate your wife and children, your brothers and sisters, so that you may help the ones you hate by becoming a friend of God through that very hatred and so receiving the freedom to benefit them.

XXXVIII. At the same time remember the one who prayed in the Spirit for the children whom the martyrs left behind because of their love for God, and asked God "to preserve the sons of those who have been put to death" (Ps. 78:11 LXX). Only bear in mind that it is not the children of the flesh who are the children of God (Rom. 9:8). Just as it is said to those of the seed of Abraham, "I know that you are the seed of Abraham" and "if you were Abraham's children, you would do what Abraham did" (Jn. 8:37, 39), so also it will be said to your children, "I know that you are the seed of Ambrose" and "if you were Ambrose's children, you would do what Ambrose did." And probably they will do it, since you will give them more help after such a death than you would if you remained with them. For then you will love them with more understanding and will pray for them more wisely, if you learn that they are your children and not merely your seed. Now have the words ready, "He who loves son or daughter more than me is not worthy of me" and "He who finds his soul will lose it, and he who loses his soul for my sake will find it" (Mt. 10:37, 39).

XXXIX. Through your eagerness for martyrdom give place to the Spirit of your Father, which speaks in those who are arrested for their religion (cf. Mt. 10:20). If you know yourselves hated and abominated and considered impious, then take up the saying "For this reason the world hates you, because you are not of this world; if you were of this world, the world would love its own" (cf. Jn. 15:19). By the One in whom you have believed endure to the end many reproaches for Christ and many dangers. Go forward by enduring, because he who endures to the end will be saved (Mt. 10:22). Know that, according to Peter, you will rejoice, "though now for a little while you may have to be grieved by various trials, so that the genuineness of your faith, more precious than gold which though perishable is tested by fire, may redound to praise and glory and honor at the revelation of Jesus Christ" (1 Pet. 1:6–7). Moreover, hear "grieved" as though it said "suffered," as is indicated by "in griefs you shall bring forth children" (Gen. 3:16). For a woman by no means experiences grief in bearing children, but rather suffering.

We may suppose that the following passage is helpful for Christ's disciples, "Do not love the world or the things in the world. If any one loves the world, love for the Father is not in him. For all that is in the world, the lust of the flesh and the lust of the eyes and the pride of life, is not of the Father but is of the world. And the world passes away, and the lust of it" (1 John 2:15–17). Therefore, do not love what is passing away; but by doing the will of God become worthy of becoming one with the Son and the Father and the Holy Spirit according to the prayer of the Savior, who said, "As I and you are one, that they also may be one in us" (cf. Jn. 17:21). How many days is it possible to gain by loving "the world or the things in the world"—and by losing or destroying one's own soul, by carrying about a conscience weighed down by a burden too heavy, weighed down by the fall of denial? (cf. 1 John 2:15; Mt. 10:39, 16:25; Mk. 8:35; Lk. 9:24; Ps. 38:4). Let us each remember how many times he has been in danger of dying an ordinary death, and let us consider that perhaps we have been preserved so that baptized with our own blood and washed of every sin we may pass our existence with our fellow contestants near the altar in heaven (cf. Rev. 6:9).

XL. But if anyone because of his love of life or his weakness in the face of sufferings or of arguments he thinks plausible should allow himself to be brought over to their side by those who try to persuade us to baser conduct, and if he should deny that there is one God and His Christ and confess demons or Fortunes, let him know that by preparing "a table for the demon" and by filling "a cup for Fortune" (Is. 65:11; Prov. 9:2) he forsakes the Lord and forgets His holy mountain in yielding to these disgraces. Isaiah described it this way, "But you who forsake me and forget my holy mountain and prepare a table for the demon and fill a cup for Fortune, I will deliver you to the sword, and all of you shall fall in the slaughter, because I called you and you did not obey, I spoke and you did not listen, but you did what was evil in my sight and chose what I did not wish. Therefore, thus says the Lord God: 'Behold, my servants shall eat, but you shall be hungry; behold, my servants shall drink, but you shall be thirsty; behold, my servants shall rejoice, but you shall be put to shame; behold, my servants shall sing for gladness of heart, but you shall cry out for pain of heart, and shall wail for anguish of spirit. For you shall leave my name to my chosen for abundance, and the Lord will destroy you' " (Is. 65:11–15). Moreover, if we understand what the table of the Lord is and wish to partake of it, let us bear in mind the verse "You cannot partake of the table of the Lord and the table of demons" (1 Cor. 10:21). And if we understand what the verse means, "I tell you I shall not drink again of this fruit of the vine until that day when I drink it new with you in the kingdom of heaven" (Mt. 26:29). And if we so wish to be found with those who drink with Jesus, let us heed the warning, "You cannot drink the cup of the Lord and the cup of demons" (1 Cor. 10:21).

Suppose someone has heard John the son of thunder (cf. Mk. 3:17) say, "He denies the Father and the Son . . . no one who denies the Son has the Father. He who confesses the Son has the Father also" (1 John 2:22–23). Will such a person not be afraid to deny the Son by saying he is not a Christian, since by denying Him he does not have the Father? And who would not be encouraged to confess himself a Christian in deeds and words so that he might have the Father also? For those who confess have the Father.

XLI. If we have passed from death to life by passing from unbelief to faith, let us not be surprised if the world hates us (cf. Jn. 5:24, 15:18; 1 John 3:14). For no one who has failed to pass from death to life but has remained in death can love those who have passed from the darkened house of death, so to speak, to the houses built of living stones and filled with the light of life (cf. 1 Pet. 2:5; Jn. 8:12; Eph. 2:20–22). Jesus laid down His soul for us (cf. 1 John 3:16); let us, then, lay ours down, not I shall say for Him, but for ourselves—and, I think it may be also, for those who will be built up by our martyrdom. A time of boasts is present for us Christians. For it says, "More than that, we boast in our sufferings, knowing that suffering produces endurance, and endurance produces character, and character produces hope, and hope is not ashamed; only, let the love of God be poured into our hearts through the Holy Spirit" (cf. Rom. 5:3–5). Let Paul say, "Suppose, humanly speaking, I fought with beasts at Ephesus" (1 Cor. 15:32). Let us say, "Suppose, humanly speaking, I was executed in Germany."[15]

XLII. If as the sufferings of Christ abound so also comfort abounds through Christ (2 Cor. 1:5), let us welcome the great encouragement of Christ's sufferings and let them abound in us, if we indeed yearn for the abundant comfort with which all who mourn will be comforted, though perhaps it will not be alike for everyone (cf. Mt. 5:4). For if the comfort were alike for everyone, it would not be written, "As the sufferings of Christ abound for us, so also our comfort abounds through Christ" (2 Cor. 1:5). Those who share in sufferings will share also in the comfort in proportion to the suffering they share with Christ. And we learn this from the one who made such statements with unshaken conviction, for "we know that as you share in our sufferings, you will also share in our comfort" (2 Cor. 1:7).

And God says through the prophet, "In an acceptable time I have heard you, and in a day of salvation I have helped you" (Is.

---

15. The Emperor Maximin won his victory over Alexander Severus on the Rhine frontier and was presumably still in Germany when Origen wrote.

49:8; 2 Cor. 6:2). What other time, then, is more acceptable than when for piety toward God in Christ we are led under guard in procession before the world, celebrating a triumph rather than being led in triumph? For the martyrs in Christ disarm the principalities and powers with Him, and they share His triumph as fellows of His sufferings, becoming in this way also fellows of the courageous deeds wrought in His sufferings (cf. Col. 2:15). These deeds include triumphing over the principalities and powers, which in a short time you will see conquered and put to shame. What other day is so much a day of salvation as the one when we gain such a deliverance from them? But I urge you, place "no obstacle in any one's way, so that no fault may be found" on your account with the presbytery or the diaconate (2 Cor. 6:3ff.).[16] But commend yourselves "in every way as the ministers of God": through great "endurance," saying, "And now, what is my endurance? Is it not the Lord?" (Ps. 39:7); in "afflictions," persuaded that "many are the afflictions of the righteous" (Ps. 34:19); in "necessities," so that we may ask for the blessedness necessary for us; in "difficult straits," so that by traveling steadily on the straitened and narrow path (cf. Mt. 7:14) we may arrive at life. If it is necessary, let us recommend ourselves also "in beatings, imprisonments, tumults, labors, watching, and fasting" (2 Cor. 6:5). For behold, the Lord is here, and His reward is in His hand to give to each according to his works (cf. Is. 40:10, 62:11; Ps. 62:12; Rom. 2:6; Rev. 2:23, 22:12).

XLIII. Now let us prove that we have yearned for "knowledge" on account of deeds befitting knowledge. Let all "purity" from every defilement of whatever kind in whatever sin be made evident in us. As sons of a forbearing God and brothers of a forbearing Christ, let us show "forbearance" in everything that happens to us; for "the man of forbearance has great understanding; but he who has a hasty temper is a fool" (Prov. 14:29). If we must commend ourselves "with the weapons of righteousness for the right hand and for the left," in commending ourselves in "honor" and not becoming conceited by it, now let us also endure "dishonor" (2 Cor. 6:7–8). If we have lived a life deserving "good repute" and have

---

16. Chapters 42 and 43 are a meditation on 2 Corinthians 6, first introduced by the citation of Isaiah 49:8.

been spoken well of, now let us also bear up under "ill repute" from the ungodly. Still more, if we have been admired as "true" by those who love truth, now let us laugh at being called "imposters." During the many dangers from which we have been delivered many said that we were "well known" by God; now let the one who wishes call us "unknown," when we are probably better known. Thus, in bearing what has happened to us we are "punished" and yet "not killed," and though "rejoicing," we resemble those who are "sorrowful" (cf. 2 Cor. 6:8–10).

XLIV. Paul speaks in one place to those who have endured at the beginning and encourages them to bear the second set of dangers they faced because of the Word with an endurance matching the first: "But recall the former days when, after you were enlightened, you endured a hard struggle with sufferings, sometimes being publicly exposed to abuse and affliction, and sometimes being partners with those so treated. For you had compassion on the prisoners, and you joyfully accepted the plundering of your property, since you knew that you yourselves had a better possession and an abiding one. Therefore do not throw away your confidence, which has a great reward. For you have need of endurance" (Heb. 10:32–36). Therefore, let us, as well, now endure a hard struggle with sufferings, being publicly exposed to abuse and affliction and joyfully accepting the plundering of our property. For we are persuaded we have a better possession that is not earthly or corporeal, but one that is invisible and incorporeal. And we look not to the things that are seen, since we realize that they are transient, while the others are eternal (2 Cor. 4:18).

XLV. Now there are some who do not understand the law by which demons live and that to remain in this thick atmosphere of earth they need the food of rising smoke, and so they keep an eye on places where there are always the smell and blood of burnt sacrifices and incense fumes. Now there are some people who, ignoring this, count sacrificing cheap, as though it were a matter of indifference. We should answer their opinion by saying that if those who give food to robbers, murderers, and the barbarian enemies of the great king have wronged the common good and are punished, how much more should those who by sacrificing give food to the servants of evil that will maintain them in this earthly region be prosecuted with the greatest justice, especially if after learning that whoever sacrifices to any god, save to the Lord only, shall be utterly destroyed (Ex. 22:20), they sacrifice to those who are to blame for the evils on earth. Indeed, I think that they will be prosecuted for the sins committed by the demons who work against men no less than the demons who work these evils, because they have fed them by sacrificing. For the demons and those who have maintained them on earth bear joint responsibility for bringing evils to men, since the demons could not hold out without the rising smoke and the foods thought to correspond to their bodies.

XLVI. Furthermore, there are some who suppose that names are merely conventional and have no relation in nature to the things for which the names stand.[17] And so they think there is no difference whether a person says "I worship the first god" or "Dios" or "Zeus," and no difference whether a person affirms "I honor and welcome the sun" or "Apollo," "the moon" or "Artemis," "the spirit in the earth" or "Demeter," and all the others the wise men of the Greeks speak of. They must be told that the subject of names is something very deep and recondite and that if someone understands it, he will see that if names were merely conventional, then the demons or any other invisible powers when summoned would not obey those who know their names and name the names that have been given. But as it is, certain sounds and syllables and expressions, aspirated or unaspirated and with a long or a short vowel, when they are spoken aloud, by some unseen nature immediately bring to us those who are summoned. If this is so and names are not merely conventional, then the first God must not be called by any other name than the ones by which the worshiper, the prophets, and our Savior and Lord Himself named Him, such as Sabaoth, Adonai, Saddai, and further, the God of Abraham, the God of Isaac, and the God of Jacob. For it says, "This is my name for ever, and thus I am to be remembered throughout all generations" (Ex. 3:15). And it is not surprising if the demons attribute their own names to the first God in order to be worshiped as the first God. But this is not the custom for anyone who worships as we do, or for the prophets, for Christ the fulfillment of the Law, or for

---

17. Cf. *Contra Celsum* I.24, V.45.

His apostles. We have introduced these considerations necessarily, lest anyone should trick us with false arguments or defile our reasoning in the least respect. We must give careful attention to them if we are to give no opportunity for interference on the part of our opponents.

XLVII. Moreover, a person will still love life, even when he has become convinced of the rational being of the soul, which has a certain kinship with God. For both are intelligible and invisible and, as the prevailing argument demonstrates, incorporeal. Why would our Maker have instilled within us a yearning for true religion and fellowship with Him, that even when we stumble preserves certain traces of the divine will, if it were impossible and unattainable for rational beings to gain what they yearn for by nature? And it is clear that just as each one of our members is constituted by nature to preserve a relation proper to it, the eyes in relation to what is visible, the ear in relation to what is audible, so also the mind preserves a relation to what is intelligible and to God, who transcends the intelligible order. Therefore, why do we hang back and hesitate to put off the perishable body, the earthly tent that hinders us, weighs down the soul, and burdens the thoughtful mind (Wis. 9:15)? Why do we hesitate to burst our bonds and to depart from the stormy billows of a life with flesh and blood (cf. Phil. 1:23; 1 Cor. 15:50)? Let our purpose be to enjoy with Christ Jesus the rest proper to blessedness, contemplating Him, the Word, wholly living. By Him we shall be nourished; in Him we shall receive the manifold wisdom and be modeled by the Truth Himself. By the true and unceasing Light of knowledge our minds will be enlightened to gaze upon what is by nature to be seen in that Light with eyes illuminated by the Lord's commandment (cf. Ps. 19:8; Eph. 1:18).

XLVIII. Long ago we heard the words of Jesus, and it is already a great while since we became disciples of the Gospel. And all of us have built ourselves a house. But where we have built, whether upon the rock by digging deep or upon the sand without a foundation, the present contest will show (cf. Mt. 7:24–28; Lk. 6:48–49). For winter has come bringing rains and floods and winds, or as Luke calls it, a "deluge." And when they break against the house, either they will not be strong enough to shake it and, consequently, the house will not fall, since it has been founded on the rock, Christ; or they will prove the building unsound, since it will fall because of what has come against it. May this be far from our buildings! Great indeed is the fall in denial or, as Luke says, "great is the ruin" of a building without a foundation (Lk. 6:49). Therefore, let us pray that we may be like the wise man who built his house upon the rock (Mt. 7:24). Let them come upon such a building—the rain from the spirits of wickedness in the heavenly places (cf. Eph . 6:12), or the floods of our enemies, the principalities and powers, or the harsh winds from the world rulers of this darkness, or the deluge of infernal spirits. And let them break themselves against our house built on the rock, so that in addition to the house's not falling and not even beginning to be shaken, they may because of us suffer the effects of their own activity rather than direct them at us. And let each one of you say when you smite the opposing spirits, "I do not box as one beating the air" (1 Cor. 9:26).

XLIX. Moreover, since the Sower has gone out to sow, let us show that our souls have received His seed neither like those along the path nor like the rocky ground nor like the thorns, but like the good soil (Mt. 13:3ff. and parallels). Thus, as much as lies in us we shall boast in the Lord that the word of Jesus has fallen neither along the path nor upon thorns. We have understood what was said, and so the Evil One has not snatched away what was sown in our hearts. And many will bear witness of us that it was not sown upon thorns, for they will see that neither the care of this world nor the deceit of wealth nor the pleasures of life have been able to thwart the word of God in our souls. For the rest people may be uncertain whether the word of God so far as it concerns us has fallen on rocky ground or on the good soil. For affliction and persecution because of the word has come; and the time of great temptation is present, when what was sown on rocky ground will be found out, as will those who have not dug deeply enough and have not accepted Jesus to the depth of their soul. But the one who understands the word bears fruit and keeps the word to the end by endurance, bearing a hundred-fold.

We hear how Scripture presents those who in a time of tribulation or persecution are offended, after appearing to receive the holy teachings with joy. And they stumble because they have no root, but believe for a while. According to Matthew the passage reads, "As for what was sown on rocky ground, this is he who hears the word and immediately receives it with joy; yet he has no root in himself, but endures for a while, and when tribulation or persecution arises on account of the word, immediately he falls away" (Mt. 13:20–21). According to Mark we read, "And these are the ones sown upon rocky ground, who, when they hear the word, immediately receive it with joy; and they have no root in themselves, but endure for a while; then, when tribulation or persecution arises on account of the word, immediately they fall away" (Mk. 4:16–17). According to Luke we read, "And the ones on the rock are those who, when they hear the word, receive it with joy; but these have no root, they believe for a while and in time of temptation fall away" (Lk. 8:13). But in teaching about those who bear fruit well Scripture says, "As for what was sown on good soil, this is he who hears the word and understands it; he indeed bears fruit, and yields, in one case a hundred-fold, in another sixty, and in another thirty" (Mt. 13:23). Or, "But those that were sown upon the good soil are the ones who hear the word and accept it and bear fruit, thirty-fold and sixty-fold and a hundred-fold" (Mk. 4:20). Or, "And as for that in the good soil, they are those who, hearing the word, hold it fast in an honest and good heart, and bring forth fruit with endurance" (Lk. 8:15).

Therefore, since, according to the Apostle, "you are God's planting, God's building" (cf. 1 Cor. 3:9), a planting in the good soil and a building on the rock, as God's building let us stand unshaken before the wintry storm, and as God's planting let us not think about the Evil One or about the tribulation or persecution that happens on account of the word or about the care of this age or about the deceit of wealth or about the pleasures of life. Rather, despising all these, let us receive the Spirit of wisdom, which is without care (Wis. 7:23). Let us hasten to the wealth that has no deceit whatever. Let us hasten to the pleasures, so to speak, of the paradise of delight, considering in each of our sufferings that this light momentary affliction is preparing for us an eternal weight of glory beyond all comparison, because we look not to things that are seen but to the things that are unseen (2 Cor. 4:17–18).

L. We also know that what was said of Abel, when he was

slain by the wicked murderer Cain, is suitable for all whose blood has been shed wickedly. For let us suppose that the verse "The voice of your brother's blood is crying to me from the ground" (Gen. 4:10) is said, as well, for each of the martyrs, the voice of whose blood cries to God from the ground.

And perhaps just as we have been redeemed by the precious blood of Jesus, who received the name above every name (cf. 1 Pet. 1:19; Rev. 5:9; Phil. 2:9), so some will be redeemed by the precious blood of the martyrs, since they too have been exalted beyond the exaltation of those who were righteous but did not become martyrs. For there is good reason to call the special kind of death that is martyrdom an exaltation, as is clear from the verse "When I am exalted from the earth, I will draw all men to myself" (Jn. 12:32). Let us, then, glorify God, exalting Him by our own death, since the martyr will glorify God by his own death. This is what we have learned from John, when he says, "This He said to show by what death He was to glorify God" (Jn. 21:19).

LI. This, then, as far as I am able and it has been possible, is my advice to you. I pray that it may prove helpful to you in the present contest. But if, especially now since you are worthy of seeing more of God's mysteries, you should have a greater and richer understanding, more effectual for what lies ahead, and should despise my words as childish and common, I should myself pray that this would be your case. For it is not most important that you be helped in your present straits by me, but that you be helped in whatever way possible. May you, indeed, be helped by words more divine, more understanding, greater than the whole of human nature, and by the wisdom of God.

ON PRAYER

I. There are realities that are so great that they find a rank superior to humanity and our mortal nature; they are impossible for our rational and mortal race to understand. Yet by the grace of God poured forth with measureless abundance from Him to men through that minister of unsurpassed grace to us, Jesus Christ, and through that fellow worker with the will of God, the Spirit, these realities have become possible for us. Indeed, the possession of the wisdom by which everything was established—for according to David God made "everything by wisdom" (cf. Ps. 104:24)—was an impossibility for human nature. But from an impossibility it became a possibility through our Lord Jesus Christ, whom God made our wisdom, our righteousness and sanctification and redemption (1 Cor. 1:30). For what man can learn the counsel of God? Or who can discern what the Lord wills? For the reasoning of mortals is worthless, and our designs are likely to fail, for a perishable body weighs down the soul, and this earthly tent burdens the thoughtful mind. We can hardly guess at what is on earth, but who has traced out what is in the heavens (Wis. 9:13–16)? Who would not admit that it is impossible for a human being to trace out what is in the heavens? Nevertheless, this impossibility has become a possibility by the boundless excellence of the grace of God (cf. 2 Cor. 9:14). For it is likely that he who was caught up into the third heaven traced out what was in those three heavens, because he heard things that cannot be told, which man may not utter (2 Cor. 12:2–4). And who could say that it is possible for a human being to know the mind of the Lord? Nevertheless, even this is given by God through Christ. [For He says, "No longer do I call you servants, for the servant does not know what his master is doing; but I have called you friends, for all that I have heard from my Father I have made known to you" (Jn. 15:14–15). He makes known to them when they are servants][18] the will of Him who is no longer their Lord. He teaches them the will of Him who wishes no longer to be Lord, but turns into a friend of those whose Lord He once was. Moreover, just as no one "among men knows a man's thoughts except the spirit of the man which is in him, so also no one knows the thoughts of God except the Spirit of God" (1 Cor. 2:11). If no one knows the thoughts of God except the Spirit of God, it is impossible for a human being to know the thoughts of God. But now consider this—how it becomes possible. "Now we," he says, "have received not the spirit of the world, but the Spirit which is from God, that we might understand the gifts bestowed on us by God. And we impart this in words not taught by human wisdom but taught by the Spirit" (1 Cor. 2:12–13).

II.1. Now, my most religious and industrious Ambrose and my most honest and manly Tatiana, from whom I vow womanish things have vanished just as they did from Sarah (cf. Gen. 18:11), you are probably puzzled as to why, when my proposed subject is prayer, I speak in my preface of things impossible for human beings made possible by the grace of God. My conviction, so far as my weakness allows, is that one of these impossible things is giving a clear account of prayer that will be accurate and religious—for what and how we ought to pray, and what we should say to God in prayer, and what times are more appropriate than others for prayer.[19] . . . [We know that Paul] was cautious about the abundance of revelations so that no one might think more of him than he saw or heard of him (cf. 2 Cor. 12:6–7). And he confessed that he did not know how to pray "as we ought." For he says, "What we ought to pray for as we ought we do not know" (Rom. 8:26). It is necessary not only to pray, but also to pray "as we ought" and to pray for what we ought. Our attempt to understand what we should pray for is deficient unless we also bring to our quest the "as we ought." Likewise, what use to us is the "as we ought" if we do not know for what we should pray?

---

18. The brackets enclose Koetschau's conjectural attempt to fill a lacuna of 3½ lines in the manuscript.

19. A lacuna of 4¹/₅ lines follows in the manuscript.

2. One of these two, I mean the "what we ought," consists of the words of prayer, while the "as we ought" refers to the disposition of the person praying. The following sayings are examples of the "what we ought": "Seek the great things and the little things will be added for you; seek the heavenly things and the earthly things will be added for you";[20] "Pray for those who abuse you" (Lk. 6:28); "Pray therefore the Lord of the harvest to send out laborers into His harvest" (Mt. 9:38; Lk. 10:2); "Pray that you may not enter into temptation" (Lk. 22:40; Mt. 26:41; Mk. 14:38); "Pray that your flight may not be in winter or on a sabbath" (Mt. 24:20; Mk. 13:8); "And in praying do not heap up empty phrases" (Mt. 6:7). Similar sayings could be added. The following sayings apply to the "as we ought": "I desire then that in every place the men should pray, lifting holy hands without anger or quarreling; also that women should adorn themselves modestly and sensibly in seemly apparel, not with braided hair or gold or pearls or costly attire but by good deeds, as befits women who profess religion" (1 Tim. 2:8–10). The following saying also teaches about the "as we ought": "So if you are offering your gift at the altar, and there remember that your brother has something against you, leave your gift there before the altar and go; first be reconciled to your brother, and then come and offer your gift" (Mt. 5:23–24). For what better gift can a rational being send up to God than the fragrant word of prayer, when it is offered from a conscience untainted with the foul smell of sin? Another example of the "as we ought" is: "Do not refuse one another except perhaps by agreement for a season, that you may devote yourselves to prayer; but then come together again, lest Satan rejoice over you[21] through lack of self-control" (1 Cor. 7:5). What this means is that the "as we ought" is thwarted unless the mysteries of marriage, which are to be honored with silence, are performed with holiness, deliberately, and without passion. The "agreement" found in the text does away with the disagreement of passion, destroys incontinence, and prevents Satan from "rejoic-

---

20. An agraphon or extracanonical saying (or sayings) of Christ. Cf. Jn. 3:12; Mt. 6:33; Lk. 12:31. Cf. Clement of Alexandria (*Strom.* I.24:158.2; *Strom.* IV.6:34.6) and Eusebius of Caesarea In Psalm 16.2, both of whom preserve only the first half. Cf. also, Origen, *Contra Celsum* VII.44.

21. Origen has this reading instead of "tempt."

ing" in evil. As well as these sayings, the following teaches about the "as we ought": "And if[22] you stand praying, forgive if you have anything against any one" (Mk. 11:25). And in Paul we find, "Any man who prays or prophesies with his head covered dishonors his head, but any woman who prays or prophesies with her head unveiled dishonors her head" (1 Cor. 11:4–5). This makes explicit the "as we ought."

3. Moreover, Paul knew all these sayings and many more from the Law and the prophets and from the fulness of the Gospel, and he was able to explain them with a skillfully woven interpretation for each. He speaks with an art not only carefully constructed but also true, since he sees even after all these insights how far short he comes of knowing what we must pray for as we ought. He adds the phrase "what we ought to pray for as we ought we do not know" to his discussion, implying that what is lacking will be supplied to a person who does not know but who fashions himself worthy of having his lack supplied. Indeed, he says, "the Spirit Himself makes special intercession with God with sighs too deep for words. And He who searches the hearts knows what is the mind of the Spirit, because the Spirit intercedes for the saints according to the will of God" (Rom. 8:26–27). The Spirit cries "Abba, Father" (cf. Gal. 4:6) in the hearts of the blessed; and He knows by careful attention our sighs in this tabernacle, sighs suitable for weighing down those who have fallen or transgressed. He "makes special intercession with God with sighs too deep for words" by accepting our sighs because of His great love and compassion for mankind. And by the wisdom in Him He sees that our soul has been humbled to dust (cf. Ps. 44:25) and imprisoned in the body of humiliation (cf. Phil. 3:21). And so He "makes special intercession with God" not by using just any "sighs," but those "too deep for words," which have words that cannot be spoken, that are not right for a human being to speak (cf. 2 Cor. 12:4). Moreover, this Spirit is not content with interceding with God, but intensifies the petition and "makes special intercession." I think this is for those who are specially victorious, as Paul says, "No, in all these things we are more than conquerors" (Rom. 8:37). Perhaps He only intercedes for those who

---

22. Origen reads "if" instead of "whenever," a variant reading found also in IX.3.

do not count as more than conquerors, but who are conquerors and not, at the other extreme, conquered.

4. The verse "I will pray with the Spirit and I will pray with the mind also; I will sing with the Spirit and I will sing with the mind also" (1 Cor. 14:15) is related to the verse "What we ought to pray for as we ought we do not know, but the Spirit makes special intercession with God with sighs too deep for words" (Rom. 8:26). For our mind would not even be able to pray unless the Spirit prayed for it as if obeying it, so that we can not even sing and hymn the Father in Christ with proper rhythm, melody, measure, and harmony unless the Spirit who searches everything, even the depths of God (1 Cor. 2:10), first praises and hymns Him whose depths He has searched out and has understood as far as He is able.[23] I also think that one of Jesus' disciples was conscious in himself of human weakness, which falls short of knowing how we ought to pray. Once he came to know this, when he heard the wise and mighty words recited by the Savior in prayer to the Father, he said to the Lord, when He had ceased praying, "Lord, teach us to pray, as John taught his disciples." The entire passage reads this way, "He was praying in a certain place, and when He ceased, one of His disciples said to Him, 'Lord, teach us to pray, as John taught his disciples' " (Lk. 11:1). . . .[24] Are we then to conclude that a man brought up in the instruction of the Law, who heard the words of the prophets and did not fail to attend the synagogue, did not know in any way at all how to pray until he saw the Lord praying "in a certain place"? It would certainly be foolish to say this. For he prayed according to the customs of the Jews, but he saw that he needed better knowledge about the subject of prayer. Moreover, what would John teach his disciples about prayer when they came to him from Jerusalem and all Judea and the surrounding country to be baptized (cf. Mt. 3:5–6), if he had not seen certain things about prayer because he was greater than a prophet (cf. Mt. 11:9)? And he apparently handed over these things secretly not to all that came to

---

23. This implies that the Spirit's knowledge of the Father is limited. Origen's doctrine of the Spirit is a puzzle. The chief passages are *De principiis* I.3; *Comm. in Joh.* II.10–11.

24. A lacuna of 2 lines, possibly citing Mt. 3:5–6.

be baptized, but to those who became his disciples in addition to being baptized.[25]

5. Such prayers as were truly spiritual, since the Spirit prays in the heart of the saints, were written down, filled with secret and marvelous teachings. In 1 Samuel (1:11–13) part of Hannah's prayer is found; for "when she continued praying before the Lord," she spoke "in her heart" (1 Sam. 1:12–13), and the whole prayer was not put in writing. In Psalms the Seventeenth Psalm is entitled "A Prayer of David"; and the Ninetieth, "A Prayer of Moses, the Man of God"; and the One Hundred and Second, "A Prayer of the Poor, when he faints and pours out his complaint before the Lord." These prayers, since they were truly prayers made and spoken by the Spirit, are also filled with the teachings of God's wisdom, so that one can say of what is recited in them, "Who is wise and will understand these things? Who is discerning and will know them?" (Hos. 14:9).

6. Therefore, the discussion of prayer is so great a task that it requires the Father to reveal it, His Firstborn Word to teach it, and the Spirit to enable us to think and speak rightly of so great a subject. That is why I, who am only a human being and in no way attribute an understanding of prayer to myself, think it right to pray for the Spirit before beginning my treatise on prayer, in order that the fullest spiritual account may be given to me and that the prayers written in the Gospels may be made clear. Now, therefore, let me begin the treatise on prayer.

PART ONE: PRAYER IN GENERAL
A. INTRODUCTION: THE WORDS FOR "PRAYER"

III.1. So far as I have been able to observe, the first mention of prayer in Scripture occurs when Jacob took flight from his brother Esau's wrath and departed for Mesopotamia according to the instructions of Isaac and Rebekah. This is how the text reads, "And Jacob prayed a prayer,[26] saying, 'If the Lord God will be

---

25. Origen here attributes to John the Baptist his own distinction between the simpler and the perfect disciples.

26. In Greek *euchē*, to be taken in the sense "vow." Here and in what follows, "prayer"

with me, and will keep me in this way that I go, and will bring me again to my father's house in safety, then the Lord shall be my God, and this stone, which I have set up for a pillar, shall be for me God's house; and of all that You give me I will give the tenth to You" (Gen. 28:20–22). . . .[27]

2. In this passage it must be noted that the word *prayer* is used to refer to the person's promise to do what the prayer announces if he obtains his requests from God. (This is because *prayer* often means something other than prayer in the usual sense.) Nevertheless, the word also occurs in contexts that accord with our customary usage. For example, in Exodus we find it used this way after the plague of frogs, which is the second of the ten plagues.[28] [Then Pharaoh ordered Moses and Aaron to pray to the Lord for him, so that He might take away from him and his people the frogs that covered everything. The text reads this way,] "Pharaoh called Moses and Aaron and said to them, 'Pray for me to the Lord, and let Him take the frogs away from me and my people; and I will let the people go to sacrifice to the Lord' " (Ex. 8:8). If someone finds it hard to believe, because the word is spoken by Pharaoh, that *pray* takes its meaning from *prayer* in its first and customary usage, let him observe the verse that follows, "Moses said to Pharaoh, 'Command me when I am to pray for you and your servants and your people, that the frogs be destroyed from you and from your people and from your houses, and left only in the river' " (Ex. 8:9).

3. I have observed that in the third plague, that of the gnats, Pharaoh does not ask for a prayer, nor does Moses pray. In the fourth plague, that of the flies, he says, "Pray for me to the Lord" (Ex. 8:28). And then Moses said, "I will go out from you and I will pray to God, and the swarms of flies will depart from Pharaoh and his servants and his people tomorrow" (Ex. 8:29). And a little further on it says, "And Moses went out from Pharaoh and prayed to God" (Ex. 8:30). Again, although in the fifth and the sixth

---

has been retained in the translation, because in his discussion Origen points out that the words *euchē* and *proseuchē* ordinarily mean "prayer," but sometimes mean "vow." To introduce the distinction into the translation would have solved the problem before Origen had a chance to discuss it.

27. A lacuna of two lines in the manuscript.

28. There follows Koetschau's conjectural attempt to fill a lacuna of two lines in the manuscript.

plagues Pharaoh does not ask for a prayer nor does Moses pray, in the seventh plague "Pharaoh sent, and called Moses and Aaron, and said to them, 'I have sinned this time; the Lord is in the right, and I and my people are in the wrong. Pray, therefore, to the Lord and let the thunders of God and the hail and fire cease' " (Ex. 9:27–28). And a little further on it says, "Moses went out of the city from Pharaoh, and stretched out his hands to the Lord, and the thunders ceased" (Ex. 9:33). (Why does it not say "and he prayed" as in the former instances, but instead, "he stretched out his hands to the Lord"? This may be more conveniently discussed elsewhere.) In the eighth plague Pharaoh says, " 'And pray to the Lord your God and let Him take this death away from me.' And Moses went out from Pharaoh and prayed to God" (Ex. 10:17–18).

4. We said that the word *prayer* is often used in a way different from the customary usage, as in the case of the passage about Jacob. Moreover, the same usage is found in Leviticus, "The Lord said to Moses, 'Speak to the children of Israel and say to them, Whenever some one prays a prayer to the Lord to the value of his life, the valuation of a male from twenty years old up to sixty years old shall be fifty double drachmas of silver in the holy weight' " (Lev. 27:1–3). And in Numbers, "And the Lord said to Moses, 'Speak to the children of Israel and say to them, Whenever a man or a woman prays a special prayer to be consecrated in purity to the Lord, he shall be separated from wine and strong drink' " (Num. 6:1–3). What follows concerns the one called a Nazirite. And then a little further on it says, "And he shall consecrate his head that same day on which he was consecrated to the Lord, for the days of the prayer" (Num. 6:11–12 LXX). And again a little further on, "This is the law of the one who has prayed for the day when he has fulfilled the time of his prayer" (Num. 6:13). And again a little further on, "And after that the one who has prayed may drink wine. This is the law of the one who has prayed, whoever prays his offering to the Lord for his prayer, except for what his hand finds according to the law of purification" (Num. 6:20–21). And toward the end of Numbers we read, "And Moses spoke to the rulers of the tribes of the children of Israel, saying, 'This is the word the Lord has commanded: Whenever a man prays a prayer to the Lord or swears an oath with a vow or binds himself by vowing his life, he

shall not break his word; he shall do according to all that proceeds out of his mouth. And whenever a woman prays a prayer to the Lord or binds herself by a vow, while within her father's house, in her youth, and her father hears of her prayers and her vows by which she has bound her life, and her father keeps silence, then all her prayers shall stand, and all the vows by which she has bound her life shall remain for her' " (Num. 30:1–4). And in what immediately follows there are laws concerning such a woman. In this same sense there is written in Proverbs,[29] ["I have a sacrifice of peace, today I pay back my prayers" (Prov. 7:14) and "A foolish son is shame to his father, prayers from a paid courtesan are not pure" (Prov. 19:13 LXX) and "It is a snare] for a man to sanctify any of his possessions too quickly, for after he has prayed, it will happen that he will change his mind" (Prov. 20:25). And in Ecclesiastes, "It is better not to pray than to pray and not to pay it" (Eccles. 5:5). And in the Acts of the Apostles, "We have four men who are under a prayer for themselves" (Acts 21:23).

IV.1. It seemed to me not without purpose to spend some time at first giving the meaning according to Scripture, since prayer means two different things. The same is true of the other word for prayer, *proseuchē*. This word, often used in the common and customary sense of prayer and as a synonym for the customary meaning of the word *euchē*, is used in what is said about Hannah in 1 Samuel. "And Eli the priest was sitting on the seat beside the doorposts of the temple of the Lord. And she with bitter soul was also praying (*prosēuksato*) to the Lord and wept bitterly. And she prayed a prayer (*ēuksato euchēn*) and said, 'O Lord of hosts, if you will indeed look upon the lowliness of your maidservant and remember me, and not forget your maidservant, and will give your maidservant a son, then I will give him to the Lord as a gift all the days of his life, and no razor shall touch his head' " (1 Sam. 1:9–11).

2. Now by comparing "she was praying (*prosēuksato*) to the Lord" and "she prayed a prayer (*ēuksato euchēn*)," one can say that if she did two things, that is "prayed to the Lord" and "prayed a

---

29. What follows is Koetschau's conjectural attempt to fill a lacuna of 1³/₅ lines in the manuscript.

prayer," then "prayed" (*proseuksato*) is used to refer to our ordinary meaning of prayer, while "she prayed a prayer" is used in the meaning of "vow" that we found in Leviticus and Numbers. For the verse "I will give him to the Lord as a gift all the days of his life, and no razor shall touch his head" is not properly speaking a prayer, but that sort of prayer which Jephthah prayed in the following passage, "And Jephthah prayed a prayer to the Lord and said, 'If you will surely give the children of Ammon into my hand, then whoever it will be who comes forth from the doors of my house to meet me when I return victorious from the children of Ammon shall be the Lord's, and I will offer him up for a burnt offering' " (Jud. 11:30–31).

B. INTRODUCTION: OBJECTIONS TO PRAYER

V.1. If then after this discussion I must first set forth, as you have requested, the plausible arguments of those who suppose that nothing is gained by prayer and that this is why it is superfluous to pray, I shall not hesitate to do this so far as I am able, using from now on the more common and simple word for prayer, *euche*.[30] [For there are some who do not even accept prayer in this sense, but laugh to scorn those who pray any kind of prayer and wish to do away with the word altogether, whatever its meaning.] The view is a base one and is not to be found defended by anyone distinguished. So much is this the case that scarcely anyone who accepts providence in some sense and establishes God over the universe fails to accept prayer. The opinion belongs either to those who are altogether atheists and deny the being of God or to those who are willing to talk about God but take away His providence. Nevertheless, the opposing Power (cf. 2 Thess. 2:4, 9) wishes to attribute the most impious doctrines to the name of Christ and to the teachings of the Son of God, and has been able to convince some that we ought not to pray. The ones who defend this opinion are those who do away with perceptible things entirely and practice neither bap-

---

30. The following is Koetschau's conjectural attempt to fill a lacuna of two lines in the manuscript.

ON PRAYER

tism nor the eucharist, explaining the Scriptures with sophisms by
saying that when they speak of prayer they mean to be teaching
something quite different.

2. Well then, here are the arguments of those who set prayers
aside—obviously, I mean those who establish God over the universe and say that providence exists; for it is not now my task to
examine what is said by those who reject God or providence altogether:

> God knows all things before they come to be (cf. Sus. 42), and nothing that is
> established will first be known to Him when it is established, and so un-
> known to Him before that. Therefore, what use is it to offer prayer to One
> who knows what we need even before we pray? For our heavenly Father
> knows what we need before we ask Him (Mt. 6:8). It is reasonable that the
> Father, since He is the Creator of everything, loves all that is, and in no way
> loathes what He has made (cf. Wis. 11:24), should govern as a savior the
> destiny of each apart from prayer. He does this like a father who defends his
> children and does not wait for them to ask him, either because they are quite
> unable to ask or through ignorance often wish to receive what will contradict
> what is to their advantage and profit. And we humans are further away from
> God than ordinary children are from the attention of their fathers.
>
> 3. And it is likely that God not only foreknows what will happen but
> also foreordains it, and that nothing can happen contrary to His foreordina-
> tion. Therefore, if someone, for example, should pray for the sun to rise, he
> would be considered a fool, if he thought that what would happen quite
> apart from his prayer had happened because of his prayer. In just this way,
> whoever supposes that things happen because of his prayer and would not
> happen at all without his praying will prove a fool. To take another example,
> suppose someone is burdened by the sun in summertime and is burning up,
> and then thinks that through prayer the sun will change to its position in
> spring so that he may enjoy temperate air. This man reaches the very height
> of madness. In just this way, if anyone thinks that the circumstances that
> necessarily happen to the human race are subject to the persuasive power of
> prayer, he would reach the height of insanity.
>
> 4. And if "sinners have become estranged from the womb" (cf. Ps. 58:3)
> and the righteous is set apart "from his mother's womb" (cf. Gal. 1:15) and it
> is said, "The elder will serve the younger, though they were not yet born and
> had done nothing either good or bad, in order that God's purpose of election
> might continue, not because of works, but because of His call" (Rom. 9:11–
> 12; Gen. 25:23), then it is in vain that we ask for the forgiveness of sins or to
> receive the Spirit of strength that we may be strong in all things with Christ
> empowering us (cf. Phil. 4:13). For if we are sinners, we have been estranged
> from the womb. And if we have been set apart from our mother's womb, the

91

noblest things will come our way even if we do not pray. What prayer did Jacob offer before he was born that it was prophesied that he should prevail over Esau and that his brother should serve him? What impiety did Esau commit before he was born that he should be hated? Why does Moses pray as he does in Psalm 90 if God is his "refuge before the mountains were established and the earth and the world fashioned" (Ps. 90:1–2)? . . .[31]

5. Moreover, in the letter to the Ephesians it is written concerning all those to be saved that the Father "chose" them "in Him," "in Christ," "before the foundation of the world" that they should be "holy and blameless before Him, having destined them in love to be His sons through Christ" (Eph. 1:3–5). Well then, any one of them has been chosen "before the foundation of the world," and it is impossible that he should fall away from his election. Therefore, he needs no prayer. Or if he has not been chosen or predestined, he prays in vain; and even if he prays ten thousand times, he will not be heard. For "those whom God foreknew He also predestined to be conformed to the image of the glory of His Son. . . . And those whom He predestined He also called; and those whom He called He also justified; and those whom He justified He also glorified" (cf. Rom. 8:29–30). Why did Josiah toil, or why did he pray and concern himself with whether he would be heard at all or not, since it had been explicitly prophesied many years before; and what he would do was not only foreknown, but had also been foretold in the hearing of many (2 Kings 22; cf. 1 Kings 13:1–3)? Why does Judas pray so that his prayer is counted as sin (Ps. 109:7), since it had been proclaimed beforehand from the times of David that he would lose his office and that another would take it instead of him (cf. Acts 1:16, 20; Ps. 109:7–8)? Since God does not change and has taken charge of the universe beforehand and remains fixed in what has already been decreed, it is obviously inconsistent to pray, supposing that His dispensation will change through prayer. This would imply that He has not foreordained, but waits to receive each person's prayer so that He may ordain because of the prayer what is suitable for the person praying, and only then orders what proves to be reasonable, though it has not been seen by Him before.

6. Let the argument I have been stating in the preceding discussion be stated in the words of the letter you have written me. "First, if God foreknows what will come to be and if it must happen, then prayer is vain. Second, if everything happens according to God's will and if what He wills is fixed and no one of the things He wills can be changed, then prayer is vain." I should think a preliminary discussion will be useful to resolve the difficulties that make people insensitive to prayer.

---

31. A lacuna of $1^3/_7$ lines in the manuscript.

ON PRAYER

VI.1. Of the things that are moved, some receive their motion from outside themselves, for example, things that are lifeless and held together in nothing more than a fixed system, and things that are moved by nature and the animating principle, since when they are moved it is not by what makes them what they are, but in a way like the things held together in nothing more than a fixed system. For stones and pieces of wood, when dug out of a quarry or having lost the power of growing, since they are held together in nothing more than a fixed system, receive their motion from outside themselves. Moreover, both the bodies of living beings and the produce of plants, when moved by someone, are not moved by what makes them living beings and plants, but like stones and pieces of wood that have lost the power of growing. Even if they are moved because all bodies are in a state of flux and are wasting away, they have this motion merely as a consequence of their wasting away. A second class of things that are moved consists of things moved by the nature or animating principle that exists within them. These are said to be moved "out of" themselves, in the opinion of those who use words with great precision. A third kind of motion is that found in living beings, which is called motion "from" themselves. And I believe that the motion of rational beings is motion "through" themselves. Now if we take motion "from" itself away from a living being, it cannot any longer be supposed to be a living being, but will be like a plant moved only by nature or like a stone hurled by something outside itself. But if something follows along by its own motion, since we call this motion "through" itself, then it must necessarily be rational.

2. Therefore, those who want to say that we have no free-dom[32] must necessarily admit something extremely foolish—first, that we are not living beings and, second, that we are not rational beings. On their view, since we are in no way moved by ourselves but by something moving outside ourselves, we may be said to do what we suppose we are doing ourselves only because of that external cause. On the contrary, let anyone pay special attention to his own experiences and see whether he will not say without blushing

---

32. In Greek *to eph'hēmin*, the technical expression of the Stoics for that which is "in our control." *Freedom* will be used in the translation throughout.

that it is he who wills, he who eats, he who walks, he who gives his assent and acceptance to certain opinions, and he who rejects others as false. And if we assume that our freedom is in no way preserved, it would be impossible for a person to assent to certain opinions, even if he builds them up with ten thousand ingenious explanations and employs persuasive arguments; and it would be similarly impossible for a person to have any convictions about human life. For who is so affected by the fact that nothing is certain or lives in such a way that he suspends judgment about everything whatsoever? Who does not strike a servant when he forms the impression that the servant has done wrong? Who is there who does not accuse a son who does not give due respect to his parents? Or who does not blame and censure the adulteress as one who has done something shameful? The truth forces itself upon us; and even if someone gives ten thousand ingenious explanations, it compels us to act and to give praise and blame, on the assumption that our freedom is preserved and that its exercise by us is subject to praise or blame.

3. If then our freedom is preserved, however vast the number of inclinations it has to virtue or to vice and, again, to what is becoming or to what is unbecoming, it, along with everything else from creation and from the foundation of the world (cf. Rom. 1:20), will be known to God before it comes to be for what sort of freedom it will be. And among all the things God foreordains in accordance with what He has seen concerning each deed of our freedom, there has been foreordained according to merit for each motion of our freedom what will meet it from providence and still cohere with the chain of future events. And so, God's foreknowledge is not the cause of everything that will come to be, even of our freedom when we are made active by our own impulse. For even if we entertain the supposition that God does not know what will come to be, we do not for this reason lose the power of acting in different ways and of willing certain things. But if God takes the order for the governance of the universe from His foreknowledge, then all the more is our individual freedom useful for the ordering of the world.

4. If, therefore, our individual freedom is known to Him and consequently foreseen by Him, then what is reasonable in accordance with each person's merit is ordered from providence, as is what he prays and what character a certain man has who believes

this way. And what He wills him to have is decided beforehand. Since such things have been decided beforehand, they have been ordered in accordance with the constitution of the universe, so that God might say:

> I will hear this man who prays intelligently because of the very prayer he prays, but I will not hear this man either because to hear him would be wrong or because he prays for what would neither profit him nor be fitting for me. And, so to speak, I will not hear this prayer of such a person, but I will hear that one.

If anyone is troubled because God, who foreknows what will happen, cannot lie, and so draws the inference that things have been established by necessity, let him be told that this very thing is definitely known to God, namely, that this particular person does not will the nobler things definitely and firmly and will so wish for the baser things that he will be incapable of turning to things that will profit him. And again God might say:

> These are the things I will do for this man praying, for it is right for me to do this for someone who prays to me blamelessly and gives himself attentively to prayer. And when he prays for such a time, I will give him these things more abundantly than what he asks or thinks (cf. Eph. 3:20), for it is right for me to conquer him with good deeds and to furnish him with more than he has been capable of asking. To a person who will turn out to be like this I will send this ministering angel, who will begin to work with him from such and such a time and will stay with him until such and such a time. And to this person who will prove better than the first I will send, so to speak, this angel more honorable than the first. And from such a man who grows weak after he has given himself over to excellent words and turns back to more material things, I shall take this better angel and fellow worker away. And when he has gone away, some worse power proportioned to the man's merit will be summoned by having found an opportunity to assail him in his carelessness, by having urged him on to such sins as these, and by having given himself as a companion for sinning.

5. This, then, is the way He who foreordains everything will speak. For example, He will say:

> Amon will beget Josiah, who will not rival his father's transgressions; but because he will chance upon that road which led of old to virtue through those who will accompany him, he will be noble and good. And he will

95

destroy the altar wickedly built by Jeroboam (cf. 2 Kings 21–23). And I know that when my Son comes to live with the human race, Judas will be noble and good to begin with, but afterwards will change and fall into human sins. Because of these sins it will be reasonable for him to suffer certain things like this.

(This foreknowledge, probably about everything but certainly about Judas and other mysteries, also belongs to the Son of God, who saw by His understanding of the revolving pattern of future events Judas and the sins he would commit against Him. This is why, even before Judas was born, with accurate perception He said through David, "O God, do not fail to hear my praise, and so forth" [Ps. 109:1, the psalm thought to refer to Judas].)

I know what will happen and how strenuously Paul will strive for true religion. Therefore, in myself before the creation of the world when I turn myself to the beginning of making the world, I will choose him and will supply him at the moment of his birth with powers that cooperate for the salvation of men, such as these. I will set him aside from his mother's womb (Gal. 1:15) and will lead him to begin with in youthful zeal, allowed because of ignorance, to persecute on the pretense of religion those who believe in my Christ, and to keep the clothes of those who stone my servant and martyr Stephen (Acts 9:5). I will do this so that when he outgrows the folly of youth, takes a new start, and turns to what is best, he may not boast before me (cf. 1 Cor. 1:29), but may say, "I am unfit to be called an apostle, because I persecuted the church of God" (1 Cor. 15:9). And when he perceives that I will be kind to him after his youthful errors committed on the pretense of religion, he will say, "But by the grace of God I am what I am" (1 Cor. 15:10). He will be held back by his consciousness of what he did against Christ while he was still young, and so will not be puffed up with elation at the abundance of revelations graciously manifested to him (cf. 2 Cor. 12:7).

VII. Now with respect to the argument about the prayer for the rising of the sun, the following must be said. Even the sun has a certain kind of freedom, since it praises God along with the moon. For it says, "Praise Him, sun and moon" (Ps. 148:3). And it is clear that the same conclusion must be reached about the moon and all the stars. For it says, "Praise Him, all you stars and light" (Ps. 148:3). Now we have said that God uses the freedom of each of us on earth and has ordered our freedom aright for some benefit to those on earth. We must suppose that the same conclusion applies to the freedom of the sun, the moon, and the stars, which is fixed, sure, firm, and wise, and that God has ordered the whole world of heaven and the course and movement of the stars in harmony with the universe. Now if it is not in vain that I pray about someone else who has freedom, how muc h more is this so when I pray about one of the free stars that move through heaven as tokens of the safety of the universe? Indeed, it is possible to say further concerning things on earth that certain kinds of impressions accrue to them from circumstances and evoke in us instability or incline us to a worse state, so that we do or say such things or others. But in the case of heavenly things what impression can accrue to them that would displace or change from a course so useful to the world any one of those beings who have such a soul fashioned by reason and equivalent to their own cause and who employ such an ethereal body?

C. THE BENEFITS OF PRAYING "AS WE OUGHT"

VIII.1. Moreover, it is not unreasonable to use such an example as the following as a way of exhorting people to pray and to turn away from neglecting prayer. Just as it is not possible to beget children without a woman and without receiving the power that serves to beget children, so no one may obtain such requests as these unless he has prayed with such and such a disposition, believes this way, has not led such a way of life before his prayer. Vain repetitions ought not be used (cf. Mt. 6:7), nor should little things be requested nor prayers made for earthly things, nor should we go to prayer with anger and with troubled thoughts. Indeed, it is not even possible to arrange the leisure needed for prayer without purification, nor is it possible for one praying to gain forgiveness of sins unless from his heart he forgives the transgressor and thinks his brother worthy to gain pardon (cf. Mt. 18:35).

2. I believe that profit often meets and joins the person who prays as he ought or who makes every effort to do so as far as he is able. First, the person who composes his mind for prayer is inevitably profited in some way. Through his very disposition for prayer he adorns himself so as to present himself to God and to speak to Him in person as to someone who looks upon him and is present.

For just as various impressions and memories of the various things of which they are the memories defile the thoughts that arise under such impressions, in the same way we must believe that remembering God is profitable. This is because we have put our trust in Him and because He knows the motions in the secret part of our soul, when it harmonizes itself to please Him as present and watching and overtaking every mind as the One who tries the hearts and searches out the reins (cf. Ps. 7:9; Jer. 11:20, 17:10; Rom. 8:27; Rev. 2:23). This is why even if we were to suppose there were no profit beyond this for someone who composed his mind for prayer, it must not be supposed that he gains something insignificant when he so harmonizes himself reverently at the time of prayer. If this happens frequently, those who have given themselves over to prayer with great constancy know by experience how many sins it prevents and how many virtuous actions it brings about. For if our remembering and considering a highly respected man who has prospered by wisdom urges us on to rival him and often thwarts impulses to a baser course of life, how much more will remembering God, the Father of the universe, along with prayer to Him, profit those who have persuaded themselves that they stand beside Him present and listening and are speaking with God?

IX.1. What I have said must now be supported from the sacred Scriptures in the following way. The person praying must stretch out "holy hands" by thoroughly purging the passion of "anger" from his soul and harboring no rage against anyone and by forgiving each the sins he has committed against him (cf. 1 Tim. 2:8; Mt. 6:12, 14; Lk. 11:4). Next, so that his mind may not be muddied by thoughts from outside, he must forget for the time being everything but the prayer he is praying. (How can such a man fail to be highly blessed?) Paul teaches this in his first letter to Timothy, when he says, "I desire then that in every place the men should pray, lifting holy hands without anger or quarreling" (1 Tim. 2:8). Moreover, in addition to them the woman, especially when she is praying, must be calm and orderly in soul, as well as body, standing in awe of God most especially when she prays, banishing from her governing mind everything that would remind her of incontinent and womanish ways, and adorning herself not with "braided hair or gold or pearls or costly attire" but with what a woman professing religion should be adorned. (I should be surprised if anyone were to doubt that a woman who prepared herself for prayer in this way would reveal her blessedness merely from such a disposition.) This is what Paul teaches in the same letter when he says, "Also that the women should adorn themselves modestly and sensibly in seemly apparel, not with braided hair or gold or pearls or costly attire but by good deeds, as befits women who profess religion" (1 Tim. 2:9–10).

2. The prophet David also says that the holy person when he prays has many other characteristics. It would not be out of place to set these down, so that what is of greatest profit may become clear to us, even if we only consider the attitude and preparation for prayer of the one who dedicates himself to God. What David says is, "To you have I lifted up my eyes, you who dwell in heaven" (Ps. 123:1) and "To you, O God, have I lifted up my soul" (Ps. 25:1). For the eyes of the mind are lifted up from their preoccupation with earthly things and from their being filled with the impression of material things. And they are so exalted that they peer beyond the created order and arrive at the sheer contemplation of God and at conversing with Him reverently and suitably as He listens. How would things so great fail to profit those eyes that gaze at the glory of the Lord with unveiled face and that are being changed into His likeness from glory to glory (cf. 2 Cor. 3:18)? For then they partake of some divine and intelligible radiance. This is demonstrated by the verse "The light of your countenance, O Lord, has been signed upon us" (Ps. 4:6). And the soul is lifted up and following the Spirit is separated from the body. Not only does it follow the Spirit, it even comes to be in Him. This is demonstrated by the verse "To you have I lifted up my soul," since it is by putting away its existence that the soul becomes spiritual.

3. We may suppose that renouncing malice is an act of the greatest virtue, since according to the prophet Jeremiah it sums up the entire Law. What he says is, "I did not command these things to your fathers when they came out of Egypt, but this command I gave them: Let no one bear malice in his heart against his neighbor" (cf. Jer. 7:22–23; Zech. 7:10). When we leave behind bearing malice in coming to pray, we keep the Savior's commandment, "If you stand praying, forgive, if you have anything against any one"

(Mk. 11:25). It is evident that when we stand praying this way, we have already obtained what is noblest.

X.1. Even if we were to suppose that no other results besides these will attend our prayers, we should nevertheless have gained what is noblest, since we should have succeeded in understanding how we ought to pray. And it is clear that whoever prays this way will be heard while he is still speaking, since he looks to the power of Him who hears—the "here am I" (cf. Is. 58:9)—and has cast aside all dissatisfaction with providence before he prays. This is made clear by the verse "If you take away from you the yoke, the pointing of the finger, and the word of grumbling" (Is. 58:9). What this means is that the person who is satisfied with what happens is free from bondage to anything that has taken place and does not point his finger against God, since He has ordered what He wills for our training. Furthermore, he does not even grumble in his secret thoughts though they are inaudible to the people around him. Such grumbling is like that of wicked servants who do not openly find fault with their masters' orders. Those who do not dare grumble out loud do so with their whole soul to revile providence for what has happened to them, even though they wish, so to speak, their dissatisfactions to escape the notice of the Lord of all. And I think this is what it says in Job, "In all these things that happened to him Job did not sin in any way before God *with his lips*" (Job 2:10). Before he was tested himself it is written, "In all these things that happened to him Job did not sin in any way before God" (Job 1:22). Moreover, the saying in Deuteronomy commands that we should not grumble, "Take heed lest there be a secret word in your heart, a transgression, and you say, the seventh year is near, and so forth" (Deut. 15:9).

2. Therefore, the man who has been profited by praying in this fashion becomes more ready to be mingled with the Spirit of the Lord, who has filled the whole world and has filled the whole earth and heaven, and who says this through the prophet, "Do I not fill heaven and earth? says the Lord" (Jer. 23:24). Moreover, through the purification that has been mentioned and through prayer he will partake of the Word of God, who stands in the midst even of those who do not know Him (cf. Jn. 1:26), who is never absent from prayer, and who prays to the Father with the person

whose Mediator He is. For the Son of God is a High Priest who makes offerings for us (cf. Heb. 2:17, 3:1, 4:14, 5:10, 6:20, 7:26, 8:1, 9:11, 10:10) and an Advocate with the Father (cf. Jn. 14:16, 26, 15:26, 16:7; 1 John 2:1). He prays for those who pray and appeals along with those who appeal. But He does not pray for servants who do not pray continuously through Him, nor will He be the Advocate with God for His own if they are not obedient to His instructions that they "ought always to pray and not lose heart." For it says, "And He told them a parable to the effect that they ought always to pray and not lose heart: In a certain city there was a judge, and so forth" (Lk. 18:1–2). And in an earlier passage, "And He said to them, 'Which of you who has a friend will go to him at midnight and say to him, "Friend, lend me three loaves; for a friend of mine has arrived on a journey, and I have nothing to set before him" ' " (Lk. 11:5–6). And a little further on, "I tell you, though he will not get up and give him anything because he is his friend, yet because of his importunity he will rise and give him whatever he needs" (Lk. 11:8). Who that believes in the mouth of Jesus that cannot lie would hesitate a moment to be persuaded to pray, when He says, "Ask, and it will be given you . . . for everyone who asks, receives" (Lk. 11:9–10; Mt. 7:7–8)? Indeed, the good Father, when we ask for the living bread, gives Him—and not the stone that His adversary wishes to give to Jesus and His disciples for food—to those who have received the Spirit of sonship (cf. Rom. 8:15) from the Father. And the Father gives a good gift, raining it down from heaven for those who ask Him (cf. Lk. 11:13; Mt. 7:11).

XI.1. Not only does the High Priest pray with those who pray genuinely, but so do the angels who rejoice in heaven over one sinner who repents more than over ninety-nine righteous persons who need no repentance (Lk. 15:7; Mt. 18:13). So do the souls of the saints who have already fallen asleep. All this is demonstrated by the story of Raphael's offering a spiritual sacrifice to God for Tobit and Sarah. For after they prayed, the Scripture says, "The prayer of both was heard in the presence of the glory of the great Raphael, and he was sent to heal the two of them" (Tb. 3:16–17). And Raphael himself, when he reveals what he had arranged for both of them as an angel under God's orders, says, "And so, when you and your daughter-in-law Sarah prayed, I brought a reminder of your prayer before the Holy One," and a little further on, "I am Raphael, one of the seven angels who present [the prayers of the saints][33] and enter into the presence of the glory of the Holy One" (Tb. 12:12, 15). Therefore, according to Raphael's words, "Prayer is good, when accompanied by fasting, almsgiving, and righteousness" (Tb. 12:8). Also think of Jeremiah, who appears in 2 Maccabees, distinguished "by his grey hair and dignity," and how "there was something marvelous, majestic, and authoritative about him" (2 Macc. 15:13). He stretched out his "right hand" and gave "to Judas a golden sword" (2 Macc. 15:15). Another saint who has fallen asleep bears witness to him by saying, "This is the man who prays much for the people and the holy city, Jeremiah, the prophet of God" (2 Macc. 15:14).

2. Now if the knowledge manifested to those worthy of it in the present time comes through a mirror and in an enigma and is to be fully revealed face to face "then" (1 Cor. 13:12), it is foolish not to suppose that it is the same way with the other virtues. Though made ready beforehand in this life, they will be perfected rightly only "then." One of the most supreme virtues according to the divine Word is the love of neighbor. And we must suppose that it is far more present in the saints who have already fallen asleep toward those struggling in life than in those who are still in human weakness and struggle alongside their inferiors. For it is not only here below that there applies to those who love the brethren the saying "If one member suffers, all the members suffer together; and if one member is honored, all the members rejoice together" (1 Cor. 12:26). Indeed, it is fitting also for the love of those outside this present life to speak about "the anxiety for all the churches. Who is weak, and I am not weak? Who is made to fall, and I am not indignant?" (2 Cor. 11:28-29). And Christ says the same thing when He confesses that with each of the saints in sickness He is sick and, similarly, that He is in prison, naked, a stranger, hungry, and thirsty (cf. Mt. 25:35–40). For who that has read the Gospel is unaware of the fact that Christ applies what happens to those who believe in Him to Himself and counts their sufferings His own?

3. If the angels of God came to Jesus and ministered to Him

---

33. The phrase is omitted from the manuscript.

(cf. Mt. 4:11), it is not right that we should suppose that the ministry of angels to Jesus was only for the short time of His bodily sojourn among men, since He is still in the midst of believers not as one sitting at table but as one serving (cf. Lk. 22:27). How many angels, then, is it likely minister to Jesus as He wishes to gather the children of Israel one by one (cf. Is. 27:12) and to collect those who are scattered (cf. Jn. 7:35, 10:16, 11:52) and to rescue those who are afraid and call upon Him (cf. Acts 2:21; Rom. 10:12–13)? More than the apostles, the angels work for the increase and spread of the Church; and that is why certain rulers of the churches are called "angels" by John in Revelation (Rev. 1:20; 2:1, 8, 12, 18; 3:1, 7, 14). For it is not in vain that the angels of God, made visible to eyes enlightened by the light of knowledge, ascend and descend upon the Son of Man (cf. Jn. 1:51).

4. At the very time of prayer the angels are reminded by the one praying of what he needs, and they accomplish what they are able to do as those who have received a universal order. The following metaphors will be useful with respect to this point and will make my idea acceptable. Imagine that a physician who has his mind set on righteousness comes to a sick man praying for health. And suppose that he knows how the patient may be healed of the disease about which he is praying. It is obvious that he will be moved to heal the man praying, perhaps supposing not in vain that this very thing is God's intention and that God has heard the prayer of the man praying for deliverance from his disease. Or imagine that a man who has more than he needs for life and is generous hears the prayer of a poor man who is making intercession to God for his needs. It is obvious that he will fulfill the requests of the poor man's prayer, and will become a minister of the Father's will. For God at the time of prayer brings the one who is able to supply the needs and is unable because of his right use of free will to ignore the man who needs such things as these, and puts him in the same place as the one praying.

5. Therefore, we must not suppose that when things like this happen, they happen as though by chance. The One who numbers all the hairs of the saints' heads (cf. Mt. 10:30; Lk. 12:7) brings together in harmony at the time of prayer the one who will be His minister by hearing the request for a good deed from the other and

the one who has made the request faithfully. In the same way we must suppose that the presence of the angels who watch over us and minister to God comes together this way with someone who prays, so that the angels may be united with him in what he asks in prayer. Moreover, each person's angel, even of the "little ones" in the Church, always beholds the face of the Father who is in heaven (cf. Mt. 18:10) and sees the divinity of Him who created us. And he prays with us and does all he can to work with us for what we pray.

XII.1. In addition, I believe that the words of the saints' prayers are filled with power, especially when praying with the Spirit they also pray with the mind (cf. 1 Cor. 14:15). Then the mind is like light rising from the understanding of the one who prays (cf. Ps. 96:11; Is. 58:10; Rom. 3:13; Jas. 3:8). It goes forth from his mouth to weaken by the power of God the spiritual poison coming from the opposing powers and entering the governing part of the mind of whose who neglect to pray and fail to heed the injunction to "pray constantly" (1 Thess. 5:17), which Paul gives in accordance with the exhortations of Jesus. For it goes forth from the soul of the one praying like an arrow shot from the saint by knowledge and reason and faith. And it wounds the spirits hostile to God to destroy and overthrow them when they wish to hurl round us the bonds of sin (cf. Ps. 8:3; Prov. 5:22).

2. And he prays "constantly" (deeds of virtue or fulfilling the commandments are included as part of prayer) who unites prayer with the deeds required and right deeds with prayer. For the only way we can accept the command to "pray constantly" (1 Thess. 5:17) as referring to a real possibility is by saying that the entire life of the saint taken as a whole is a single great prayer. What is customarily called prayer is, then, a part of this prayer. Now prayer in the ordinary sense ought to be made no less than three times each day. This is evident from the story of Daniel, who prayed three times a day when such great peril had been devised for him (Dan. 6:13). And Peter went up to the housetop about the sixth hour to pray; that is when he saw the sheet descending from heaven let down by four corners (Acts 10:9, 11). He was offering the middle prayer of the three, the one referred to before him by David, "In the morning may you hear my prayer,[34] in the morning

34. Both the Septuagint and the Hebrew text have "voice."

I will offer to you and I will watch" (Ps. 5:3). And the last time of prayer is indicated by "The lifting up of my hands is an evening sacrifice" (Ps. 141:2). Indeed, we do not even complete the night-time properly without that prayer of which David speaks when he says, "At midnight I rise to praise you because of your righteous ordinances" (Ps. 119:62). And Paul, as it says in the Acts of the Apostles, prayed "about midnight" with Silas in Philippi and sang a hymn to God so that even the prisoners heard them (Acts 16:25).

XIII.1. Now if Jesus prays and does so not in vain, since He gets what He asks for in prayer when He might not have done so apart from prayer, which of us would neglect to pray? Mark says that "in the morning, a great while before day, He rose and went out to a lonely place, and there He prayed" (Mk. 1:35). And Luke says, "He was praying in a certain place, and when He ceased, one of His disciples said to Him" (Lk. 11:1) and elsewhere, "And all night He continued in prayer to God" (Lk. 6:12). And John records His prayer, saying, "When Jesus had spoken these words, He lifted up His eyes to heaven and said, 'Father, the hour has come; glorify your Son that the Son may glorify you'" (Jn. 17:1). The same evangelist writes that the Lord said that He knew "you hear me always" (Jn. 11:42), and this shows that the one who prays "always" is "always" heard.

2. But why should I draw up a long list of those who have gained the greatest favors from God through praying the way they ought, since it is open to anyone to collect more examples from Scripture for himself? For Hannah ministered to the birth of Samuel, who has been ranked with Moses (cf. Jer. 15:1; Ps. 99:6); when she believed she was barren, she prayed to the Lord (cf. 1 Sam. 1:9ff.). And Hezekiah, still childless,[35] when he learned from Isaiah that he would die, prayed he would be adopted into the Savior's genealogy (cf. Mt. 1:9–10; 2 Kings 20:1ff.; Is. 38:1ff.). Moreover, when the people were about to be destroyed by a single decree because of Haman's plot, the prayer Mordecai and Esther offered with fasting was heard and engendered in addition to the feasts prescribed by Moses a day of rejoicing given the people by Mordecai (cf. Esther 3:6, 7, 4:16, 17, 9:26–28). Then, too, Judith

---

35. The Septuagint of Isaiah 38:19 implies that Hezekiah was childless. Cf. *Contra Celsum* VIII.46.

by offering a holy prayer prevailed over Holofernes with God's help; and one woman of the Hebrews brought shame upon the house of Nebuchadnezzar (cf. Jdt. 13:4–9). And a moist whistling wind (Song of Three Childr. 27) did not permit the fiery flame to take effect, and Ananias, Azarias, and Misael were worthy to be heard and gain their request. And the lions in the Babylonians' den had their mouths stopped because of Daniel's prayer (Dan. 6). And Jonah did not despair of being heard from the belly of the whale that had swallowed him, but left the belly of the whale and fulfilled what was lacking in his prophecy to the Ninevites (cf. Jon. 2:3–4).

3. If one of us remembers with gratitude the benefits he has received and wishes to offer God praise, how many of them would each of us have to recount in detail? For souls that have become for the most part barren, when they perceive the sterility of their own governing reason and the barrenness of their own mind, through persistent prayer they conceive from the Holy Spirit saving words filled with visions of the truth; and they give birth to them. And because there are vast hosts of the opposing power who war against us and wish to exterminate us from faith in God, how many enemies march against us? But if we take courage from the fact that they call upon chariots and they call upon horses, while we call upon the name of the Lord (Ps. 20:7), then we shall see that in truth a horse is a vain hope for salvation (Ps. 33:17). Moreover, the one who trusts in praising God (the name Judith is translated "praise") often cuts in pieces even the chief captain of the Adversary, that deceptive and plausible word, who makes many even of those who suppose they are believers cower in fear. And what must we say about all those who, when they have repeatedly fallen into temptations hard to overcome and more burning than any flame, have suffered nothing from them, but have passed through them entirely unharmed, not even getting as they ordinarily would the harm of the smell of the hostile fire (cf. Song of Three Childr. 27)? Still more, among how many wild beasts made savage against us, evil spirits and savage men, have some fallen and have stopped their mouths with prayers, since they have not been able to strike their teeth against those of us who have become members of Christ (cf. 1 Cor. 6:15, 12:27)? For often the Lord has crushed together the fangs

of the lions for each one of the saints, and they have been set at naught like water that runs away (Ps. 58:6–7). And we know that fugitives from God's orders who have been swallowed up by death, which at first prevails over them, have been saved through repentance from so great an evil, since they did not despair of being able to be saved even though they had been made captive in the belly of death (cf. Jon. 2:1–2). For death has prevailed and swallowed them up, but again God wiped away every tear from every face (Is. 25:8).

4. I think that it was necessary for me to say all this after listing those who have benefited from prayer. For I wish to turn those who yearn for the spiritual life in Christ away from praying for little and earthly things and to urge those who read this treatise on to the mysteries of which what I said before were types. For every prayer for the spiritual mysteries reserved beforehand for us is always perfected by the person fighting not according to the flesh (cf. 2 Cor. 10:3) but putting to death the deeds of the body by the Spirit (cf. Rom. 8:13), since those who seek for the spiritual meaning by careful examination are preferred above those who set before their minds on the basis of the obvious and literal meaning the benefits that will come to those who pray. And we must train ourselves not to be childless or barren when we hear the spiritual Law as spiritual people, so that by putting aside barrenness and sterility we may be heard as Hannah and Hezekiah were and so that we may be delivered as Mordecai, Esther, and Judith were from the spiritual enemies sent by the Evil One to plot against us. And since Egypt is an iron furnace (cf. Deut. 4:20; Jer. 11:4; Origen *In Jer. hom.* IX.2) referring symbolically to the entire earthly realm, everyone who flees the evil of human life and is not inflamed by sin or filled with fire in his heart like a furnace must give thanks no less than those who were tested in the "moist" fire (Song of Three Childr. 27). Moreover, the one who has been heard when he prays and says, "Do not deliver the soul that has praised you to the wild beasts" (Ps. 73:19 LXX–Ps. 74:19) and who has suffered no harm from the adder and serpent because through Christ he has trod upon them and has trampled down the lion and the dragon (cf. Ps. 91:13) by using the noble power given by Jesus to tread upon serpents and scorpions and over all the power of the enemy (Lk.

10:19) and has been in no way injured by such great forces—this one must give thanks more than Daniel, since he has been delivered from more fearsome and harmful wild beasts. In addition, the one who has been persuaded of what sort of whale the one that swallowed up Jonah was a type and who has understood what Job said, "Let him curse it who curses that day, who is about to conquer the great whale" (Job 3:8)—if he should ever find himself through some disobedience in the belly of the whale, let him repent and pray, and he will come out of there. And if he comes out and is faithful in obeying the orders of God, he will be able by the kindness of the Spirit to prophesy to those who are now Ninevites on the brink of destruction and be for them a cause of salvation, since he did not despair of the kindness of God or seek that God should remain in His severity toward them when they repented.

5. That mighty deed Samuel is said to have accomplished through prayer is something that everyone who genuinely relies on God can accomplish spiritually even now, since he has become worthy of being heard. For it is written, "Now therefore stand still and see this great thing, which the Lord will do before your eyes. Is it not wheat harvest today? I will call upon the Lord, that He may send thunder and rain," and then a little further on it says, "So Samuel called upon the Lord, and the Lord sent thunder and rain that day" (1 Sam. 12:16–18). For every saint and genuine disciple of Jesus is told by the Lord, "Lift up your eyes, and see how the fields are already white for harvest. He who reaps receives wages, and gathers fruit for eternal life" (Jn. 4:35–36). In this time of harvest the Lord does "a great thing" before the eyes of those who hear the prophets. For when the one adorned with the Holy Spirit calls to the Lord, God gives from heaven thunder and rain that waters the soul, so that he who once was in evil may stand in great awe of the Lord and His minister of goodness, manifested as venerable and august by the requests that are heard. And Elijah, who shut up heaven for the wicked for three and a half years, later opened it (cf. 1 Kings 17:18; Lk. 4:25; Jas. 5:17–18). This, too, is always accomplished for everyone who through prayer receives the rain of the soul, since the heavens were previously deprived of it because of his sin.

ON PRAYER

D. What We Should Pray

XIV.1. Now that I have explained the benefits that come to the saints through prayers, let me consider the saying "Seek the great things, and the little things will be added for you. And seek the heavenly things, and the earthly things will be added for you."[36] Now every symbol and type by comparison with what is true and spiritual is "little" and "earthly." Apparently, the divine Word summons us to imitate the prayers of the saints that we may ask them according to the truth of which they accomplished the types, I mean the "heavenly" and "great" things that have been indicated by earthly and little things. What the saying means is "You who wish to be spiritual, seek through your prayers heavenly and great things, so that in getting them as heavenly you may inherit the kingdom of heaven and in getting them as great you may enjoy great good things. And as for the earthly and little things you need for your bodily necessities, the Father will supply you with them in proportion as you need them."

2. Now since the Apostle in 1 Timothy used four terms for four things directly related to the discussion of prayer, it will be useful to set down his statement and to see whether we rightly comprehend each of the four precisely understood. This is what he says, "First of all, then, I urge that supplications, prayers, intercessions, and thanksgivings be made for all men, and so forth" (1 Tim. 2:1). I think that *supplication* is a prayer offered with entreaty to get something a person lacks, while *prayer* is something nobler offered by a person with praise and for greater objects. And I think that *intercession* is a petition for certain things addressed to God by someone who has some greater boldness, while *thanksgiving* is a statement of gratitude made with prayers for receiving good things from God, either when it is a great thing that is received and acknowledged with gratitude or when the greatness of the benefit is one that appears only to the one who has benefited.

3. The following are examples of the first, supplication: Gabriel's word to Zechariah, when he is apparently praying for the

---

36. Cf. II.2.

birth of John. This is the way it goes, "Do not be afraid, Zechariah, for your supplication is heard, and your wife Elizabeth will bear you a son, and you shall call his name John" (Lk. 1:13). Next, what is written in Exodus at the time the Golden Calf was made, as follows, "And Moses made supplication before the Lord God and said, 'O Lord, why does your wrath rage against your people, whom you have brought forth out of the land of Egypt with great power?' " (Ex. 32:11). Next, in Deuteronomy, "And I made supplication before the Lord a second time as before; forty days and forty nights I neither ate bread nor drank water because of all the sins which you had committed" (Deut. 9:18). Next, in Esther, "Mordecai made supplication to God, calling to remembrance all the works of the Lord, and said, 'O Lord, Lord, King who rule over all things' " (Esther LXX; English Apocrypha 13:8–9). Next, Esther herself, "She made supplication to the God of Israel and said, 'O Lord our King' " (Esther LXX; English Apocrypha 14:3).

4. The following are examples of the second, prayer: In Daniel, "Then Azarias stood and offered this prayer; in the midst of the fire he opened his mouth and said" (Song of Three Childr. 2). Next, in Tobit, "And I prayed in anguish saying, 'You are righteous, O Lord, and all your deeds and all your ways are mercy and truth, and you render true and righteous judgement forever' " (Tb. 3:1–2). But since those of the circumcision have placed an obelus[37] over the passage in Daniel, because it is not found in the Hebrew text, and since they reject the book of Tobit as not in the Old Testament, I shall list in addition the passage about Hannah in 1 Samuel, "And she prayed to the Lord, and wept bitterly. And she prayed a prayer and said, 'O Lord of hosts, if you will indeed look on the lowliness of your maidservant, and so forth' " (1 Sam. 1:10–11). Next, in Habakkuk, "A prayer of Habakkuk the prophet, with music, 'O Lord, I have heard your voice and been afraid. O Lord, I have considered your works and been amazed. In the midst of the two living creatures you will be known; as the years draw near you will be recognized' " (Hab. 3:1–2 LXX). This gives an especially clear definition of prayer, because it is offered with praise

---

37. A mark used by grammarians in the ancient world to indicate something in the text that was to be omitted.

by the one praying.[38] Moreover, in Jonah, "Jonah prayed to his Lord God from the belly of the whale and said, 'I called to the Lord my God in my affliction, and He heard me. Out of the belly of hell you heard the voice of my cry. You cast me into the depths of the heart of the sea, and the floods circled me' " (Jon. 2:1–3).

5. The following are examples of the third, intercession: In the writings of the Apostle, where he quite reasonably assigns prayer to our control, but intercession to that of the Spirit, since He is better and has boldness with the One to whom He makes intercession. What he says is, " For what we should pray for as we ought we do not know, but the Spirit Himself makes special intercession for us to God with sighs too deep for words. And He who searches the hearts knows what is the mind of the Spirit, because the Spirit intercedes for the saints according to the will of God" (Rom. 8:26–27). For the Spirit "makes special intercession" and "intercedes," but we pray. It seems to me that what Joshua says about the sun standing still at Gibeon is an intercession, "Then spoke Joshua to the Lord in the day when the Lord gave the Amorites into the hands of Israel, when He crushed them in Gibeon, and they were crushed before the children of Israel. And Joshua said, 'Let the sun stand still at Gibeon, and the moon in the valley of Elom' " (Josh. 10:12). And in Judges I think Samson made an intercession when he said, "Let my soul be swallowed up with the Philistines." This was when "he bowed with all his might; and the house fell upon the lords and upon all the people that were in it" (Judg. 16:30). Even if it is not written that Joshua and Samson interceded, but only that they "said," their words are apparently intercessions. We must suppose this to be different from prayer, if we listen accurately to the terms. An example of thanksgiving is the voice of our Lord, when He says, "I give thanks to you, O Father, Lord of heaven and earth, that you have hidden these things from the wise and understanding and revealed them to babes" (Mt. 11:25; Lk. 10:21). For "I give thanks" (*ekshomologoumai*) is a synonym of "I thank" (*eucharistō*).

6. Then, too, it is not foolish to offer supplication, intercession, and thanksgiving also to the saints. Moreover, two of them, I

---

38. Origen's remark may reflect his realization that the different words in the Bible do not always reflect the definitions of them he has given.

mean intercession and thanksgiving, may be addressed not only to the saints but also to other people, while supplication may be addressed only to the saints if someone is found to be a Paul or a Peter so as to help us by making us worthy of receiving the authority given them to forgive sins (cf. Mt. 9:6; Jn. 20:23). An exception may be made if we wrong someone, even if he is not a saint; then we are permitted, conscious of our sin against him, to supplicate even such a person, so that he may pardon us for wronging him. If these kinds of prayer are to be offered to holy men, how much more must thanksgiving be addressed to Christ, who has benefited us so greatly by the will of the Father? Moreover, intercession must be addressed to Him, as Stephen says, "Lord, do not hold this sin against them" (Acts 7:60). Imitating the father of the lunatic we shall say, "I pray you, Lord, have mercy on my son"—or on me, or on any one at all (cf. Mt. 17:15; Lk. 9:38).

XV.1. Now if we are to take prayer in its most exact sense, perhaps we should not pray to anyone begotten, not even to Christ Himself, but only to the God and Father of all, to whom even our Savior Himself prayed, as we have explained,[39] and to whom He taught us to pray.[40] For when He heard "teach us to pray," He did not teach us to pray to Himself, but to the Father by saying "Our Father in heaven, and so forth" (Lk. 11:1ff.; Mt. 6:5ff.). For if, as is demonstrated by other arguments, the Son is a being and subject distinct from the Father,[41] it follows that prayer should be addressed to the Son and not to the Father, or to both, or to the Father alone. Anyone at all would agree that the first possibility, to the Son and not to the Father, is completely absurd, and would have to be maintained against the obvious facts. And if we prayed to both, then it is obvious that we should offer our requests in the plural, saying in our prayer, "*You all* supply and do good and furnish and save, and so forth." The very expressions betray the absurdity of this alternative, nor can anyone find in Scripture prayers addressed in the plural. Consequently, the remaining possibility is that we

---

39. Cf. XIII.1.

40. Cf. *Contra Celsum* V.4, VIII.13, V.11.

41. "Being" translates *ousia*, a term that Origen uses without reference to the later dogmatic distinction between *ousia* and *hypostasis* established at the Council of Constantinople in 381.

should pray only to the God and Father of all, yet not without the High Priest, who was appointed "with an oath" according to the verse, "He has sworn and will not change His mind, You are a priest forever after the order of Melchisedek" (Ps. 110:4; Heb. 7:20–21).

2. And so, when the saints give thanks to God in their prayers, they acknowledge through Christ Jesus the favors He has done. And if it is true that one who is scrupulous about prayer ought not to pray to someone else who prays, but rather to the Father whom our Lord Jesus taught us to address in prayers, it is especially true that no prayer should be addressed to the Father without Him, who clearly points this out Himself when He says, "Truly, truly, I say to you, if you ask anything of the Father, He will give it to you in my name. Hitherto you have asked nothing in my name; ask, and you will receive, that your joy may be full" (Jn. 16.23–24). Now He did not say "ask me" or simply "ask the Father." On the contrary, He said "If you ask anything of the Father, He will give it to you in my name." For until Jesus taught this, no one asked the Father in the name of the Son. And what Jesus said was true, "Hitherto you have asked nothing in my name." And also true was His saying, "Ask, and you will receive, that your joy may be full."

3. Let us suppose someone thinks that we should pray to Christ Himself and argues that we are permitted to do so because it says that He is worshiped in the text from Deuteronomy, which admittedly refers to Christ, "Let all the angels of God worship Him" (Deut. 32:43 LXX; Heb. 1:6). Let him be told that even the Church, which is called Jerusalem by the prophet, is worshiped by kings and queens, who are her nursing mothers and foster fathers. This is said in the following passage, "Behold, I will lift up my hand to the nations, and raise my signal to the peoples; and they shall bring your sons in their bosom, and your daughters they shall carry on their shoulders. Kings shall be your foster fathers, and their queens your nursing mothers. With their faces to the ground they shall worship you, and lick the dust of your feet. Then you will know that I am the Lord, and you will not be ashamed" (Is. 49:22–23).

4. Christ said, "Why do you call me good? No one is good but God the Father alone" (cf. Mk. 10:18; Lk. 18:19; Mt. 19:17). Would He not also say:

> Why do you pray to me? You should pray only to the Father, to whom I pray myself. This is what you learn from the holy Scriptures. For you must not pray *to* the High Priest appointed on your behalf by the Father (cf. Heb. 8:3) or *to* the Advocate who is charged by the Father with praying for you (cf. 1 John 2:1). Rather you must pray *through* the High Priest and Advocate, who is able to sympathize with your weaknesses, since He has been tempted in every respect as you are, and yet tempted without sin (Heb. 4:15) because of the Father's gift to me. Learn, then, how great a gift you have received from my Father, when you received the Spirit of sonship (Rom. 8:15) by becoming regenerate in me, so that you are called sons of God and my brothers. For you have read the proclamation concerning you that I made to the Father through David, "I will proclaim your name to my brethren, in the midst of the Church I will praise you" (Ps. 22:22; cf. Heb. 2:12). It is not reasonable for those who are deemed worthy of one and the same Father to pray to a brother. You must pray only to the Father with me and through me.

XVI.1. Since we hear Jesus saying this, let us pray to God through Him, all of us saying the same things and not divided about the way we pray. Are we not divided if some of us pray to the Father and some to the Son, since those who pray to the Son, whether with or without the Father, sin through lack of instruction and great simplicity because they have not examined or inquired into the matter? Therefore, let us pray as to a God, and let us intercede as with a Father. Let us make supplication as of a Lord, and let us give thanks as to a God, a Father, and a Lord, though in no sense Lord of a servant. For a father may reasonably be supposed also lord of a son, and He is Lord of those who have become sons through Him. Just as He is not God of the dead, but of the living (Mt. 22:32; Mk. 12:27; Lk. 20:38), so He is not Lord of base slaves, but of those who to begin with were in fear because of their childishness, but who have been made noble and afterwards serve more blessedly by love than they did in fear. For the marks of God's servants and of His sons are visible in the soul only to the One who sees their hearts.

2. Therefore, everyone who seeks earthly or little things from

God disobeys God, who does not know how to give anything earthly or little, and fails to obey His order to seek heavenly and great things. But suppose someone replies that corporeal things were given the saints in answer to prayer, and that even the saying in the Gospel teaches that earthly and little things "will be added" for us. He must receive the following answer. Imagine that someone gives us a corporeal object, it does not matter what. We should not say that he gave us the shadow of the object. (For he would not offer to give two things, an object and a shadow, but his offer is to give an object, and our reception of the object's shadow follows from the gift of the object.) In just the same way, if we consider with our minds raised to nobler aspirations those gifts God chiefly gives us, we shall say that what follows upon the great and heavenly spiritual gifts are corporeal things that pertain to them, since they are given to each of the saints for the common good (1 Cor. 12:7) or in proportion to our faith (Rom. 12:6) or as the Giver wills (1 Cor. 12:11). And He wills wisely, even if we are not able to give the reason for each of the things given or an account worthy of the Giver.

3. Hannah's soul, then, when it was transformed from sterility, bore greater fruit than her body did when it conceived Samuel[42] (1 Sam. 1:19–20). And Hezekiah gave birth to divine children more of his mind than of his body, since his bodily children were born of bodily seed. And Esther, Mordecai, and the people were delivered more from spiritual plots than from Haman and his fellow conspirators. [And Judith] cut in pieces the power of the Prince, who wished to destroy her soul, more than she did the power of Holofernes. Who would not acknowledge that the spiritual blessing that overtakes all the saints and that is described by Isaac to Jacob, when he says, "May God give you of the dew of heaven" (Gen. 27:28), is what came upon Ananias and those with him more than the corporeal dew that overcame Nebuchadnezzar's fire? It was the mouths of invisible lions more than the ones perceived that were shut for the prophet Daniel so they were unable to do anything against his soul. All of us who have read about them in Scripture have understood this. Who is there who has escaped the

---

42. Cf. the list in XIII.2.

belly of the whale that swallows up every fugitive from God but has been subdued by Jesus our Savior, that does not become like Jonah a saint filled with the Holy Spirit?

XVII.1. We must not be surprised if to all those who receive, so to speak, the objects that cast such shadows, the shadow is not always given, even though some do receive the shadow. This is clearly proved by those who study the problems of sun dials and the account given of shadows with respect to the body that gives light, since it varies according to latitude.[43] Thus, in some latitudes sundials cast no shadow at a certain time; in others, so to speak, they cast short shadows, and in others shadows longer than in the first. Now since it is the purpose of the One who gives to bestow the chief gifts according to certain ineffable and mysterious proportions that harmonize with those who receive them and with the times, it is no great surprise if when the chief gifts are given, sometimes absolutely no shadows come along for those receiving them, while sometimes shadows not of all but of a few come along; sometimes they are smaller by comparison with others, and sometimes greater. Now neither the presence nor the absence of the shadows of objects delights or saddens the one who seeks the sun's rays, since he has the most necessary thing when he receives its light, even if he is deprived of a shadow, or if he has a longer or a shorter shadow. In the same way when spiritual gifts are present with us and we are enlightened by God for the complete possession of true goods, let us not split hairs about so shabby a thing as a shadow. For all material and corporeal things, whatever they are, are reckoned a fleeting and feeble shadow, since they can in no way be compared to the saving and holy gifts of the God of all. For what comparison is there between corporeal wealth and the wealth with all speech and all knowledge (1 Cor. 1:5)? And who would be so mad as to compare health of flesh and bone with a healthy mind, a robust soul, and well-ordered thoughts? If all these are put in harmony by the Word of God, they make bodily sufferings nothing but an insignificant scratch, indeed less than a scratch.

2. The person who understands what beauty that bride has who is loved by the "bridegroom," the Word of God—and I mean

---

43. Reading the conjectural emendation *klimata* instead of *sōmata*.

the soul when it blooms with a beauty beyond heaven and beyond the universe—he will be ashamed even to honor by the same word "beauty" the corporeal beauty of a woman, a boy, or a man. For flesh does not contain beauty in the proper sense, since it is all ugliness. "All flesh is grass"; and its glory, which is shown in the so-called beauty of women and boys, is compared to a flower according to the prophetic word "All flesh is grass, and all its glory like a flower of grass. The grass has withered, and the flower has fallen; but the Word of the Lord stands forever" (Is. 40:6). Moreover, who would any longer call what is constantly spoken of by people noble birth in its true sense, once he has known the noble birth of the sons of God? And how will the mind that has contemplated the unshakable kingdom of Christ (cf. Heb. 12:28) fail to despise as worth nothing every kingdom on earth? And the one who has seen as clearly as he can—so far as the human mind still bound to the body is capable—the army of angels and the chief captains of the Lord's power among them, and archangels, thrones, dominions, principalities, and heavenly powers, and who has gained the power of being honored equally with them by the Father (cf. Lk. 2:13; Josh. 5:14; Col. 1:16; Lk. 20:36)—how will he fail, even if he is feebler than a shadow, to despise by comparison what foolish men marvel at and count them the meanest things of all and worth nothing? And even if all these things are given him, he will despise them so as not to be deprived of the true principalities and the more divine powers. We must pray, therefore, we must pray for the things that are chiefly and truly great and heavenly. And we must leave to God what concerns the shadows that accompany the chief goods, since He knows what we need because of our mortal body before we ask Him (Mt. 6:8).

PART TWO: THE LORD'S PRAYER

XVIII.1. I have spoken sufficiently in the preceding examination on the subject of prayer and have done so as far as I have been capable of receiving it according to the grace given by God through His Christ. (And my hope is that it has been given also in the Holy Spirit; if so, you who read this treatise will judge of its inspiration.)

117

Now I come to the next challenge and wish to contemplate the prayer written by the Lord as a model and the power with which it is filled.

2. First of all, it must be observed that Matthew and Luke seem to many to have written down the same prayer, sketched out to show how we ought to pray. The verses of Matthew have it in the following form: "Our Father in heaven, hallowed be your name, your kingdom come, your will be done, on earth as in heaven. Give us today our daily bread. Forgive us our sins, as we forgive our debtors. And lead us not into temptation, but deliver us from the Evil One" (Mt. 6:9–13). Luke's version reads, "Father, hallowed be your name, your kingdom come. Give us day by day our daily bread. And forgive us our sins, for we ourselves forgive everyone who is indebted to us. And lead us not into temptation" (Lk. 11:2–4).

3. Now it must be said to those who hold the opinion I have mentioned that first, the words, even if they have a close resemblance to one another, nevertheless appear to differ in the two versions, as I shall explain when I examine them carefully. Second, it is impossible that the same prayer should be spoken in two places. The first is on the mountain where "seeing the crowds, He went up . . . and when He sat down, His disciples came to Him. And He opened His mouth and taught" (Mt. 5:1–2). This first version is found written by Matthew in the context of the proclamation of the beatitudes and of the commandments that follow. The second is in "a certain place" in which "He was praying," and "when He ceased," He spoke the prayer to one of the disciples who asked to be taught to pray "as John taught his disciples" (Lk. 11:1). For how can we admit that the same words were spoken in a prolonged speech without a prior request and also proclaimed at the request of a disciple? Yet perhaps someone will say in reply that the prayers have the same force as a single prayer spoken one time in a prolonged speech and another time in answer to the request of a disciple, who was apparently absent when He spoke the prayer in Matthew's version or failed to understand what was said then. On the whole, it is better to suppose that the prayers are different, even though they have certain parts in common. I looked also in Mark,

lest a prayer having the same force had by chance escaped my notice, but I found no trace of a prayer there.

XIX.1. Now since, as I have said in the previous discussion, the one praying must first place himself in a certain settled disposition and then pray with this attitude, let us see what our Savior says about praying, immediately before the prayer found in Matthew. These are his words, "When you pray, you must not be like the hypocrites; for they love to stand and pray in the synagogues and at the street corners, that they may be seen by men. Truly, I say to you, they have received their reward. But when you pray, go into your room and shut the door and pray to your Father who is in secret; and your Father who sees in secret will reward you. And in praying do not heap up empty phrases as the Gentiles do; for they think that they will be heard for their many words. Do not be like them, for your Father knows what you need before you ask Him. Pray then like this . . ." (Mt. 6:5–9).

2. Our Savior often shows Himself an opponent of the love of glory as something involving a destructive passion. He did so here when He forbade them to try to accomplish what hypocrites do at the time of prayer. For hypocrites work hard at boasting before men of their piety or generosity. We must remember our Lord's saying, "How can you believe, who receive glory from one another and do not seek the glory that comes from the only God?" (Jn. 5:44). And so we must despise the glory that comes from men, even if it may be supposed a good thing; and we must seek the proper and true glory, which comes only from Him who glorifies the person worthy of glory in a way fitting for Himself, and does so beyond the worth of the one glorified. Thus, that very thing which is supposed to be good and praiseworthy is defiled when we act that we may receive glory from men or that we may be seen by men (cf. Mt. 6:2, 5). And consequently we receive no reward from God for this. Now every one of Jesus' words is without deceit; and, if pressed, we must say that they are still more without deceit when He speaks with His accustomed oath. And He says the same thing about those who seem to do good to their neighbor for human glory or who pray "in the synagogues and at the street corners that they may be seen by men. Truly, I say to you, they have received their

reward" (Mt. 6:5). For just as the rich man, according to Luke, has received "good things" in his own human "lifetime" and because of having received them is incapable of getting them any longer after the present life, so the man who receives his "reward" for giving something to someone or by prayers, since he has not sown to the Spirit but to the flesh, will reap corruption and will not reap eternal life (cf. Lk. 16:25; Gal. 6:8). The man who gives alms "in the synagogues and in the streets" with a "trumpet" before him, that he may be glorified by men, reaps to the flesh (Mt. 6:2). So does the man who loves "to stand and pray in the synagogues and at the street corners," that he may appear to men a religious person and may be supposed holy by those who see him (Mt. 6:5).

3. Moreover, everyone who travels on the broad and open road that leads to destruction (cf. Mt. 7:13), a road that has nothing right and straight but is full of twists and turns (for straight stretches are for most of the way blocked off), stands on it praying badly "at the street corners"; and through fondness for pleasure he is found not in one but in many streets (Mt. 6:5). And in these streets those who die like men (cf. Ps. 82:7) because they have fallen away from the Godhead stand glorifying and blessing those whom they suppose to have the same false religion as themselves. And there are many who always appear when they pray to be lovers of pleasure rather than lovers of God (2 Tim. 3:4). By praying drunkenly in the midst of banquets and carousings they truly "stand and pray at the street corners." For everyone who lives by pleasure and loves the open road has fallen from the narrow and straitened road of Jesus Christ, which has no twists or turns at all (cf. Mt. 7:13–14).

XX.1. Let us suppose there is a difference between church and synagogue. (In its proper sense the church has no spot or wrinkle or any such thing [Eph. 5:27], but is holy and blameless. Into it enters no bastard or eunuch or one castrated [cf. Deut. 23:1–2], no, not even an Egyptian or Edomite, unless when children have been born to them for three generations they may with difficulty be able to fit into the church [Deut. 23:7–8]. No Moabite or Ammonite may enter, unless the tenth generation is fulfilled and the time accomplished [Deut. 23:3]. But the synagogue was built by "a centurion" before the coming of Jesus and the time when He bore witness that the Son of God had never found anyone having such faith, "not even in Israel" [Lk. 7:9; Mt. 8:10].) Thus, the one who loves "to pray in the synagogues" is not far from the "street corners." But the saint is not like this. For he does not love to pray, but has true affection[44] for it. And he does not pray in the synagogues, but in the churches, not in the street corners, but in the straightness of the narrow and straitened road. And he prays not that he may appear to men, but that he may appear before the Lord God (Deut. 16:16). For he is a male, understanding the acceptable year of the Lord (Is. 61:2; Lk. 4:19) and keeping the commandment, "three times a year all your males shall appear before the Lord your God" (Deut. 16:16).

2. We must listen carefully to the expression "they may appear," since nothing that appears is good (cf. Ignatius, Rom. 3), because it exists only in appearance and not in truth and because it forms the images of erroneous impressions inaccurately and falsely. For example, the actors[45] of the plays in the theaters are not what they say they are, but they are seen according to the parts they happen to be playing. In the same way, those who pretend to the false appearance of good are not righteous but only actors of righteousness, "hypocrites," and they act in their own theater, "the synagogues and street corners." But the person who is not an actor, but has put away everything foreign to him, and who makes himself ready to give delight in that theater far surpassing the one just mentioned, enters into his own "room" to the wealth treasured up there, since he has shut up for himself the treasures of wisdom and knowledge (cf. Mt. 6:6; Col. 2:3; 1 Tim. 6:18–19). And without turning or gaping in any way toward what is outside, he shuts up every "door" of the senses that he may not be held by the senses, or his mind glutted by their impressions. And he prays to the Father, who does not shun or abandon such a hidden place, but dwells in it together with the presence of His Only Begotten Son. For He says, "I and the Father will come and make our home with him" (cf. Jn. 14:23). It is obvious that if we pray this way, we make intercession with the Righteous One, who is not only our God, but also our

---

44. The word in Greek is *agapei* and is contrasted with *philei*.
45. In Greek, *hypokritai*, which means both "actors" and "hypocrites."

Father, who does not abandon His sons, but is present with us in the secret place, observes it, and brings greater treasure into the "room," if we shut its door.

XXI.1. Moreover, when we pray, let us not "heap up empty phrases," but let us discuss divine truths. Now we heap up empty phrases when we fail to find fault with ourselves or the words we offer in prayer and when we speak of corrupt deeds, words, or thoughts, things that are lowly, blameworthy, and foreign to the incorruptibility of the Lord. Thus, the one who heaps up empty phrases in his prayers is by his condition in a worse synagogue than those I have mentioned and in a more dangerous road than those who are at the street corners, since he preserves not a trace even of the pretense of good. For according to the text of the Gospel only "the Gentiles" heap up empty phrases, since they have no impression of the great and heavenly requests and offer every prayer for bodily and outward things. The person who asks for the things here below from the Lord who dwells in the heavens and above the heights of the heavens is like a Gentile heaping up empty phrases.

2. And it seems to be the case that the man who speaks much "heaps up empty phrases," and the man who heaps up empty phrases speaks much. For nothing that pertains to matter and bodies is one, but everything that we suppose to be one is split, cut up, and divided into more than one, thus losing its unity. And the good is one, but shameful things are many; and truth is one, but lies are many; and true righteousness is one, but there are many ways of counterfeiting it; and the wisdom of God is one, but many are the wisdoms—doomed to pass away—of this age and of the rulers of this age (1 Cor. 2:6); and the word of God is one, but many are the words foreign to God. Therefore, no one will escape sin when words are many; and no one who thinks he will be heard, when words are many, can be heard (cf. Prov. 10:19). Consequently, we must not make our prayers like those of the Gentiles, who heap up empty phrases or speak with many words or do anything at all like a serpent (cf. Ps. 57:5 LXX–Ps. 58:4). For the God of the saints, since He is their Father, knows what His sons need (cf. Mt. 6:8), because such things are worthy of the Father's knowledge. And if someone does not know God, he does not know the things of God, and does not know what he needs. He is entirely mistaken about

what he supposes he needs. But he who has seen the better and more divine things he needs, the things known by God, will obtain what he has seen and what is known to the Father, even before he asks. Now that I have discussed what Matthew says before his version of the prayer, let me go on to contemplate what is revealed by the prayer itself.

XXII.1. *Our Father in heaven* It is right to examine what is said in the Old Testament quite carefully to see whether any prayer may be found in it calling God "Father." Up till now, though I have looked as carefully as I can, I have not found one. I do not mean that God was not called Father or that those who are supposed to have believed in God were not called sons of God; but nowhere have I found in a prayer the boldness proclaimed by the Savior in calling God Father. It is often possible to see God called Father and those who have drawn near to the Word of God sons. For example, it says in Deuteronomy, "You have deserted God who begot you and have forgotten God who nourishes you" (Deut. 32:18) and again, "Is He not your Father, who possessed you and made you and created you?" (Deut. 32:6), and again, "Sons, in whom there is no faith" (Deut. 32:20). And in Isaiah, "Sons have I begotten and raised up, but they have rejected me" (Is. 1:2). And in Malachi, "A son will honor his father, and a servant his lord. If then I am a Father, where is my honor? And if I am a Lord, where is my fear?" (Mal. 1:6).

2. But even if God is called Father and those who are begotten by the word of faith in Him are called sons, the certainty and immutability of sonship cannot be seen in the Old Testament. Indeed, the passages I have listed indicate that those called sons are guilty, since according to the Apostle, "so long as the heir is a child, he is no better than a servant, though he is lord of all, but he is under guardians and trustees until the date set by the father" (Gal. 4:1–2). And "the fulness of time" (Gal. 4:4) is present in the coming of our Lord Jesus Christ, when those who wish receive the adoption of sons, as Paul teaches in these words, "For you did not receive the spirit of bondage to fall back into fear, but you have received the Spirit of sonship in which we cry, 'Abba, Father!' " (Rom. 8:15). And in John, "But to all who received Him, He gave power to become children of God, to those who believe in His name" (Jn.

1:12). And because of the "Spirit of sonship" we have learned in the general letter of John concerning those born of God that "no one born of God commits sin, for His seed remains in him, and he cannot sin because he is born of God" (1 John 3:9).

3. If, therefore, we understand what the verse written in Luke means, "When you pray, say, 'Father' " (Lk. 11:2), we shall hesitate to offer this address to Him if we have not become genuine sons, lest we should somehow be guilty of the charge of impiety in addition to our other sins. What I mean is this. Paul says in 1 Corinthians, "No one can say 'Jesus is Lord' except by the Holy Spirit, and no one speaking by the Spirit of God ever says 'Jesus be cursed!' " (1 Cor. 12:3). He names the same person "the Holy Spirit" and "the Spirit of God." Now what it means to say "Jesus is Lord" by the Holy Spirit is not entirely clear, since multitudes of hypocrites use the expression, as well as a great many heretics and sometimes even demons, when conquered by the power in the name. But no one will dare declare that any of these say "Jesus is Lord" by the Holy Spirit. Moreover, he would not even be shown to say "Jesus is Lord," since the only ones who say "Jesus is Lord" in its true sense are those who serve the Word of God and make public proclamation in whatever they do that they have no other Lord. If it is such people that say "Jesus is Lord," perhaps everyone who sins curses the divine Word by transgressing and shouts through his deeds "Jesus be cursed!" Therefore, just as one sort of person says "Jesus is Lord," while the one with the opposite disposition says "Jesus be cursed," so, too, "everyone who is born of God" and does not sin because he partakes of God's seed, which turns him away from all sin, through his deeds says "Our Father in heaven." And the Spirit bears witness with their spirit that they are "children of God," His "heirs," and "fellow heirs with Christ," when by suffering with Him they hope with good reason to be glorified with Him (cf. Rom. 8:16–17). And so that they may not say "Our Father" only half way, such people add to their works their heart, which is the fount and origin of good works and which believes to righteousness, while the mouth joins in harmony and confesses to salvation (cf. Rom. 10:10).

4. Therefore, all their deeds, words, and thoughts, formed by the Only Begotten Word according to Him (cf. Gal. 4:19; Rom.

8:29; 2 Cor. 3:18), have come to imitate the image of the invisible God (Col. 1:15; 2 Cor. 4:4; cf. *Contra Celsum* VIII.17) and have come to be after the image of the Creator (Col. 3:10), who makes the sun rise on the evil and on the good, and sends rain on the just and on the unjust (Mt. 5:45), so that the image of the Man from heaven (1 Cor. 15:49), who is Himself the image of God, is in them. The saints, therefore, are an image of an image (cf. 1 Cor. 11:7), since the Son is the image (Col. 1:15). And they model His sonship by being conformed not only to Christ's glorious body (Phil. 3:21), but also to the one in the body.[46] And they become conformed to the One in a glorious body, when they are transformed by the renewal of their mind (Rom. 12:2). Now if these are the sort of people who say "Our Father in heaven" in everything, it is obvious that "he who commits sin," as it says in the general letter of John, "is of the devil; for the devil has sinned from the beginning" (1 John 3:8). And just as the "seed" of God remaining in the person "born of God" (1 John 3:9) explains why the one formed according to the Only Begotten Word cannot sin, so also the "seed" of the devil is present in everyone who "commits sin." And so long as it is present in his soul, it does not permit the person who has it to gain the ability to do right. But since "the reason the Son of God appeared was to destroy the works of the devil" (1 John 3:8), it is possible by the coming of the Word of God to our soul for the works of the devil to be overthrown, the evil seed placed within us to be utterly destroyed, and for us to become children of God.

5. Therefore, let us not suppose that the Scriptures teach us to say "Our Father" at any appointed time of prayer. Rather, if we understand the earlier discussion of praying "constantly"[47] (1 Thess. 5:17), let our whole life be a constant prayer in which we say "Our Father in heaven," and let us keep our commonwealth (Phil. 3:20) not in any way on earth, but in every way in heaven, the throne of God, because the kingdom of God is established in all those who bear the image of the Man from heaven (1 Cor. 15:49) and have thus become heavenly.

XXIII.1. Now when He is said to be the Father of the saints in heaven, we must not suppose that He is circumscribed by any

---

46. Presumably Origen means the Incarnate Lord before His exaltation.
47. Cf. Chapter XII.

corporeal shape and dwells in heaven. The reason is that God would be found contained as something less than heaven, since heaven would contain Him; and it is necessary to hold the conviction that everything is contained and held together by Him through the ineffable power of His divinity. And generally speaking, the literal expressions of Scripture, which are supposed by the simple to say that God is in a place, must be understood in a sense suitable to lofty and spiritual ideas about God. The point applies to the following passage in John, "Now before the feast of the Passover, when Jesus knew that His hour had come to depart out of this world to the Father, having loved His own who were in the world, He loved them to the end," and a little further on, "Knowing that the Father had given all things into His hands, and that He had come from God and was going to God" (Jn. 13:1, 3). And in another passage, "You heard me say to you, 'I go away, and I will come to you.' If you loved me, you would have rejoiced, because I go to the Father" (Jn. 14:28). And again, another passage, "But now I am going to Him who sent me; yet none of you asks me, 'Where are you going?' " (Jn. 16:5). Now if these passages must be understood in a spatial sense, so must the following one, "Jesus answered and said to them, 'If a man loves me, he will keep my word, and my Father will love him, and we will come to him and make our home with him" (cf. Jn. 14:23).

2. Surely this statement does not refer to the idea of a change of place with respect to the Father and the Son toward the one who loves Jesus' word, nor can it be understood in a spatial sense. Rather, the Word of God, by condescending to us and by being humbled, as it were, in regard to His own worth, when He is present with men, is said to change places from this world to the Father. The result is that we also see Him in His perfection, returning from the emptying with which He emptied Himself (Phil. 2:7) alongside us, to His own fulness (cf. Col. 1:19, 2:9; Eph. 1:23). And we, too, using Him as a guide, are fulfilled and delivered from all emptiness. Therefore, let the Word of God leave the world and go away "to the One who sent Him," and let Him go "to the Father." We must also seek to understand in a more mystical sense the statement at the end of John's Gospel, "Do not hold me, for I have

not yet ascended to my Father" (Jn. 20:17). If we understand the ascent of the Son to the Father with holy insight and in a way suitable to God, we shall realize it is the ascent of mind rather than of body.

3. I think it was necessary to add this discussion to the consideration of "Our Father in heaven" in order to refute the lowly notion about God held by those who suppose that He is in heaven in a spatial fashion and to say that no one should allow that God is in a corporeal place, since it would follow that He is Himself corporeal. The most impious doctrines are implied by the belief that God is corporeal; and He will be thought to be divisible, material, and corruptible. For every body is divisible, material, and corruptible. Or let them say to us, not just by way of an unconsidered feeling but by way of a claim to perceive clearly, how it is possible to avoid the conclusion that He is of a material nature. Now since even before the corporeal coming of Christ, many passages of Scripture seem to say that God is in a corporeal place, it does not seem to me foolish to list a few of them in order to remove what distracts those people from the truth, who on account of their own experience, so far as it goes, circumscribe the God of all in a small and narrow place. First, in Genesis it says, "Adam and Eve heard the sound of the Lord God walking in the garden in the cool of the day, and Adam and his wife hid themselves from the presence of the Lord God among the trees of the garden" (Gen. 3:8). We shall ask those who are unwilling to approach the treasures of Scripture and do not even give the first knock at its door (cf. Lk. 13:25) the following question. The Lord God, who fills heaven and earth (cf. Jer. 23:24) and who in their opinion uses in a bodily fashion heaven as a throne and earth as the stool of His feet (cf. Mt. 5:34–35; Is. 66:1)—are they able to imagine Him enclosed in a place so small by comparison with the whole heaven and earth that the garden they suppose was corporeal was not filled by God, but was so much greater than He that it contained Him while He was walking, since the sound of His footsteps was heard? And it would be even more foolish according to them for Adam and Eve, ashamed before God because of their transgression, to try to hide themselves "from the presence of the Lord God among the trees of the garden." And it does not even

127

say that they wanted to hide themselves, but that they actually "hid themselves." And how according to them could God inquire of Adam, "Where are you?" (Gen. 3:9)?

4. I have given a more extended treatment of this in my commentary on Genesis. For the moment, lest I should completely pass over so great a problem, let me be content with bringing to mind what is said by God in Deuteronomy, "I will dwell in their midst, and I will walk among them" (cf. Deut. 23:14; Lev. 26:12; Ezek. 37:27; 2 Cor. 6:16). His walking among the saints is just like His walking in the garden, since everyone who sins hides himself from God, flees His coming, and is removed from boldness. For this is how "Cain went away from the presence of God, and dwelt in the land of Nod, opposite Eden" (Gen. 4:16). Therefore, He dwells in heaven the same way He dwells among the saints or in every saint who also bears the image of the Man from heaven (1 Cor. 15:49) or in Christ, in whom are all the luminaries and the stars of heaven destined for salvation (cf. Phil. 2:15; Rev. 1:20; Gen. 1:14, 16; Wis. 13:2). Or because of the saints in heaven He also dwells there in accordance with the verse, "To you have I lifted up my eyes, O you that dwell in heaven" (Ps. 123:1). And in Ecclesiastes, "Do not hasten to offer a word before the presence of God, for God is in heaven above, and you upon earth below" (Eccles. 5:2). He wants to show the difference between those who are still in the body of humiliation (Phil. 3:21) and those who are with the angels, exalted by the help of the Word to be with the holy powers and with Christ Himself. And it is not absurd for Him to be, properly speaking, the Father's throne, since He is called allegorically "heaven" (cf. Heb. 1:8); and His Church, called "earth," is the stool of His feet.

5. I have added a few passages from the Old Testament that are thought to describe God in a place in order by the power given me to persuade the reader in every way to hear the sacred Scripture in a more lofty and spiritual sense, when it appears to teach that God is in a place. And it was right to add this discussion to the words "Our Father in heaven," since they show that the being of God is distinct from everything generated. And those who do not share His being, nonetheless have a certain glory of God and His power and, so to speak, an emanation of the Godhead (cf. Wis. 7:25).

XXIV.1. *Hallowed be your name* The one who prays either describes what has not yet happened or what he thinks, having happened, will not remain or be kept safe.[48] This is clear because in Matthew and Luke, when we are commanded to say "hallowed be your name," the implication of the text is that the name of the Father has not yet been hallowed. But someone might say, how could a person think that the name of God could be hallowed as though it had not already been hallowed? Let me consider the meaning of the "name" of the Father and of its hallowing.

2. Now a name is a designation that sums up and describes the particular quality of the one named. For example, Paul the Apostle has a certain quality all his own, both of soul by which he is what he is, and of mind by which he can contemplate certain things, and of body by which he is a certain way. Thus, the special character of these qualities, which is incompatible with anyone else, is indicated by the name "Paul": for no one else is exactly like Paul in these respects. But in the case of human beings, since their individuating qualities are subject to change, their names are rightly changed according to Scripture. For when the quality of "Abram" was changed, he was called "Abraham" (Gen. 17:5). And when "Simon" was changed, he was called "Peter" (Mk. 3:16; Jn. 1:42). And when "Saul" stopped persecuting Christ, he was named "Paul" (Acts 13:9). In the case of God, however, who is Himself unchangeable and always remains unaltered, there is always a single name—that, we may say, spoken of Him in Exodus, "I AM" (Ex. 3:14) or something that would have the same significance. Since, then, all of us suppose something about God and have some ideas about Him, but not all of us understand what He is (for rare and, if it can be said, rarer than rare are those who understand His holiness in all respects), it follows that we are rightly taught that the idea about God in us is holy, so that we may see the holiness of the One who creates, exercises His providence, judges, chooses, abandons, welcomes, turns away, thinks worthy of a prize, and punishes each one according to his worth.

3. For in these activities and those like them, so to speak, the

---

48. Adopting the conjectural emendations *ho euchomenos . . . eite men*, instead of *hote men . . . hote de*.

special quality of God is characterized, which is what I suppose the "name" of God means in the Scriptures. For example, in Exodus, "You shall not take the name of the Lord your God in vain" (Ex. 20:7). And in Deuteronomy, "Let my speech be expected as rain, and let my words come down as dew, as the gentle rain upon the tender grass, and as the showers upon the herb, for I have called upon the name of the Lord" (Deut. 32:2–3). And in Psalms, "They will remember your name in all generations" (Ps. 45:17). Now the one who fits his idea of God to things he ought not takes "the name of the Lord in vain." But the one who is able to utter speech "like rain," which works together with those who hear it for the production of the fruits of their souls, and who can give encouraging words "like dew," bringing extremely profitable "gentle rain" in words with the force of edification upon the hearers or most effectual showers—this man can do all this because of the name. Since he understands that he needs God to bring all this to perfection, he calls Him to his side as the true provider of what I have mentioned. And everyone who sees clearly will, as well, remember the things concerning God rather than learn them for the first time, even if he thinks he hears them from someone or supposes that he finds out the mysteries of true religion.

4. Just as the one who prays must understand what is being said here and must ask that the name of God be hallowed, so also in the Psalms it is said, "Let us exalt His name together" (Ps. 34:3). The prophet commands us with all harmony in the same mind and will to attain to the true and lofty knowledge of the special character of God. For this is what it is to exalt the name of God "together." When someone partakes of an emanation of the Godhead, through being drawn up by God and having conquered his enemies, unable then to exult at his fall, he exalts the very power of God in which he partakes. This is shown in Psalm 30 by the verse, "I will exalt you, O Lord, for you have drawn me up and have not let my foes rejoice over me" (Ps. 30:1). And someone exalts God when he dedicates a house to Him in himself, since the title of the psalm reads this way, "A Psalm. A Son at the dedication of the house of David" (Ps. 30).

5. Moreover, in regard to the fact that "hallowed be your name" and the following petitions are in the imperative mood, it

must be said that quite frequently the translators[49] used imperatives instead of optatives. For example, in Psalms, "*Let* the lying lips *be* dumb, which speak lawlessness against the righteous" (Ps. 31:18) instead of "may they be." And, "*Let* the creditor *search out* all that he has . . . *let* him *have* no protector" in Psalm 109 about Judas (Ps. 109:11–12). For the entire psalm is a request that certain things may happen to Judas. Now Tatian did not realize that the verb "become" in the imperative mood does not always signify a wish, but sometimes must be understood according to its form as a true imperative. As a result he drew the most impious conclusions about the verse where God says, "Let there be light" (Gen. 1:3), by supposing He was praying that there be light rather than giving a command, "since," says Tatian because of his godless ideas, "God was in darkness."[50] I must say to him how, then, shall we understand, "Let the earth put forth vegetation" and "Let the water under heaven be gathered together" and "Let the waters bring forth swarms of living creatures" and "Let the earth bring forth living creatures" (Gen. 1:11, 9, 20, 24)? Must we conclude that God prays that "the water under heaven be gathered together" so as to stand on a firm foundation or that "the earth put forth" so that He may partake of its produce? What need has He of fish, birds, or animals—like His need of light—that He should pray for them? And if in the case of God it is foolish for Him to pray for them and so the verses are imperatives, how can we avoid saying the same thing about the verse "let there be light" and construe it not as a wish but as an imperative? It seemed to me necessary in my discussion of the imperatives in the Lord's Prayer to call to mind Tatian's different interpretations because of those who have been deceived by accepting his impious teaching, some of whom I have encountered.

XXV.1. *Your kingdom come* If the kingdom of God according to our Lord and Savior's word "does not come with signs to be observed, nor will they say, 'Lo, here it is!' or 'There!'" but "the kingdom of God is within us" (Lk. 17:20–21)—for the Word is

---

49. I.e., of the Septuagint.
50. Cf. *Contra Celsum* VI.51.

very near, in our mouth and in our heart (cf. Deut. 30:14; Rom. 10:8)—then it is clear that the one who prays that the kingdom of God may come prays that the kingdom of God may spring up in him, bear fruit, and be rightly perfected. This is because every saint is ruled by God, obeys the spiritual laws of God, and dwells in himself as in a well-ordered city. The Father is present with him, and Christ rules with the Father in his perfected soul in accord with the verse we called to mind a little earlier,[51] "We will come to him and make our home with him" (Jn. 14:23; cf. Mt. 13:23; Mk. 4:20; Lk. 8:15). (And I think that the kingdom of God may be understood to be the blessed condition of the governing mind and the right ordering of wise thoughts, while the kingdom of Christ is the saving words that go forth to those who hear and the deeds of righteousness and the other virtues that are accomplished.) For the Son of God is Word and Righteousness (cf. 1 Cor. 1:30). But every sinner is under the tyranny of the Prince of this age (cf. Ignatius; Eph. 19:1; 1 Cor. 2:6, 8; 2 Cor. 4:4), since every sinner is made a friend of the present evil age because he does not hand himself over to the One who gave "Himself for our sins to deliver us from the present evil age" and to deliver us "according to the will of our God and Father," according to the verse in the letter to the Galatians (Gal. 1:4). And the one who by voluntary sin is under the tyranny of the Prince of this age is also ruled by sin. That is why we are commanded by Paul no longer to be subjected to sin that wishes to rule over us. We are so ordered through the following words, "Let not sin therefore reign in your mortal bodies, to make you obey their passions" (Rom. 6:12).

2. Now someone will say in regard to both petitions, "hallowed be your name" and "your kingdom come," that if someone prays to be heard and is at some time heard, then obviously there will come a time for him when, according to what has just been said, the name of God will be hallowed and consequently the kingdom of God established. And if this will come to pass for him, how could he any longer pray appropriately for what is already present as though it were absent and say "hallowed be your name, your kingdom come"? This is the answer to be given. The one who prays

---

51. Cf. Chapter XXIII.1.

to get the word of knowledge and the word of wisdom (cf. 1 Cor. 12:8) always prays appropriately for them, since by being heard he will always receive more visions of wisdom and knowledge. But he will know "in part" only as many as he can understand in the present. And the perfect, which does away with "that which is in part," will "then" appear, when the mind contemplates intelligible things "face to face" apart from sense perception (cf. 1 Cor. 13:9–12). In just this way for each of us the perfect hallowing of God's name and the perfect establishment of His kingdom is not possible unless there also comes the perfection of knowledge, of wisdom, and, probably, of the other virtues. We are on the road to perfection, if straining forward to what lies ahead we forget what lies behind (cf. Phil. 3:14). As we make continual progress, the highest point of the kingdom of God will be established for us when the Apostle's word is fulfilled, when Christ with all His enemies made subject to Him will deliver "the kingdom to God the Father . . . that God may be all in all" (1 Cor. 15:24, 28). Therefore, let us pray "constantly" (1 Thess. 5:17) with a character being divinized by the Word, and let us say to our Father in heaven, "hallowed be your name, your kingdom come."

3. One further point must be made about the kingdom of God. Just as there is no partnership of righteousness and iniquity, no fellowship of light with darkness, and no agreement between Christ and Beliar (2 Cor. 6:14–15), so the kingdom of sin cannot coexist with the kingdom of God. If, therefore, we wish to be ruled by God, let not sin rule in any way in our bodies (cf. Rom. 6:12); and let us not obey its commands, when it summons our soul to the works of the flesh and to what is alien to God. Rather, let us put to death the members that are on earth (cf. Col. 3:5); and let us bring forth the fruits of the Spirit (cf. Gal. 5:22; Jn. 15:8, 16), so that the Lord may, as it were, walk about in us as in a spiritual garden (cf. Gen. 3:8; 2 Cor. 6:16), ruling alone over us with His Christ sitting in us at the right hand of the spiritual power we pray to obtain and seated until all His enemies in us become the stool of His feet and every rule and authority and power is destroyed from us (cf. 1 Cor. 15:24; Mt. 26:64; Mk. 14:62; Lk. 22:69; Ps. 110:1; Is. 66:1). For it is possible that this will come to pass for each one of us and that the last enemy, death, will be destroyed, so that also in our case Christ

will say, "O death, where is your sting? O hell, where is your victory?" (1 Cor. 15:55, 26). Now, then, let our "corruptible" put on holiness in purity and all spotlessness, and let it put on "incorruption." And let "this mortal," when death has been destroyed, clothe itself with the Father's immortality (cf. 1 Cor. 15:53–54), so that we who are ruled by God may now be partakers of the good things of regeneration and resurrection (cf. Mt. 19:28).

XXVI.1. *Your will be done on earth as in heaven* Luke, after "your kingdom come," omits this petition and puts next, "give us day by day our daily bread." So, let us examine in accordance with the previous discussion the words just cited, which are found only in Matthew. While we who pray are still on earth, since we understand that the will of God is done in heaven by all His own in heaven, let us pray that in everything the will of God may be done by us on earth just as it is done by them. This will happen when none of us do anything contrary to His will. And when the will of God is established "as in heaven" so also for us "on earth," then we shall inherit the kingdom of heaven (cf. Mt. 25:34), having been made like those in heaven, since like them we have borne the image of the Man from heaven (1 Cor. 15:49). And those who come after us "on earth" will pray to be made like us who have come to be "in heaven."

2. Moreover, the words "on earth as in heaven," found only in Matthew, can be taken to apply to each one of the petitions, so that what we are commanded to say in the prayer is, "Hallowed be your name on earth as in heaven, your kingdom come on earth as in heaven, your will be done on earth as in heaven." For the name of God has been sanctified by those in heaven, and the kingdom of God has been established for them, and the will of God has been done by them. And all these things, while lacking to us on earth, can become ours if we fashion ourselves worthy of gaining God's hearing concerning all of them.

3. Now someone may ask about "your will be done on earth as in heaven" and say, "How has the will of God been done in heaven, where there are spirits of wickedness (cf. Eph. 6:12) that explain why the sword of God will drink its fill in heaven?" (cf. Is. 34:5). If we pray that God's will be done on earth as in heaven, may we not be praying inadvertently that the opposing spirits should remain on

earth where they have come from heaven? For there are many wicked spirits on earth because of the victorious spirits of wickedness that are in the heavenly places (cf. Eph. 6:12). But suppose someone were to interpret heaven allegorically and say that it is Christ, while the earth is the Church. (For who is so worthy to be the Father's "throne" as Christ? And what is so like a "stool of His feet" as the Church? [Cf. Heb. 1:8; Ps. 45:7; Acts 7:49; Is. 66:1, and chapter 23.4]) In this way he will readily solve the questions raised by saying that each member of the Church must pray that he may make way for the Father's will in just the same way that Christ made way for it, when He came to do His Father's will (cf. Jn. 4:34) and perfected it completely. For it is possible for the one united to Him to become one Spirit with Him (cf. 1 Cor. 6:17), thereby making way for His will so that as it has been perfected in heaven it may so be perfected on earth. For, according to Paul, "He who is united to the Lord is one Spirit" (1 Cor. 6:7). And I think this interpretation will not be easily despised by any one who considers it quite carefully.

4. But someone contradicting it will cite the passage at the end of Matthew in which the Lord after the resurrection says to the eleven disciples, "All authority in heaven and on earth has been given to me" (Mt. 28:18). Having authority over what is in heaven, He says that authority on earth has been added. This is because what is in heaven was enlightened even before by the Word, while it is "at the close of the age" that what is on earth will be established as heaven by imitating what the Savior has already taken through the authority given the Son of God. Therefore, we may infer that through prayers He wishes to take His disciples as His fellow workers with the Father, so that like the things in heaven that had been subjected to truth and to the Word, He might correct the things on earth by the authority He received on earth as in heaven and might lead them to the blessed perfection of things subject to His power. In light of this the one who wishes heaven to be the Savior and earth the Church, and who says that heaven is the First Born of all creation (Col. 1:15) on whom the Father rests as on a throne, will find that it is the Man, whom He put on, when he had been made that power's own through humbling himself and becoming obedient to death (Phil. 2:8), that said after the resurrection,

"All authority in heaven and on earth has been given to me" (Mt. 28:18). This is because the Man corresponding to the Savior received authority over the things in heaven as things belonging to the Only Begotten, so that he might share with Him, being mingled with His divinity and united with Him.

5. But the second difficulty has not yet been solved—how can the will of God be in heaven, when the spirits of wickedness in heavenly places (cf. Eph. 6:12) wrestle against those on earth? Putting it this way suggests how the question can be solved. Now the one who, though still on earth, has his commonwealth in heaven (Phil. 3:20) lays up treasure in heaven (Mt. 6:20; Lk. 12:34), has his heart in heaven, and bears the image of the Man from heaven (1 Cor. 15:49)—he is no longer on earth, not because of place but because of free will; nor is he of the world below, but of that heaven which is even better than this worldly heaven. In just the same way the spirits of wickedness who live in heavenly places (cf. Eph. 6:12) have their commonwealth on earth, and through the things they plot in wrestling against men, they lay up treasure on earth (cf. Mt. 6:19); they bear the image of the man of dust (cf. 1 Cor. 15:49), who is the same as the first of the works of the Lord, created to be made sport with by the angels (Job 40:19 LXX). And so they are not heavenly nor do they dwell in heavenly places because of their wicked disposition. Therefore, when it is said, "Your will be done on earth as in heaven," we must not suppose that they are in heaven, since by their mind's intent they have fallen with the one who fell from heaven like lightning (cf. Lk. 10:18).

6. And perhaps when our Savior says that we ought to pray that the Father's will be done as in heaven so on earth, He does not command that there be prayers for those in the place "earth," so that they may be like those in the heavenly place. Rather, He commands the prayer because He wishes that everything "on earth," that is, the baser things and those allied with earthly things, should be made like the nobler things and those that have their commonwealth in heaven (Phil. 3:20), that is, everything that has become "heaven." For the one who sins, wherever he may be, is "earth," and will be somehow with his kindred unless he repents (cf. Gen. 3:19). But the one who does God's will and does not disobey the saving spiritual laws is "heaven." If then we are "earth"

because of sin, let us pray that also for us God's will may be disposed for correction, just as it overtook those before us who became or were "heaven." And if we are reckoned by God not "earth" but "heaven," let us ask that the will of God may be fulfilled on earth as in heaven, I mean for the baser people so that they may, so to speak, make earth heaven with the result that there will no longer be any earth, but all will become heaven. For if the will of God is done on earth as in heaven, understood as I have said, then earth does not remain earth. Let me put it more clearly by using another example. If the will of God is done for the incontinent just as for the continent, the incontinent will be continent. Or if the will of God is done also for the unjust as for the just, then the unjust will be just. Therefore, if the will of God is done also "on earth" as it is "in heaven," we shall all be "heaven." And although flesh, which has no profit, and blood, which is akin to it, cannot inherit the kingdom of heaven (cf. Jn. 6:63; 1 Cor. 6:9–10, 15:50), they will be chosen to inherit it, if they change from flesh, earth, dust, and blood to a heavenly form of being.

XXVII.1. *Give us today our daily bread*, or, in Luke's version, *Give us day by day our daily bread*   Since there are some who suppose that we are told to pray for corporeal bread, it is right to refute their false opinion and to establish the truth concerning "daily bread." It must be said to them: How can the One who says we must ask for heavenly and great things have us ask for bread to be given for our flesh, since that is not a heavenly thing nor is the request for it a great thing? It would be as though He had forgotten His own teaching and ordered us to offer supplication to the Father for an earthly and small thing.

2. Now I shall follow the Teacher Himself and shall bring forward what He teaches about bread as almost irrefutable evidence. In the Gospel of John He says to those who came to Capernaum to seek Him, "Truly, truly, I say to you, you seek me, not because you saw signs, but because you ate your fill of the loaves" (Jn. 6:26). For the one who has eaten of "the loaves" blessed by Jesus and has been filled by them seeks rather to comprehend the Son of God more accurately and hastens to Him. That is why He rightly gives the order, "Do not labor for the food that perishes, but for the food that endures to eternal life, which the Son of Man will

give to you" (Jn. 6:27). Those who heard this inquired about it and said, " 'What must we do, to be doing the works of God?' Jesus answered them, 'This is the work of God, that you believe in Him whom He has sent' " (Jn. 6:28–29). "God sent His Word and healed them" (Ps. 107:20), as it is written in Psalms, obviously referring to the sick. Those who believe in the Word do "the works of God," which are "food that endures to eternal life." And He says, "My Father gives you the true bread from heaven. For the bread of God is He who comes down from heaven and gives life to the world" (Jn. 6:32–33). The true bread is He who nourishes the true Man, made in the image of God; and the one who has been nourished by it will come to be in the likeness of Him who created him (cf. Gen. 1:26–27; Col. 3:9–10). And what is more nourishing to the soul than the Word, or what is more honorable than the Wisdom of God to the mind that holds it? What more rightly corresponds to a rational nature than truth?

3. But if someone objects to this and says that He would not have taught us to ask for "daily bread" if He meant something else, let him hear that even in the Gospel according to John sometimes He speaks about it as though it were something other than Himself, and sometimes as though He were Himself "bread." An example of the first is, "Moses gave you bread from heaven, not the true bread, but my Father gives you the true bread from heaven" (cf. Jn. 6:32). An example of referring it to Himself is what He says to those who said to Him, "Give us this bread always": "I am the bread of life; he who comes to me shall not hunger, and he who believes in me shall never thirst" (Jn. 6:34–35). And a little further on, "I am the living bread which came down from heaven; if anyone eats of this bread, he will live forever; and the bread which I give for the life of the world is my flesh" (Jn. 6:51).

4. Now all food is called "bread" in Scripture, as is clear from what is written about Moses, "For forty days I neither ate bread nor drank water" (cf. Deut. 9:9). How manifold and varying, then, is the nourishing Word, since not everyone can be nourished by the solid and vigorous food of divine teachings. That is why, when He wishes to offer food for an athlete, suitable for the more perfect, He says, "The bread which I shall give for the life of the world is my flesh" (Jn. 6:51), and a little further on, "Unless you eat the flesh of

the Son of Man and drink His blood, you have no life in you; he who eats my flesh and drinks my blood has eternal life, and I will raise him up at the last day. For my flesh is true food, and my blood is true drink. He who eats my flesh and drinks my blood abides in me, and I in him. As the living Father sent me, and I live because of the Father, so he who eats me will live because of me" (Jn. 6:53–57). This is the "true food," the "flesh" of Christ, existing as the Word become flesh according to the verse "The Word became flesh" (Jn. 1:14). And when we eat and drink Him, He also has dwelt in us (cf. Jn. 1:14). And when He is distributed (cf. Jn. 6:11), there is fulfilled the verse, "We have beheld His glory" (Jn. 1:14). "This is the bread which came down from heaven, not such as the fathers ate and died; he who eats this bread will live forever" (Jn. 6:58).

5. And Paul in addressing the Corinthians as "babes" and as people "behaving like ordinary men" (cf. 1 Cor. 3:1, 3) says, "I fed you with milk, not solid food; for you were not ready for it; and even yet you are not ready, for you are still of the flesh" (1 Cor. 3:2–3). And in Hebrews he says, "You need milk, not solid food; for everyone who lives on milk is unskilled in the word of righteousness, for he is a child. But solid food is for the perfect, for those who have their faculties trained by practice to distinguish good from evil" (Heb. 5:12–14). And I think that the verse, "One believes he may eat anything, while the weak man eats only vegetables" (Rom. 14:2) refers not primarily to his corporeal food, but to the words of God that nourish the soul. The first one, who is most faithful and perfect, can partake of all of them, as is indicated by "one believes he may eat anything." But the other one, who is weaker and less perfect, is content with the simpler teachings and with those that do not produce much vigor, as Paul wishes to indicate when he says, "The weak man eats only vegetables."

6. And I think that what is said by Solomon in Proverbs teaches that the one who cannot receive the more vigorous and greater teachings because of his simplicity and yet does not stumble in his thinking is better than the one who is quicker and sharper and applies himself to these matters more fully, but does not see clearly the meaning of peace and of the harmony of the universe. This is what the verse says, "Better is a dinner of vegetables with friend-

ship and grace than a fatted calf with hatred" (Prov. 15:17). And so we often accept a common and more simple dinner with a good conscience, when we are entertained by those unable to offer us any more, in preference to words lifted on high against the knowledge of God (cf. 1 Cor. 10:5), which proclaim with great persuasiveness a teaching foreign to the Law and the prophets given by the Father of our Lord Jesus (cf. Mt. 5:17, 7:12, 22:40; Lk. 16:16). Therefore, lest we should be sick through lack of food for the soul or die because of a famine of the Lord's Word (cf. Amos 8:11; Rom. 14:8; Gal. 2:19), let us ask the Father for the "living bread," who is the same as the "daily bread." Let us obey our Savior as teacher, believing and living more worthily.

7. Now I must consider what "daily" (*epiousion*) means. The first point to know is that the expression "daily" is not employed by any of the Greeks or of the wise, nor is it in colloquial use among the common people. Rather, it seems to have been invented by the evangelists. At least Matthew and Luke agree in using it without any difference. The translators of the Hebrew Scriptures did the same thing in other cases. For what Greek ever used the expression *enōtizou* or *akoutisthēti* instead of "receive in the ears" and "he makes you hear" (cf. Job 33:1, 31:34, 16:37; Is. 1:2)? Now something like the expression "daily" is that written by Moses, when God says, "You shall be to me a people for possession" (*periousios*) (cf. Ex. 19:5–6). It seems to me that both these words have been formed with reference to "being" (*ousia*), the one pointing out bread that has come together for "being" and the other meaning a people dwelling around "being" and sharing in it.

8. Those who say that substance (*hypostasin*) chiefly pertains to incorporeal things[52] customarily refer "being" in its strict sense to incorporeal things, since they exist steadfastly and neither admit any addition nor suffer any loss. (For this is the property of bodies, which are subject to increase and diminution because they are in flesh and need something to enter so as to sustain and nourish them. And whenever more comes in at a certain time than goes out, increase takes place; while whenever less comes in, diminution takes place. And perhaps when something receives nothing at all coming

---

52. The Platonists.

in, it is, so to speak, in a state of absolute diminution.) But those who think that "being" refers primarily to bodies and only to incorporal things secondarily[53] give the following definitions of "being." "Being is the prime material (*hylē*) and source of things that exist, either the material and source of bodies or the material and source of things named. Or being is the prime unqualified substratum that either subsists before things have existence or receives all changes and alterations, while it by definition remains itself unaltered, or endures through all alteration and change." According to these men, being by definition is without quality or shape and does not even have a fixed size, while it is present in every quality as a kind of prepared figure. By way of differentiation they say that qualities are energies and actions by which motions and relations take place. And they say that being by definition does not partake of any of these things, but is potentially inseparable from any one of them, since it is nevertheless receptive of all the energies of what acts in whatever way it does act and change. For the force existing in being and pervading it throughout is the cause of every quality and of the arrangements concerning it. They say that being is throughout changeable and throughout divisible, and that every being can be mingled with every other and nevertheless be a unity.

9. Now in inquiring about "being" because of "daily" bread and a people "for possession," I concluded that different meanings of "being" can be distinguished. And in the preceding discussion I argued that the bread for which we should ask is spiritual. Therefore, it is necessary to understand the being in the same sense as the bread, so that just as corporeal bread distributed to the body of the person to be nourished goes into his being, so also "the living bread which came down from heaven" and is distributed to the mind and the soul gives a share in its own power to the person who provides himself food from it. And thus the bread we ask will be "daily" in the sense that it will be "for our being." Moreover, just as the person nourished becomes empowered in differing ways according to the quality of the food, which may be solid and suitable for athletes or like milk or vegetables, so also it follows that the Word of God is given either as milk suitable for children or as vegetables fit

---

53. The Stoics.

for the sick or as meat special for those taking part in the contests. And the different ones, each nourished in proportion to how he places himself in the power of the Word, are able to do differentthings and become different kinds of people. Of course, there is something supposed to be food that is poisonous, and another that causes disease, and another that cannot even be distributed. All these must be transferred by analogy to different sorts of teaching that are supposed to be nourishing. Therefore, "daily bread," that is, "bread for being," is what corresponds most closely with a rational nature and is akin to Being itself. It procures at one time health, vigor, and strength to the soul; and since the Word of God is immortal, it shares its own immortality with the one who eats it.

10. Now this "daily bread for our being" seems to be given another name in Scripture, namely "the tree of life"; for the one who stretches out his hand and takes from it "will live forever" (Gen. 3:22). And by a third name this tree is called the Wisdom of God by Solomon, as follows, "She is a tree of life to all who lay hold of her, and to those who rely on her as on the Lord she is steadfast" (Prov. 3:18). And since the angels are nourished by the Wisdom of God and empowered to fulfill their special tasks by their contemplation of the truth with Wisdom, it is said in Psalms that the angels are also nourished, while the people of God who are called "Hebrews" share with the angels and, as it were, are fellow guests at their banquet. This is what is reported in the verse "Man ate of the bread of the angels" (Ps. 78:25). Surely our mind is not so impoverished as to think that the angels are nourished by always partaking of some corporeal bread such as is recounted to have come down from heaven on those who had come out of Egypt, and to think that this was the bread the Hebrews shared in with the angels, the ministering spirits of God.

11. It is not out of place while we are inquiring about "daily bread for our being," the tree of life, the Wisdom of God, and the food common to holy men and angels to note also the passage in Genesis about the three men who were entertained by Abraham and partook of three measures of fine meal kneaded to make bread baked in the ashes (Gen. 18:2–6). Perhaps the story is written to be understood in a merely figurative way, since the saints are able sometimes to partake of spiritual and rational food not only together

with men but also with the more divine powers, either because it profits them or because it shows what great nourishment they have been empowered to get for themselves. And the angels take delight in being nourished in such a manifestation and become more ready to assist them in every way and to inspire them thereafter in their comprehension of more and greater aspects of Him who gladdens and, so to speak, feeds them with nourishing teachings previously prepared. And it is not surprising that a man should feed angels, since Christ, too, agrees to stand at the door and knock (Rev. 3:20) so as to come in to the one who opens for Him and to eat with him from what he has. And after that, according to His own power as Son of God, He will share His own food with the one who first entertained Him.

12. Therefore, the one who partakes of "daily bread for our being" is strengthened in his heart and becomes a son of God (cf. Ps. 104:15; Jas. 5:8; 1 Thess. 3:13). But the one who shares in "the dragon" is no other than the spiritual "Ethiopian," who is himself changed into a snake because of the "snares of the dragon" (cf. Ps. 74:13–14; Rev. 12:3–17, 13:2, 4, 11, 16:13, 20:2). As a result, even if he says he wishes to be baptized, he hears the Word reproaching him, "Serpents, brood of vipers! Who warned you to flee from the wrath to come?" (Mt. 3:7; Lk. 3:7). And concerning the dragon's body that the Ethiopians dined upon, David says this, "You broke the heads of the dragons on the water. You crushed the head of the dragon. You gave him as food to the peoples, the Ethiopians" (Ps. 73:13–14 LXX–74:13–14). And since the Son of God exists in being and since the Adversary also exists, if it is not inconsistent that each of them becomes food for different people, why should we hesitate to accept the notion that in the case of all the nobler and baser powers and in the case of men each one of us can be nourished from all of them? Thus, when Peter was about to join in fellowship with the centurion Cornelius and with those assembled with him in Caesarea, and afterwards was going to give a share in the words of God to the Gentiles, he saw the vessel let down by four corners from heaven, in which were all kinds of animals, reptiles, and wild beasts of the earth (cf. Acts 10:11–12). And when he was ordered to rise, kill, and eat, after refusing, he said, "[You know] that nothing common or unclean has ever entered my mouth" (Acts

10:14). But he was commanded to call no man common or unclean, because what has been cleansed by God should not be called common by Peter (cf. Acts 10:28). The verse says, "What God has cleansed, you must not call common" (Acts 10:15, 11:9). Surely, then, the food that is clean and unclean according to the Law of Moses, distinguished by the names of a great many animals, has the higher meaning of different characters of rational beings. And the Law teaches that some foods are suitable for us, while others are the opposite until God cleanses them and makes them all nourishing, even those of every kind (cf. Mt. 13:47).

13. Now if this is so and there is such a difference between foods, there is one that stands out above all the others mentioned, "the daily bread for our being" about which we must pray that we be made worthy of it, and that nourished by God the Word, who was in the beginning with God (cf. Jn. 1:1), we may be made divine. But someone will say that *epiousion* ("daily for our being") is formed from "come upon" (*epienai*), so that we are commanded to ask for bread appropriate to the age to come, in order that God may take it ahead of time and give it to us now. As a result the bread that will be given tomorrow, so to speak, is given "today," since "today" refers to the present age and "tomorrow" to the one to come. Nevertheless, so far as I can judge, the former interpretation is better. So let me examine the next question, which concerns the "today" found in Matthew and the "day by day" found in Luke. Now it is the frequent custom of Scripture to call the whole age "today." For example, "He is the father of the Moabites up to today" (Gen. 19:37) and "He is the father of the Ammonites up to today" (Gen. 19:38) and "This story has been spread among the Jews up to today" (Mt. 28:15). And in Psalms, "Today if you hear His voice, harden not your hearts" (Ps. 95:7–8). And in the book of Joshua an extremely clear example is found in the verse, "Do not rebel from the Lord in the days today" (cf. Josh. 22:16, 18). And if the whole of this age is "today," perhaps "yesterday" is the preceding age. I have come to suppose that this is what is meant in Psalms and in Paul's letter to the Hebrews. In Psalms it says, "A thousand years in your sight are but as yesterday when it is past" (Ps. 90:4). (Perhaps this is the famous millennium that is compared to "yesterday" and distinguished from "today.") And in the Apostle's letter it

is written, "Jesus Christ yesterday and today, the same also forever" (Heb. 13:8). There is nothing surprising in God's reckoning the whole age as the span of one of our days, and I think that it is even less in His sight.

14. We must also inquire whether the words written about feasts or public festivals that take place according to days or months or seasons or years may be given a higher reference to ages (cf. Gal. 4:10). For if the Law has a shadow of the things to come (cf. Heb. 10:1), it is necessary that the many sabbaths are a "shadow" of many days of some kind and that new moons are fixed at intervals of time and accomplished by the conjunction of I do not know what moon and what sun. And if the first month and the tenth until the fourteenth day and the feast of unleavened bread from the fourteenth until the twenty-first day (cf. Ex. 12:2, 3, 6, 15, 18) have a "shadow of things to come," who is wise enough (cf. Hos. 14:9) and so much a friend of God (cf. Jas. 2:23) as to see the first of many months and the tenth day and so forth? And what should I say about the feast of the seven weeks (cf. Deut. 16:9ff.) and the seventh month when the day of the new moon is sounded with trumpets and on the tenth is the day of atonement (cf. Lev. 16:29ff., 23:24, 27–28)? These things are known only to God who gave the laws. Who has entered into the mind of Christ far enough to understand the seventh years when the Hebrews' servants were freed, debts were forgiven, and the holy land allowed to rest unfarmed (cf. Ex. 2:1–2; Lev. 25:4–7, 10–17; Deut. 15:1–3)? There is also a feast more important than the one that takes place every seven years called the Jubilee (cf. Lev. 25:8ff., 27:17ff.). But no one can imagine with any clarity how great it is or what true laws are fulfilled in it, save the one who has contemplated the Father's purpose in ordering all the ages according to His unsearchable judgments and His inscrutable ways (cf. Rom. 11:33).

15. By comparing two verses from the Apostle I have often been perplexed as to how this is the "end of the ages" in which Jesus "has appeared once for all . . . to put away sin," if there are to be ages succeeding this one. Here are the two verses. In Hebrews, "But now He has appeared once for all at the end of the ages to put away sin by the sacrifice of Himself" (Heb. 9:26). And in Ephesians, "That in the coming ages He might show the immeasurable

riches of His grace in kindness toward us" (Eph. 2:7). If I may hazard a guess at so great a puzzle, I think that just as the end of the year is the last month after which the beginning of another month takes place, so perhaps when many ages have been accomplished as, so to speak, a year of ages, the end is the present age, after which certain ages to come will take place, whose beginning is the age to come. And in those ages to come God will show the riches "of His grace in kindness," since the worst sinner, who has blasphemed the Holy Spirit and been ruled by sin from beginning to end in the whole of this present age, will afterwards in the age to come be brought into order, I know not how.

16. Therefore, let us imagine someone who sees these things and understands in his mind a week of ages. His purpose is to contemplate a holy sabbath rest, having understood also a month of ages, to see the holy new moon of God and a year of the ages, to recognize the feasts of the year when every male must appear before the Lord God (cf. Deut. 16:16; Col. 2:16) and the years of such great ages corresponding to them, to comprehend the holy seventh year and the seven weeks of ages. As a result of his prolonged meditation he sings hymns to the One who gave such great laws. How can such a person think that the least portion of an hour in a day of so great an age is of little importance? How can he fail to do everything so that after his preparation here he may become worthy of getting the "daily bread for his being" in the day that is called "today" and also "day by day"? (And it is now clear from the preceding discussion what "day by day" means.) The one who prays "today" to God, who is from infinity to infinity, not only about "today" but also somehow about "day by day" will be able to obtain from Him who is able to give more abundantly than all that we ask or think (Eph. 3:20), if I may speak in hyperboles, what exceeds what no eye has seen, what exceeds what no ear has heard, what exceeds what the heart of man has not conceived (cf. 1 Cor. 2:9).

17. It seems to me that it was necessary to discuss these matters so that "today" and "day by day" may be understood when we pray to be given our "daily bread" from His Father. And if we press our inquiry deeper and ask about "ours" in the latter book (Luke) where it is not said "give us today our daily bread" but "give us day

by day our daily bread," then it becomes a question of how this bread can be ours. Now the Apostle teaches that "whether life or death or the present or the future," all are the saints' (cf. 1 Cor. 3:22). And the statement does not necessarily refer to the present.

XXVIII.1. *And forgive us our sins, as we forgive our debtors,* or in Luke's version, *And forgive us our sins, for we ourselves forgive everyone who is indebted to us*   Now concerning debts the Apostle says, "Pay everyone their debts, taxes to whom taxes are due, fear to whom fear, revenue to whom revenue, honor to whom honor. Be indebted to no one in anything, except to love one another" (Rom. 13:7–8). Therefore, we are indebted, since we have certain responsibilities not only in giving but also in gentle speech and in certain kinds of deeds. Moreover, we are "indebted" to have a certain kind of disposition toward others. Since we are indebted in these ways, either we pay what is ordered by the divine Law by discharging it in full or, if we do not pay them because we despise the wholesome Word, we remain in debt.

2. A similar understanding must apply to our debts to our brothers, both those who have been regenerated with us according to Christ's word of true religion and those who have the same mother or father as we do. There is also a debt to citizens and another common to all men, a particular one for strangers and another particular one for those old enough to be our fathers, another in regard to any whom it would be reasonable to honor as sons or as brothers. Therefore, the person who does not do what is necessary for his debts to be paid in full to his brothers remains a debtor for what he has failed to do. In this way if we come short of anything that falls due as an obligation to others from the Spirit of wisdom that loves men, the debt becomes greater. Moreover, we are in debt to ourselves in respect of the things that concern us, to the body to use it not for the wasting away of its flesh through love of pleasure. And we are indebted also to the soul to apply great care to it and to take forethought about the sharpness of the mind and about our speech that it may be without sting, useful, and in no way idle (cf. Mt. 12:36). And whenever we fail to pay the debts owed us by ourselves, our penalty becomes heavier.

3. And beyond all this, since we are the workmanship and fashioning of God (cf. Eph. 2:10), we are indebted above all to

preserve a certain disposition toward Him and a love from all our heart, from all our strength, and from all our mind (cf. Mk. 12:30; Lk. 10:27; Mt. 22:37; Deut. 6:5, 13:3). If we do not accomplish this successfully, we remain debtors of God, since we have sinned against the Lord. And in such circumstances who will pray for us? For "if a man in sinning sins against a man, they will pray for him. But if he sins against the Lord, who will pray for him?" as Eli says in 1 Samuel (1 Sam. 2:25). Moreover, since Christ bought us with His own blood, we are His debtors, just as every servant is a debtor for the amount of money given for him to the one who bought him. We also have a debt to the Holy Spirit, in whom we were sealed for the day of redemption (Eph. 4:30). And we pay this debt when we do not grieve Him and do not bear fruits that grieve Him; these we avoid when He is present in us and gives life to our soul (cf. Jn. 15:8, 16, 6:63; 1 Pet. 3:18; 2 Cor. 3:6). And even though we do not know exactly who the angel is assigned to each of us, who sees the Father's face in heaven (cf. Mt. 18:10), nevertheless it is evident upon consideration that we are debtors for certain things to him. And if we are in a theater of the world both of angels and of men, we must know that, just as the person in a theater is a debtor to say or to do certain things in the view of the spectators and if he fails to do them is punished for having insulted the whole theater, so also we are debtors to the whole world, both to all the angels and to the human race, for those things that we shall learn from Wisdom if we are willing.

4. Apart from these more general responsibilities, a widow cared for by the Church has a debt, a deacon another, a presbyter another, and a bishop an extremely heavy debt for which payment is demanded by the Savior of the whole Church and punishment exacted if he does not pay it (cf. 1 Tim. 5:3, 16, 17). And the Apostle names a debt common to man and wife when he says, "Let the husband pay his debt to his wife, and likewise the wife to her husband." And he adds, "Do not refuse one another" (1 Cor. 7:3, 5). Why should I speak of all the debts we have, when it is open to those who read this treatise to apply what has been said to their own circumstances? Either we shall be held fast by these debts when we fail to pay them, or we shall be freed by paying them. At any rate, there is not a single hour of night or day in life when we are not in debt.

5. Now when he is in debt someone either pays or refuses payment. And it is possible in our lifetime to pay, but it is also possible to refuse payment. And some people are in debt to no one for anything (cf. Rom. 13:8). Some pay most debts and are in debt for a few things, while others pay a few and are in debt for the greater part. And perhaps there is someone who pays nothing, but is in debt for everything. Nevertheless, even the person who pays everything so as not to be in debt for anything accomplishes this at a certain time, since he needs release for his former debts. The one who tries very hard to become like this from a certain time, so that he is in debt for none of the things that might remain unpaid when they fall due, can rightly get this release. But those unlawful deeds that are marked in the governing mind become the bond that stands against us (Col. 2:14). From it we shall be judged as from books brought forward, so to speak, by all those who have taken written testimony, when we shall all stand before the judgment seat of Christ that each one may receive good or evil according to what he has done in the body (Rom. 14:10; 2 Cor. 5:10). The verse in Proverbs also refers to these debts, "Do not give yourself for security if you respect your person. For if you have nothing with which to pay, they will take your bed from under your ribs" (Prov. 22:26–27 LXX).

6. If we are in debt to so many people, it is inevitable that there are people in debt to us. Some are in our debt since we are men, others since we are citizens, others since we are fathers or sons. And in addition wives are in debt to us if we are husbands, and friends if we are friends. Therefore, whenever any of our numerous debtors are somewhat lax about paying what they owe us, we should act kindly toward them and not hold a grudge, remembering our own debts and how often we have put them off, not only when they are owing to men but even when they are owing to God Himself. For if we remember the debts we have not paid but have refused to pay when the time came to do one thing or another to our neighbor, we shall be gentler toward those liable to us who have not paid their debt. This will be especially so if we do not forget our transgressions against God and our speaking wickedness loftily (cf. Ps. 73:8) whether through ignorance of the truth or through dissatisfaction with the circumstances that have come our way.

7. But if we are unwilling to become gentler toward those liable to us, we shall experience what the man who refused to forgive his fellow servant a hundred denarii did. He had been previously forgiven according to the parable in the Gospel, and the master in anger made him pay what had been forgiven, saying to him, "You wicked and slothful servant, should you not have had mercy on your fellow servant, as I had mercy on you? Throw him into prison till he pays all his debt" (cf. Mt. 18:33–34, 25:26). And the Lord draws the moral, "So also the heavenly Father will do to every one of you, if you do not forgive your brother from your heart" (Mt. 18:35). Surely, those who have sinned against us must be forgiven when they say they repent, even if our debtor does this many times. For it says, "If your brother sins against you seven times in the day, and turns to you seven times and says, 'I repent,' you must forgive him" (Lk. 17:3–4). And we are not harsh to those who do not repent. Rather, such people are evil to themselves, for he who ignores instruction hates himself (Prov. 15:32). Nevertheless, in the case of such people healing must be sought in every way possible, even for the person so completely perverted that he is not even conscious of his own evils and is drunk with a drunkenness more deadly than that caused by wine, the drunkenness that comes from the darkness of evil (cf. Prov. 20:1; Is. 28:1, 7; Mt. 24:49).

8. Luke says "Forgive us our sins," since sins are associated with our debts if we have not paid them. He says the same thing as Matthew, but does not seem to leave room for the person who wishes to forgive debtors only if they repent. He says that our Savior has given the law that we ought to add to our prayer, "For we ourselves forgive every one who is indebted to us" (Lk. 11:4). Surely, we all have authority to forgive sins against ourselves. This is clear from "as we forgive our debtors" (Mt. 6:12) and from "for we ourselves forgive every one who is indebted to us." But consider the person inspired by Jesus as the apostles were and who can be known by his fruits (cf. Mt. 7:16, 20; Lk. 6:44) as someone who has received the Holy Spirit and become spiritual by being led by the Spirit as a son of God to do everything by reason (cf. 1 Cor. 2:14–15; Rom. 8:14; Gal. 5:18). This person forgives whatever God forgives and retains sins that cannot be healed, serving God

like the prophets by speaking not his own words but those of the divine will (cf. Jn. 20:23). So he, too, serves God, who alone has authority to forgive.

9. And in the Gospel of John the words about the power of forgiveness given the apostles read as follows, "Receive the Holy Spirit. If you forgive the sins of any, they are forgiven; if you retain the sins of any, they are retained" (Jn. 20:22–23). If someone were to take this in an unexamined sense, he might charge the apostles with not forgiving all that might be forgiven and with retaining the sins of some that they might be retained with God because of the apostles. But it is useful to take an example from the Law so that the forgiveness of men's sins by God through men may be understood. The priests in the Law in the case of certain sins are prohibited from offering a sacrifice to gain people forgiveness for the transgressions for which sacrifices are made. For though the priest has authority to make an offering for certain inadvertent sins or transgressions, nevertheless he does not offer a burnt offering and a sin offering (cf. Ps. 40:6) for adultery, deliberate murder, or any other graver fault. Therefore, it is in the same way that the apostles and those like the apostles, since they are priests according to the great High Priest, have received knowledge of God's healing and know, since they are taught by the Spirit, for what sins sacrifice must be offered and when and how; and they know for what sins it is wrong to do this. Thus, Eli the priest, when he knew that his sons Hophni and Phinehas were sinning, realizing he could in no way contribute to the forgiveness of their sins, acknowledged it as a hopeless case and said, "If a man sins against a man, they will pray for him; but if he sins against the Lord, who will pray for him?" (1 Sam. 2:25).

10. I do not know how some arrogate to themselves powers that exceed the priestly dignity; perhaps they do not thoroughly understand priestly knowledge. These people boast they are able to pardon even idolatry and to forgive adultery and fornication, supposing that through their prayers for whose who have dared these things even mortal sin is loosed. For they do not read that "there is a sin which is mortal. I do not say that one is to pray for that" (1 John 5:16). We must not leave out that most courageous Job, who offered sacrifice for his sons, saying, "It may be that my sons have thought

evil against God in their minds" (Job 1:5 LXX). He offered the sacrifice when it was doubtful his sons had sinned and for sins that had not reached the lips.

XXIX.1. *And lead us not into temptation, but deliver us from the Evil One*   The petition "but deliver us from the Evil One" is omitted by Luke. If the Savior orders us to pray for things that are not impossible, it seems to me worth asking how we are commanded to pray not to enter into temptation, when the whole of men's life on earth is temptation. We are in temptation by the very fact that we are on earth, surrounded by flesh that wars against the Spirit, the mind of which is hostile to God, since it can in no way submit to God's Law (cf. Jas. 4:1; 1 Pet. 2:11; Gal. 5:17; Rom. 8:7).

2. We learn from Job that the whole of human life on earth is temptation. He says, "Is not the life of men on earth a temptation?" (Job 7:1 LXX). And in Psalm 17 the same point is demonstrated by the verse "By you I shall be delivered from temptation" (Ps. 17:30 LXX–18:30). Moreover, Paul wrote to the Corinthians not that they would not be tempted, but that God would favor them with not being tempted beyond their power. He says, "No temptation has overtaken you that is not common to man. God is faithful, and He will not let you be tempted beyond your strength, but with the temptation will also provide the way of escape, that you may be able to endure it" (1 Cor. 10:13). For whether the wrestling is against the flesh that lusts and wars against the Spirit (cf. Eph. 6:12; Gal. 5:17; Jas. 4:1; 1 Pet. 2:11) or against the soul of all flesh (cf. Lev. 17:11), which is synonymous with the governing mind that dwells in the body and is called "heart," no matter what kind it is, the wrestling is for people tempted with human temptations. And even imagine that our contests are for firmly planted and more perfect athletes, who no longer wrestle against flesh and blood, but against the principalities and the powers and the world rulers of this present darkness and the spirits of wickedness that have already been trampled under foot (Eph. 6:12). And imagine that these athletes are not tested by merely human temptations. Even then we are not delivered from temptation.

3. Then how is it our Savior commands us to pray not to enter into temptation, since God somehow tempts everyone? For Judith says, not only to the elders at that time but also to all who read her

book, "Remember what He did with Abraham, and how He tempted Isaac, and what happened to Jacob in Mesopotamia in Syria, while he was keeping the sheep of Laban, his mother's brother. For He has not tried us with fire, as He did them, to search their hearts, nor has He taken revenge upon us; but the Lord scourges those who draw near to Him, in order to admonish them" (Jdt. 8:26–27). And David shows in a general way what happens to all the righteous when he says, "Many are the afflictions of the righteous" (Ps. 34:19). And the Apostle in Acts says, "Through many tribulations we must enter the kingdom of God" (Acts 14:22).

4. And unless we understand something that has escaped the notice of the many concerning praying not to enter into temptation, it is time to say that the apostles sometimes prayed and were not heard. How many thousand sufferings did they experience throughout their lifetimes with far greater labors, with far more beatings, with countless imprisonments, and often near death (cf. 2 Cor. 11:23)? Paul on his own received at the hands of the Jews the forty lashes less one, was beaten with rods three times, was stoned once, was shipwrecked three times, was adrift at sea a night and a day (cf. 2 Cor. 11:24–25). He was a man in every way afflicted, perplexed, persecuted, and struck down (cf. 2 Cor. 4:8–9); and yet he confessed, "To the present hour we hunger and thirst, we are ill-clad and buffeted and homeless, and we labor working with our hands. When reviled, we bless; when persecuted, we endure; when slandered, we try to conciliate" (1 Cor. 4:11–13). Now if the apostles did not gain the answers to their prayers, what hope is there for someone quite inferior to them of gaining God's hearing when he prays?

5. In Psalm 26 it says, "Prove me, O Lord, and tempt me, try with fire my reins and my heart" (Ps. 26:2). Now someone who has not carefully inquired into the purpose of our Savior's command might reasonably suppose that this verse from the psalm contradicts what our Lord taught about prayer. But who ever supposed that he was beyond human temptations by having fulfilled the tally of those he knew?[54] And what time is there when he can presume he does not have to struggle to keep from sinning? Is someone poor?

---

54. Adopting Oulton's conjectural emendation of *anthrōpinōn* instead of *anthrōpous*.

Let him take care lest he steal and profane the name of the Lord (Prov. 30:9). Is someone rich? Let him not be disdainful, for he can become filled with a lie and lifted up to say, "Who sees me?" (Prov. 30:9, 24:32 LXX). Indeed, not even Paul, who was rich with all speech and all knowledge (1 Cor. 1:5), was freed from the danger of sinning by exalting himself because of this; but he needed a thorn of Satan to harass him to keep him from being too elated (cf. 2 Cor. 12:7). And even if someone has a clean conscience and has taken wing from evils, let him read what is said of Hezekiah in 2 Chronicles. He is said to have fallen "from the loftiness of his heart" (2 Chron. 32:25–26).

6. And since I have not said much about the poor man, if someone disdains the poor man's temptation as no temptation at all, let him know that the Plotter plots to bring down the poor and needy (Ps. 37:14), especially since, according to Solomon, "The poor man does not stand up to threatening" (Prov. 13:8 LXX). And why must I say how many have taken their place in punishment with the rich man in the Gospel (cf. Lk. 16:22–24) because they have not administered corporeal wealth rightly, and how many have fallen away from the heavenly hope (cf. Col. 1:5) by bearing their poverty basely and living more slavishly and more lowly than is fitting among saints (cf. Eph. 5:3)? Nor are those between these two extremes of wealth and poverty freed entirely from sinning because of their moderate possessions.

7. But the person who is healthy and wholesome in body sometimes supposes that he is beyond all temptation because of that very health and wholesomeness. But to what others does the sin of destroying God's temple (cf. 1 Cor. 3:17) belong than to those who are healthy and wholesome? Because it is obvious to everyone, no one will venture to speak of this subject. But will someone who is sick have escaped provocations to destroy God's temple, since he has leisure at that time and full opportunity to receive thoughts of unclean things? And why must I say how many things besides these trouble him, if he does not keep his heart with all vigilance (Prov. 4:23)? For many, conquered by their pains and not knowing how to bear their diseases with courage, disgrace their souls rather than their bodies when they are sick. And many by fleeing contempt have fallen into eternal shame, since they have been ashamed of bearing Christ's name nobly.

8. Now someone may think he rests untempted when he is glorified by men. But how can we avoid the hard saying, "They have received their reward" from men (Mt. 6:2), which was proclaimed to those who were exalted by glory from the multitude as though it were a good thing? And how can we avoid the rebuke, "How can you believe, who receive glory from one another and do not seek the glory that comes from the only God?" (Jn. 5:44). And why should I list the prideful offenses of those supposed well born and the flattering subjection to their supposed superiors adopted because of their ignorance by the so-called base born—a subjection that separates from God those who feign genuine affection, but do not have love, the noblest of human possessions?

9. Therefore, as was said before, the whole life of man on earth is temptation (cf. Job 7:1). Therefore, let us pray to be delivered from temptation not by avoiding temptation (for that is impossible, especially for those on earth), but by not being defeated when we are tempted. Now I suppose that the person defeated in temptation enters *into* temptation, since he is caught fast in its meshes. The Savior entered those meshes because of those who had been caught in them before. According to what is said in Song of Songs, "looking through the meshes" He answers those who have been caught by them before and who have entered into temptation; and He says to those who are His bride, Arise, come away, my love, my fair one, my dove" (cf. Song 2:9–10). And to prove that every time is a time of temptation for men, I shall add this: Not even the person who meditates on the Law of God day and night (Ps. 1:2) and trains himself to accomplish the saying "The mouth of the righteous will exercise itself in wisdom" (Prov. 10:31)—not even he has been freed from temptation.

10. Why should I also say how many in devoting themselves to the study of the sacred Scriptures have misconstrued what is proclaimed in the Law and the prophets and have devoted themselves to godless and impious teachings or to foolish and ridiculous ones? What a vast multitude there is of those who stumble in this way, even though they do not seem guilty of the charge of neglecting Scripture. And many have suffered the same fate with respect to the Epistles and the Gospels by fabricating through their own stupidities a Son or a Father other than the one understood according to truth and explained in theology by the saints. For the person

who does not think the truth about God or His Christ has fallen away from the true God and His Only Begotten Son. By supposing what his stupidity has fabricated to be the Father and the Son, he does not really worship. This happens to him because he has not understood that there is a temptation in reading the Scriptures and has not stood armed and ready for the struggle that meets him even there.

11. Therefore, we must pray not that we be not tempted (for that is impossible), but that we be not encompassed with temptation, which is what happens to those who are enmeshed in it and conquered. Thus, it is written outside the prayer, not to enter into temptation (Lk. 22:40; Mt. 26:41; Mk. 14:38). The verse can probably be clearly understood from the previous discussion. And in the prayer we must say to God the Father, "Lead us not into temptation." So it is worth seeing how we must understand God to bring one who has not prayed or who has not been heard "into temptation." For, since someone who enters into temptation is conquered, it is absurd to suppose that God leads anyone into temptation as if He were giving him up to be conquered. And the same absurdity remains no matter how we interpret the verse "Pray that you may not enter into temptation" (Lk. 22:40). For if falling into temptation is an evil we pray not to suffer, how can it fail to be foolish to think that the good God, who cannot endure evil fruit (cf. Mt. 7:18), encompasses anyone with evils?

12. Now it is useful in this matter to add what Paul says in his letter to the Romans, "Claiming to be wise, they became fools, and exchanged the glory of the immortal God for images resembling mortal men or birds or animals or reptiles. Therefore God gave them up in the lusts of their hearts to impurity, to the dishonoring of their bodies among themselves," and a little further on, "For this reason God gave them up to dishonorable passions. Their women exchanged natural relations for unnatural, and the men likewise gave up natural relations with women, and were consumed with passion, and so forth," and a little further on, "And since they did not see fit to acknowledge God, God gave them up to an unfit mind and to impure conduct" (Rom. 1:22–24, 26–28). Surely, all this must be taken into consideration by those who cut the Godhead in two; and those who suppose that the good Father of our Lord is

156

someone other than the God of the Law must be told this: Suppose the good God leads into temptation the one who does not gain his prayer. And suppose the Father of the Lord gives up those who had previously committed any sin "in the lusts of their hearts to impurity, to the dishonoring of their bodies among themselves" (Rom. 1:24). And suppose, as they themselves say, that because He is free from the imputation of judging and punishing, He gives them up "to dishonorable passions" and "to an unfit mind and to improper conduct" (Rom. 1:26, 28). Assuming all this, would those so condemned not have been "in the lusts of their hearts" even if they had not been given up to them by God? Would they not have fallen into "dishonorable passions" even if they had not been given up to them by God? Would they not have fallen into an "unfit mind" quite apart from being given up to it by God?

13. Now I know very well that these problems are extremely troubling to the people I am talking about, and that is why they fabricate a God other than the Creator of heaven and earth, since they find many such statements in the Law and the prophets and take offense at a God who they think could not be good if He utters such words. And so, because of the perplexities about "lead us not into temptation" that led me to add the verses from the Apostle's writings, let me now see whether I can find reasonable solutions for the absurdities. I think that God orders every rational soul with a view to its eternal life. And the soul always preserves free choice; and on its own responsibility it either comes to be in nobler things, advancing step by step to the summit of goods, or descends from failing to pay attention in diverse motions to one flood or another of evil. Thus, since a quick and too brief healing causes some to think lightly of the diseases into which they have fallen, as though they were easy to heal, and since this results in their falling into the same diseases a second time after they have been healed, God in such cases will reasonably overlook the evil as it increases to a certain point, even disregarding it when it progresses so far in them as to be incurable. His purpose is that they may become satiated by long exposure to evil, and by being filled with the sin they desire may so perceive the harm they have taken. Then they hate what they previously welcomed; and since they have been healed more firmly, they are able to profit from the health of their souls, which is theirs

by the healing. Consider the following example. Once the "mixed multitude" that was among the children of Israel "had a strong craving; and the children of Israel also sat down and wept and said, 'Who will give us meat to eat? We remember the fish we ate in Egypt for nothing, the cucumbers, the melons, the leeks, the onions, and the garlic; but now our soul is dried up, and there is nothing at all but this manna to look at' " (Num. 11:4–6). And then a little further on, "And Moses heard them weeping throughout their families, every man at his door" (Num. 11:10). And again a little further on the Lord says to Moses, "And say to the people, 'Consecrate yourselves for tomorrow, and you shall eat meat, for you have wept in the hearing of the Lord, saying, "Who will give us meat to eat? For it was well with us in Egypt." Therefore the Lord will give you meat to eat, and you shall eat meat. You shall not eat one day, or two days, or five days, or ten days, or twenty days, but a whole month, until it comes out at your nostrils and becomes loathesome to you, because you have rejected the Lord who is among you, and have wept before Him, saying, "Why did we come forth out of Egypt?" ' " (Num. 11:18–20).

14. Let us see whether we can introduce the story as a useful parallel for solving the absurdity we have found in "lead us not into temptation" and in the verses from the Apostle's writings. The mixed multitude that was among the children of Israel had a strong craving and wept, and the children of Israel with them. And it is clear that as long as they did not have the things they craved, they could not have their fill of them or cease from their passion. But God, who is benevolent and good, in giving them what they desired did not wish to give it in such a way that any craving should be left in them. Therefore, He says they will not eat meat one day; for the passion would have remained in their soul, which was on fire and ablaze with it, if they had partaken of meat for so short a time. Indeed, He does not give them what they crave for two days. But wishing to make it satiating to them, as if He were not promising but threatening the one able to understand with what He was intending to give them, He says:

> You shall spend not just five days eating meat, nor double that, nor double that sum; but you shall, by eating meat for a whole month, eat long enough for what you supposed good to come out at your nostrils with a loathsome

sensation and for the craving for it to become blameworthy and shameful. My purpose is to free you from life, when you will no longer have cravings. If you go out this way, since you will be pure of craving and will remember by what pains you were freed from it, you will be able never again to fall into it. Or if it should ever happen that in long periods of time you forget what you have suffered because of your craving, if you do not take heed for yourselves and receive the Word, who perfectly frees you from every passion, then you will fall into evil. Craving once more the realm of becoming, you will ask to get what you crave a second time. But if you come to hate what you crave, then this is how you will turn back to noble things and to the heavenly food that those who grasp for baser things despise.

15. Something like this, then, is what those experienced who exchanged "the glory of the immortal God for images resembling mortal men or birds or animals or reptiles" (Rom. 1:23). By forsaking God they are given up "in the lusts of their hearts to impurity, to the dishonoring of their bodies" (Rom. 1:24). For they have lowered to a body without soul or sense the name of Him who gives to all sentient and rational beings not only the power of sentience, but also of sensing rationally, and to some even the power of sensing and thinking perfectly and virtuously. And it is reasonable that such people, by forsaking God and being forsaken by Him in return, should be given up by Him to "dishonorable passions," receiving "the due penalty for their error" (Rom. 1:26–27) by which they loved itching pleasure. For the due penalty for their error becomes theirs when they are given up to dishonorable passions, rather than when they are cleansed by the wise fire (cf. Is. 4:4; Mal. 3:2) and made to pay in prison for each of their debts up to the last penny (cf. Mt. 5:25–6; Lk. 12:58–59). For in being given up to the dishonorable passions, not only those that are natural but also many of those that are unnatural, they are defiled and coarsened by the flesh, just as though they no longer had a soul or mind, but had become entirely flesh. But in the fire and the prison they do not receive "the due penalty of their error," but they gain a beneficence for cleansing them of the evils in their error. This is accompanied by saving pains that follow those who love pleasure. And so they are freed from all the filth and blood by which they had been so stained and defiled that they could not even think of being saved from their own destruction. Thus, God shall wash away the filth of the sons and daughters of Zion, and will cleanse the blood from

their midst by a spirit of judgment and by a spirit of burning (Is. 4:4). For He goes forth like a refiner's fire and like fullers' soap (Mal. 3:2–3), washing and cleansing those who need such healing remedies because they were unwilling to acknowledge God in a fitting way. But when they are given up to these remedies, they will hate willingly "the unfit mind" (Rom. 1:28). For God does not wish that the good should belong to anyone by necessity but willingly, since there are perhaps some who by their long association with evil will come by toil and pain to understand its ugliness and will turn away from it as something falsely supposed beautiful.

16. Set beside this the question whether God hardened Pharaoh's heart (cf. Ex. 7:3, 22, 8:19, 9:12, 35, 10:1, 20, 27, 11:10) so that he might be able to say what he did when no longer hardened, "The Lord is in the right, and I and my people are in the wrong" (Ex. 9:27). Nevertheless, he needed to be hardened still more and suffer still more, lest by ceasing from the hardening too quickly he should despise the hardening as an evil and deserve to be hardened many times more. Therefore, suppose that "nets are spread for the birds not unjustly," according to what is said in Proverbs (Prov. 1:17), but that God rightly leads them "into the snare," according to the verse, "You have led us into the snare" (Ps. 66:11). And suppose that not even the meanest of birds, the sparrow, falls "into the snare" without the Father's will (cf. Mt. 10:29; Lk. 12:6), even though the bird falling into the snare falls into it because it has not made good use of the power of its wings for raising itself up. On these grounds let us pray that we do nothing to deserve being led into temptation by God's righteous judgment, since everyone so led is also given up by God "in the lusts of his heart to impurity" (Rom. 1:24), every one of them is given up "to dishonorable passions" (Rom. 1:26), every one of them "since he did not see fit to acknowledge God" is given up "to an unfit mind" and to improper conduct (Rom. 1:28).

17. Now the use of temptation is something like this. What our soul has received escapes everyone's knowledge but God's— even our own. But it becomes evident through temptations, so that we no longer escape the knowledge of what we are like. And in knowing ourselves we are also conscious, if we are willing, of our own evils; and we give thanks for the good things that have been

160

made evident to us through temptations. And the fact that the temptations that come to us are meant to show us who we are or to make known the secret things in our hearts is established by a verse in Job spoken by the Lord and by one in Deuteronomy. They read, "Do you think that I have answered you for any other reason than that you may be revealed as righteous?" (Job 40:8 LXX). And in Deuteronomy, "He humbled you and let you hunger and fed you with manna . . . and He led you . . . in the wilderness . . . with its biting serpent and scorpion and thirst . . . so that . . . you might know what was in your heart" (Deut. 8:3, 2, 15, 2).

18. If we are also willing to be reminded from the narratives of the Bible, let it be known that Eve's easy deception and the unsoundness of her reasoning did not come about when she listened to the serpent and disobeyed God, but was in existence even before she was tested. And this was why the serpent approached her, since he perceived by his own subtle judgment her weakness (cf. Gen. 3:1, 6). Moreover, not even in the case of Cain did wickedness begin when he killed his brother (Gen. 4:8). For even before that God, who knows the heart (cf. Acts 15:8, 1:24), had no regard for Cain and his sacrifice (Gen. 4:5). But his evil was made evident when he slew Abel. Moreover, if Noah had not become drunk by drinking the wine he had cultivated and had not become naked, neither the rashness of Ham and his impiety toward his father nor the reverence and respect of his brothers for their parent would have been made evident (Gen. 9:20–23). And the plot of Esau against Jacob has its apparent occasion in taking away the blessing. But before this Esau's soul had "roots" of his being immoral and irreligious (cf. Gen. 27:41; Deut. 29:18; Heb. 12:15–16). And we should not have known the splendor of Joseph's continence, prepared so as not to be captive to any lust, if his mistress had not become enamored of him (cf. Gen. 39:7ff.).

19. Therefore, in the times of relief between temptations let us stand firm for their onset, and let us be prepared for everything that can happen, so that whatever comes to pass, we may not be tested as though unready, but may be revealed as those who have disciplined themselves with extreme care. For when we have accomplished all we can by ourselves, God will fulfill what is lacking because of human weakness. In everything He works for good with

those who love Him, those who are foreseen for whatever they will be by themselves, according to His foreknowledge, which cannot be false (cf. Rom. 8:28).

XXX.1. It seems to me that Luke through "lead us not into temptation" has also implicitly taught "deliver us from the Evil One." And it is likely that the Lord spoke in a shorter way to the disciple, since he had already been helped, but in a plainer way to the multitude, who needed clearer teaching. And God delivers us from the Evil One not when the Enemy who wrestles against us (cf. Eph. 6:11–12) has in no way attacked us through any of his crafts and any of the servants of his will, but when we are gaining the victory with courage by standing firm against what happens to us. This is how we have understood the verse "Many are the afflictions of the righteous, and He will deliver them out of them all" (Ps. 34:19). For God delivers us from afflictions not when we are no longer in affliction (even if Paul says "we are afflicted in every way" [2 Cor. 4:8], as though there were never a time when we were not afflicted), but when in our affliction we are not crushed because of God's help (cf. 2 Cor. 4:8). "To be afflicted," according to a colloquial usage of the Hebrews, has the meaning of a critical circumstance that happens to us without our free choice, while "to be crushed" implies our free choice and that it has been conquered by affliction and given into its power. And so Paul is right when he says, "We are afflicted in every way but not crushed" (2 Cor. 4:8). I suppose the verse in Psalms is like this, "In affliction you have given me room" (Ps. 4:1). For the sense of joy and good cheer that comes to us in critical times from God by the cooperation and presence of the Word of God, who encourages and saves us, is called "room."

2. Therefore, the deliverance of everyone from the Evil One must be understood in a similar way. God delivered Job not because the devil did not take authority to encompass him with certain kinds of temptations (for he did take it), but because "in all these circumstances" Job sinned in no way before the Lord, but was revealed to be righteous (Job 1:22). The devil said, "Does Job fear the Lord for naught? Have you not built a fence around what is outside and what is inside his house and around all that is his round about? Have you not blessed his works and made his possessions many upon earth? But put forth your hand and touch all that he

has, and surely he will curse you to your face" (Job 1:9–11). But the devil was put to shame for having spoken falsely against Job. For when Job suffered so many things, he did not, as the Adversary had said, "curse God to His face"; but even when he was given up to the Tempter, he continued blessing the Lord. And he rebuked his wife, when she said, "Speak one word to the Lord and die" (Job 2:9 LXX). He reproved her by saying, "You have spoken as one of the foolish women. If we receive good at the hand of the Lord, shall we not endure evil?" (Job 2:10 LXX). And a second time concerning Job "the devil said to the Lord, 'Skin for skin. All that a man has he will give for his life. But truly, put forth your hand and touch his bones and his flesh, and he will curse you to your face'" (Job 2:4–5 LXX). But the devil was conquered by the athlete of virtue and proved to be a liar. For though he suffered extreme hardships, Job endured, sinning in no way "with his lips" before God (Job 2:10). Job wrestled and conquered twice, but he did not enter such a struggle a third time. For it was necessary for three wrestlings to be kept for the Savior. This threefold wrestling is written in the three Gospels (Mt. 4:1–11; Lk. 4:1–13; Mk. 1:12–13), where our Savior as man is understood to have conquered the Enemy three times.

3. Therefore, so that we may with understanding ask God not to lead us into temptation and to deliver us from the Evil One, let us examine these matters with great care and search them out by ourselves. And so, through hearing God let us become worthy of being heard by Him. Let us beseech Him when we are tempted that we be not put to death and be not set on fire by the fiery arrows of the Evil One when they are hurled against us (cf. 2 Cor. 6:9; Eph. 6:16). All whose hearts have become "like an oven," according to one of the twelve prophets (Hos. 7:6), are set on fire. But those are not set on fire who by the shield of faith quench all the fiery arrows sent against them by the Evil One, whenever they have in themselves rivers of water welling up to eternal life (cf. Jn. 4:14, 7:38) that do not allow the arrow of the Evil One to prevail, but easily destroy it by the flood of divine and saving thoughts impressed from contemplations of the truth upon the soul of the one who trains himself to be spiritual.

Part Three: Special Directions

XXXI.1. It does not seem to me out of place after these discussions to finish this treatise on prayer by speaking in an introductory way about the disposition and the posture one ought to have in praying, the place where one ought to pray, the direction in which one ought to look barring any chance circumstance, the suitable and special time for prayer, and anything else similar. The question of disposition must be referred to the soul, that of the posture to the body. Thus, Paul, as I said earlier in the treatise,[55] describes the disposition and says that we must pray "without anger or quarreling"; and he describes the posture by the phrase "lifting holy hands" (1 Tim. 2:8). He seems to me to have taken this from Psalms, where it calls "the lifting up of my hands an evening sacrifice" (Ps. 141:2). Concerning place Paul says, "I desire then that in every place the men should pray" (1 Tim. 2:8). Concerning direction, in the Wisdom of Solomon it says, "To make it known that one must rise before the sun to give you thanks, and must pray to you at the dawning of the light" (Wis. 16:28).

2. Then, it seems to me that the person who is about to come to prayer should withdraw for a little and prepare himself, and so become more attentive and active for the whole of his prayer. He should cast away all temptation and troubling thoughts and remind himself so far as he is able of the Majesty whom he approaches, and that it is impious to approach Him carelessly, sluggishly, and disdainfully; and he should put away all extraneous things. This is how he should come to prayer, stretching out his soul, as it were, instead of his hands, straining his mind toward God instead of his eyes, raising his governing reason from the ground and standing it before the Lord of all instead of standing. All malice toward any one of those who seem to have wronged him he should put away as far as any one would wish God to put away His malice toward him, if he had wronged and sinned against many of his neighbors or had done anything whatever he was conscious of being against right reason. And although there are a great many different positions for the body, he should not doubt that the position with the hands

---

55. Chapter IX.1.

outstretched and the eyes lifted up is to be preferred before all others, because it bears in prayer the image of characteristics befitting the soul and applies it to the body. I mean that this position must be preferred barring any chance circumstance. For under certain circumstances it is allowed to pray properly sometimes sitting down because of some disease of the feet that cannot be disregarded or even lying down because of fever or some such sickness. And because of circumstances, for example, if we are at sea or if affairs do not permit us to withdraw to offer the prayer that is owed, it is right to pray acting as though we were not doing it.

3. And kneeling is necessary when someone is going to speak against his own sins before God, since he is making supplication for their healing and their forgiveness. We must understand that it symbolizes someone who has fallen down and become obedient, since Paul says, "For this reason I bow my knees before the Father, from whom every family in heaven and on earth is named" (Eph. 3:14–15). And spiritual kneeling is called this because every single existing creature at the name of Jesus has fallen down before God and humbled himself to Him. The Apostle seems to me to indicate this by the phrase "That at the name of Jesus every knee should bow, in heaven and on earth and under the earth" (Phil. 2:10). For it is not at all necessary to suppose that the bodies in heaven should be formed in such a way as to have corporeal knees, since their bodies have been demonstrated to be spherical by those who have investigated such matters accurately. The person who is unwilling to accept this and who yet accepts the functional character of each of the body's members, lest anything should have been created by God in vain, will stumble on both implications of his view, unless he behaves impudently toward the Word. Either he will say that the limbs of the body are in vain and have not been brought into being by God for their proper use, or he will say that entrails and the rectum fulfill their proper functions even in heavenly beings. And anyone would behave extremely foolishly if he supposed that like statues they have only the appearance of human beings, but no longer preserve the appearance beneath the surface. This is what I have to say in my examination of kneeling and in looking at the verse "At the name of Jesus every knee should bow, in heaven and on earth and under the earth" (Phil. 2:10). Moreover, the verse in

the prophet says the same thing, "To me every knee shall bow" (Is. 45:23).

4. Now concerning the place, let it be known that every place is suitable for prayer if a person prays well. For "in every place you offer incense to me . . . says the Lord" (Mal. 1:11) and "I desire then that in every place the men should pray" (1 Tim. 2:8). But everyone may have, if I may put it this way, a holy place set aside and chosen in his own house, if possible, for accomplishing his prayers in quiet and without distraction. In addition to the general considerations he will use in assessing such a place, he should examine whether any transgression or anything contrary to right reason has been done in the particular place where he prays. For in that case he has made not only himself but also the place for his personal prayer the kind that God's watching care would flee. In examining further the question of the place I must venture an opinion that may be somewhat harsh, but that cannot be disdained by one who assesses it carefully. With respect to the place where sexual intercourse takes place, not unlawful intercourse but that permitted by the Apostle's word "by way of concession, not of command" (1 Cor. 7:6), we must inquire whether it is holy and pure to God. For if it is impossible to have leisure for prayer as we should unless someone dedicates himself to this "by agreement for a season" (1 Cor. 7:5), then perhaps the same consideration should apply, if possible, to the place.

5. And a place of prayer, the spot where believers assemble together, is likely to have something gracious to help us, since angelic powers are placed near the throngs of believers, as well as the powers of our Lord and Savior Himself, and the spirits of the saints—I think both of those who have already fallen asleep and clearly of those who are still alive, even though it is not easy to say how. Concerning angels we must reason this way. Suppose the angel of the Lord encamps around those who fear Him, and delivers them (Ps. 34:7); and suppose Jacob tells the truth not only about himself but also about all those who rely on God when he says to the understanding person, "The angel who delivers me from all these evils" (Gen. 48:16). It is likely, then, that when a great number of people are assembled genuinely for the glory of Christ, each one's angel, who is around each of those who fear Him,

encamps with that man whom he is believed to guard and order. As a result, when the saints are gathered together, there is a double Church, one of men and the other of angels. And if Raphael says that he offered only the prayer of Tobit for a "reminder" (Tb. 12:12, 3:16–17), and after him that of Sarah, who later became Tobit's daughter-in-law when she married Tobias, what must we say when a great many journey together with the same mind and the same purpose and are made one body in Christ? Concerning the Lord's power that is present with the Church Paul says, "When you are assembled, and my spirit is present with the power of the Lord Jesus" (1 Cor. 5:4). He means that the power of the Lord Jesus is united not only with the Ephesians[56] but also with the Corinthians. And if Paul, while still clothed in a body, supposed that he was taking part in Corinth by his own spirit, we must not reject the opinion that in the same way the blessed ones who have departed come to the churches in the spirit more quickly than someone who is still in the body. Therefore, let no one disdain prayers in the churches, since they have something exceptional for the person who assembles in them genuinely.

6. Just as the power of Jesus, the spirit of Paul and of those like him, and the angels of the Lord who encamp around each one of the saints accompany on their journey those who genuinely gather together and assemble with them, so we must conjecture that if someone is unworthy of a holy angel and gives himself to the devil as an angel by his sins and by the wickedness he commits, despising God, then such a person, even if there are only a few like him, will not for long escape the notice of the angels' providence, which watches over the Church in the service of God's will and brings the transgressions of such a person to the knowledge of the many. And if such people become a multitude and if they assemble for human associations, busying themselves with something more corporeal, they will not be watched over. This is demonstrated in Isaiah, where the Lord says, "Not even if you come to appear before me . . . I will turn away my eyes from you. Even if you make many prayers, I will not hear you" (Is. 1:12, 15). And perhaps, corresponding to the double order of holy people and

---

56. Paul is presumed to have written 1 Corinthians from Ephesus.

blessed angels I have already mentioned, there is, as well, a double assembly of wicked men and evil angels. Of an assembly of such beings it might be said by the holy angels and the sacred men, "I have not sat in the assembly of vanity, and I will never enter with transgressors. I have hated the church of the wicked, and I will never sit with the impious" (Ps. 26:4–5).

7. Therefore, I think that those in Jerusalem and in all Judea were subject to their enemies because of their many sins, since the peoples who deserted the Law were deserted by God, the shielding angels, and the salvation that comes from holy men. Thus, whole assemblies were then left to fall into temptations, so that even what they thought they had was taken from them (cf. Lk. 8:18; Mt. 13:12, 25:29; Mk. 4:25; Lk. 19:26). And like the fig tree that was cursed and taken away to its roots because it did not give fruit to Jesus when He was hungry (Mk. 11:20–21, 13–14; Mt. 21:18–19), they were withered and lost what little power of life in faith they had. It seemed to me necessary to say all this in my discussion of the place of prayer and my commendation of what is exceptional about the place where the saints assemble together with great reverence.

XXXII. Now concerning the direction in which one ought to look when he prays, a few things must be said. Since there are four directions, north, south, west, and east, who would not immediately acknowledge that it is perfectly clear we should make our prayers facing east, since this is a symbolic expression of the soul's looking for the rising of the true Light. But suppose someone wishes instead to offer intercessions in whatever direction the doors of the house face according to the opening of the house, saying that having a view into heaven is more inviting than looking at a wall; and suppose it should happen that the opening of the house is not toward the east. In this case let the person be told that the buildings of men arbitrarily face in certain directions or have openings in certain directions, but by nature the east is preferred over the other directions, and what is by nature must be ranked ahead of what is arbitrary. Moreover, why should the person who wishes to pray on a plain pray for this reason toward the east rather than toward the west? If in that case the east must reasonably be preferred, why should this not be done everywhere? So much for that.

ON PRAYER

XXXIII.1. It seems to me I should go on to discuss the topics of prayer and then bring this treatise to a close. It seems to me there are four topics that need to be sketched out and that I have found scattered in the Scriptures. Each person should organize his prayer according to these topics. This is what they are: In the beginning and the preface of the prayer something having the force of praise should be said of God through Christ, who is praised with Him, and by the Holy Spirit, who is hymned with Him. After this each person should place general thanksgivings, bringing forward for thanksgiving the benefits given many people and those he has himself received from God. After thanksgiving it seems to me that he ought to blame himself bitterly before God for his own sins and then ask, first, for healing that he may be delivered from the habit that brings him to sin and, second, for forgiveness of the sins that have been committed. And after confession, the fourth topic that seems to me must be added is the request for great and heavenly things, both private and general, and concerning his household and his dearest. And, finally, the prayer should be concluded with a doxology of God through Christ in the Holy Spirit.

2. As I said before, I have found these topics scattered in the Scriptures. First, giving praise may be found in the following words from Psalm 104, "O Lord my God, how greatly are you magnified! You are clothed with praise and majesty, who cover yourself with light as with a garment, who stretch out the heaven like a curtain. He lays the beams of His chambers on the waters; He makes clouds a place for Him to walk; He walks on the wings of the winds; He makes the winds His messengers and flaming fire His ministers; He lays the foundation of the earth for its stability; it shall not be shaken forever and ever. The deep like a garment is His covering. The waters will stand above the mountains; at your rebuke they will flee; at the sound of your thunder they will be afraid" (Ps. 104:1–7). And most of this psalm contains praise of the Father. And it is possible for anyone to collect more examples for himself and to see how frequently the topic of praise is found scattered in Scripture.

3. As for thanksgiving, let me cite the example found in 2 Samuel of David's proclamation after the promises made to him through Nathan. David is amazed at God's gifts and thanks Him

for them in these words, "Who am I, O Lord my Lord, and what is my house, that you have loved me thus far? And I was made little in your sight, my Lord, and you have spoken of your servant's house for a great while to come. But this is the law of man, O Lord my Lord. And what more can David say to you? And now you know your servant, O Lord. Because of your servant, you have done it, and according to your heart you have done all this greatness of yours to make it known to your servant so that he may magnify you, O Lord my Lord" (2 Sam. 7:18–22 LXX).

4. An example of confession is, "Deliver me from all my transgressions" (Ps. 39:8). And in other verses, "My wounds grow foul and fester because of my foolishness, I am utterly bowed down and prostrate; all the day I go about mourning" (Ps. 38:5–6).

5. An example of request is found in Psalm 28, "Take me not off with sinners, and do not destroy me with those who work injustice" (Ps. 27:3 LXX–28:3). Other examples are like this one.

6. And having begun with praise it is right to conclude the prayer by ending with praise, hymning and glorifying the Father of all through Jesus Christ in the Holy Spirit, to whom be glory forever (cf. Rom. 16:27; Heb. 13:21; Gal. 1:5; 2 Tim. 4:18).

XXXIV. And so, my brother Ambrose and my sister Tatiana, most zealous for learning and most genuine in your religion, these are the results, so far as I have been able, of my wrestlings with the subject of prayer and with the prayer in the Gospels, together with the passage before it in Matthew. If you strain forward to what lies ahead and forget what lies behind (Phil. 3:13) and if you pray for me in my studies, I am not without hope that from God the Giver I can become capable of additional and more divine insights into all these matters and that having received them I shall be able to discuss the same points more nobly, more loftily, and more clearly. Nevertheless, for the time being read this with forbearance.

ON FIRST PRINCIPLES: BOOK IV

CHAPTER ONE:

.THAT THE SCRIPTURES ARE DIVINELY INSPIRED[57]

1. Since in our discussion of such great and special matters it is of no avail to hand over the conclusions of the investigation to human senses and to our common understanding and, so to speak, give a visible account of invisible things, we must also take up the witnesses of the divine Scriptures to demonstrate the points we have made. And so that these witnesses may have certain and undoubted credibility whether in the matters we have already discussed or in those now to be treated, it seems necessary first to show that they are divine Scriptures, that is that they are inspired by the Spirit of God. Therefore, concerning this point we shall mark out as briefly as possible the passages from those sacred Scriptures that especially move us to this opinion, passages, that is, first from Moses, the lawgiver of the Hebrew nation, and then from the words of Jesus Christ, the author and head of the Christian religion and teaching.

Although a great many lawgivers were eminent among Greeks and barbarians, as well as numberless teachers or philosophers who promised they were declaring the truth, we remember no lawgiver so influential that he was able to inspire the minds of other nations with zeal either to adopt his laws willingly or to defend them with the entire effort of their minds. Therefore, no one was able to introduce and to implant what seemed to him the truth even in one nation, to say nothing of many other foreign nations, in such a way

---

57. The *Philocalia* has a text parallel to Rufinus's translation for chapters I.1 through III.11 Significant differences will be noted by supplying a translation of the *Philocalia* at the relevant points.

that his knowledge or his belief should reach everyone. Moreover, it cannot be doubted both that the lawgivers wanted all men to observe their laws if possible, and that the teachers wanted everyone to know what seemed to them the truth. But since they knew that they were entirely incapable of this and that they did not have such great power as to rouse even foreign nations to observe their laws or doctrines, they did not even dare to undertake such a project at all, lest what had been begun but could not be finished should mark them out as men without foresight. Nevertheless, in every part of the world, in all of Greece and in every foreign nation, there are numberless throngs of people who have left their ancestral laws and those they supposed gods, and who have dedicated themselves to the observance of Moses' Law and to the discipleship and worship of Christ. And they have done this not without finding an immense hatred stirred up against them from those who worship idols, with the result that they are often afflicted with tortures by these people and sometimes are led away to death. Nevertheless, they embrace and guard fast the word of Christ's teaching with all their desire.

2. Anyone can see in how short a time this religion has grown, making progress by the penalties and deaths exacted of its adherents, still more by the plundering of their possessions and by every kind of suffering endured by them. And it is all the more amazing that while their teachers are neither very capable nor very many, nevertheless, this word is preached throughout the whole world (cf. Mt. 24:14) so that Greeks and barbarians, wise and foolish (cf. Rom. 1:14) uphold the religion of Christ's teaching. Because of this it cannot be doubted that it is not because of human powers or abilities that the word of Christ Jesus grows strong with all authority and persuasion in the minds and souls of all. Moreover, these very things were predicted by Him and confirmed by Him with divine oracles. This is evident when He says that "you will be dragged before governors and judges for my sake, to bear testimony before them and the Gentiles" (Mt. 10:18; Mk. 13:9). And again, "This Gospel will be preached to all nations" (Mk. 13:10; Mt. 24:14). And again, "On that day many will say to me, 'Lord, Lord, did we not eat and drink in your name, and cast out demons in your name?' And I shall say to them, 'Depart from me, you evildoers, I

never knew you' " (Mt. 7:22; Lk. 13:26). If these things had been said by Him and yet had not come to pass as they had been predicted, perhaps they would seem to fall short of the truth and to have no authority. But as it is, since the things that had been predicted by Him have in fact come to pass, even though they were predicted with such great power and authority, then it is made evident with the greatest clarity that it is truly God who was made man and delivered saving teachings to men.

3. Indeed, what need is there to say that the prophets before Him predicted in regard to Him that "princes shall not depart from Judah nor leaders from his loins, until the one comes for whom it (that is, the kingdom) is kept safe, and until the expectation of the Gentiles comes" (Gen. 49:10 LXX)? For it is perfectly clear from the narrative itself and from what can be examined at the present day that from the time of Christ no further kings arose among the Jews. Moreover, all those Jewish pomps in which they used to boast as much as possible and in which they used to exult, that is, the beauty of the temple, the magnificent altars, and all those priestly ornaments and garments of the high priests—all of them have been destroyed together. For the prophecy has been fulfilled that said, "The children of Israel shall dwell many days without king or prince. There will be neither sacrifice nor altar, nor priesthood nor oracle" (Hos. 3:4).

And so, we use these witnesses against those who apparently maintain the verses spoken in Genesis by Jacob that refer to Judah, but who say that a prince from the tribe of Judah does remain to this day, namely the one who is head of their nation and whom they call the patriarch. And they say that there cannot fail those of his seed to remain until the coming of that Christ whom they represent for themselves. But suppose what the prophet says is true, that "the children of Israel shall dwell many days without king or prince. There will be neither sacrifice nor altar nor priesthood" (Hos. 3:4). And note that the temple has been overthrown and that no sacrifices are offered, no altar may be found, no priesthood is established. It most certainly follows that "princes" have departed "from Judah and a leader from his loins, until the one comes for whom it is kept safe," as it was written (Gen. 49:10 LXX). Thus, it is clear that the One for whom it was kept safe has come, in whom is also "the expectation of the Gentiles." And this is seen obviously fulfilled by the multitude of those from different nations who have believed in God through Christ.

4. Moreover, in the song of Deuteronomy the election of a foolish nation because of the sins of the former people is prophetically described for the future, and that election is no other than the one that has taken place through Christ. For this is what it says, "They have stirred me to jealousy with their idols; so I will stir them to jealousy; I will provoke them with a foolish nation" (Deut. 32:21). It is, then, quite plain to understand how the Hebrews, who are said to have stirred God to jealousy by those that are not gods and to have provoked Him with their idols, have been themselves provoked to jealousy by "a foolish nation," which God chose through the coming of Christ Jesus and His disciples. For the apostle says, "For consider your call, brethren; not many of you were wise according to worldly standards, not many were powerful, not many were of noble birth; but God chose what is foolish in the world . . . even things that are not, to bring to nothing things that are," so that Israel according to the flesh (for so it is named by the Apostle [1 Cor. 10:18] "might not boast in the presence of God" (1 Cor. 1:26–29).

5. And what need is there to mention what is prophesied of Christ in the Psalms, especially in the one with the title "A song for the beloved," where it is reported that His tongue is "the pen of a scribe who writes quickly," that He is "beautiful in appearance beyond the sons of men" because "grace is poured upon His lips" (Ps. 45:1–2). Moreover, the proof of the "grace poured upon His lips" is that although He accomplished His teaching in a short time (for He taught only a year and a few months), nevertheless the whole world has been filled with His teaching and with faith in His religion. For "in His days righteousness sprang up and an abundance of peace" enduring to the end, which is called "the taking away of the moon." "And He has dominion from sea to sea, and from the River to the ends of the earth!" (Ps. 72:7–8). Moreover, a sign was given to the house of David, for "a virgin" had conceived and borne "Immanuel," which is interpreted "God with us" (Is. 7:13–14; Mt. 1:23). And what the same prophet said has been fulfilled. "God is with us. Know this, O nations, and be con-

quered" (Is. 8:8–9). For we who are from the nations have been conquered and overcome, and we who bend our necks beneath His grace stand forth as a kind of spoils of His victory. Moreover, the place of His birth was predicted by Micah the prophet, who said, "And you, O Bethlehem, land of Judah, are by no means least among the rulers of Judah; for from you shall come a ruler who will govern my people Israel" (Mic. 5:21; Mt. 2:6). Also, the weeks of years up to the time of Christ the leader that Daniel the prophet predicted were fulfilled (Dan. 9:24). No less, there is also present the one predicted by Job who "would destroy the giant monster" (Job 3:8 LXX) and who gave authority to His intimate disciples "to tread upon serpents and scorpions, and over all the power of the enemy, with nothing from him to hurt them" (Lk. 10:19). Moreover, if anyone considers the journeys of Christ's apostles to different places in which, sent by Him, they preached the Gospel, he will find that what they dared to undertake shows something beyond the human and that their ability to accomplish what they dared shows it was from God. If we consider how men hearing them introduce a new teaching were able to receive them or, on the other hand, that often those who wanted to bring the disciples destruction were restrained by a certain divine power that was present with them, then we shall find nothing in this that can be explained by human powers, but the whole achieved by divine power and providence, by signs manifest beyond doubt, and by miracles bearing witness to their word and teaching (cf. Heb. 2:4; Acts 5:12).

6. Now that these points have been briefly demonstrated, I mean the divinity of Jesus Christ and the fulfillment of everything that had been prophesied of Him, I think it has also been proved at the same time that the very Scriptures that prophesied of Him were divinely inspired, the ones concerning either His coming or the authority of His teaching or its reception by all nations. To this must be added that, whether it is the prediction of the prophets or the Law of Moses that is asserted to be divine and divinely inspired, the claim is put in the clearest light and is proved by the fact that Christ came to this world. For before what had been predicted by them was fulfilled, even though the predictions were true and inspired by God, nevertheless they could not be demonstrated to be

true to the degree that they were not yet proved fulfilled. But the coming of Christ makes clear that what they had said was true and divinely inspired, since before that it might have been held as uncertain whether the conclusion of what had been predicted would be fulfilled. Moreover, if someone considers the prophetic writings with all the diligence and reverence they are worth, while he reads and examines with great care, it is certain that in that very act he will be struck in his mind and senses by some more divine breath and will recognize that the books he reads have not been produced in a human way, but are words of God. And in himself he will discern that the books have been written not by human art or mortal eloquence but, if I may say so, by the elevated style of God. And so, the splendor of the coming of Christ, by illuminating the Law of Moses with the radiance of truth, removed that veil which had been placed over the letter, and laid open for all who believe in Him the good things that were hidden covered within (cf. 2 Cor. 3:15–16).

7. It would, however, be too laborious to list one by one how or when the predictions made by the prophets in time past have been fulfilled, so that we might seem in this way to give complete assurance to those who doubt, especially when it is possible for anyone who wishes to gain a more careful knowledge of them to assemble proofs more fully from the books of the truth themselves. But if those who are less trained in divine teachings should see fit to object that the meaning that transcends the human is not immediately evident on the surface of the letter, there is nothing surprising about that, because divine matters are brought down to men somewhat secretly and are all the more secret in proportion to anyone's disbelief or unworthiness.[58] For although it is certain that everything that exists or happens in this world is ordered by God's providence, nevertheless certain things show quite openly that they are arranged by the governance of providence, while others are unfolded in so obscure and incomprehensible a fashion that the

---

58. The *Philocalia* completes the paragraph more briefly as follows: "The creative reason of the providential God is not so clear in regard to things on earth as in regard to the sun, the moon, and the stars, and not so clear in regard to human events as in the souls and bodies of animals, since the purpose and the cause of their motions, impressions, and natures, and the structures of their bodies have been for the most part discovered by those who study such matters."

reason of divine providence lies hidden deep within them. As a result there are sometimes people who do not believe that these matters have reference to providence, since that reason is hidden from them through which the works of divine providence are ordered by a certain ineffable art. Nevertheless, that reason is not equally obscure in everything. For even among humans themselves it is contemplated, less by one, more fully by another; while whoever it is that dwells in heaven knows more than any human being. And the reason of bodies is evident in one way, that of trees in another, that of animals in another, but that of souls is hidden in still another way. And in what way the diverse motions of rational minds are ordered by divine providence lies hidden for the most part to human beings and even, I think, to the angels, though not to such a degree.

But just as divine providence is not refuted, especially for those who are sure of its existence, because its works or operations cannot be comprehended by human capacities, so neither will the divine inspiration that extends through the entire body of sacred Scripture be called into question because the weakness of our understanding is not strong enough to discover in each different verse the obscure and hidden meanings. This is because the treasure of divine wisdom is hidden in the baser and rude vessel of words, as the Apostle points out when he says, "But we have this treasure in earthen vessels" so that the strength of divine power may shine forth all the more, provided no dross of human eloquence is mixed with the truth of the teachings (cf. 2 Cor. 4:7). For if our books had enticed people to believe because they were written with rhetorical art or philosophical skill, doubtless our faith would be supposed to depend on the art of words and on human wisdom rather than on the power of God (cf. 1 Cor. 2:4–5). But as it is, everyone knows that the word of this preaching has been received by great multitudes in almost the whole world in such a way that they have understood what they came to believe to depend not on plausible words of wisdom, but on the demonstration of the Spirit and of power (1 Cor. 2:4). Since we have been brought by a heavenly power, indeed by a more than heavenly, to faith and belief that we should worship as ours one God, the Creator of all, let us strive ourselves to advance earnestly by leaving the elementary doctrines of Christ, which are the first beginnings of knowledge; and let us go on to perfection so that the wisdom that is delivered to the perfect may also be delivered to us (cf. Heb. 6:1; 1 Cor. 2:6). For this is what the one to whom the preaching of this wisdom was entrusted promises when he says, "Yet among the perfect we impart wisdom, although it is not a wisdom of this world or of the rulers of this world, who are doomed to pass away" (1 Cor. 2:6). By this he makes it clear that this wisdom of ours, so far as beauty of speech goes, has nothing in common with the wisdom of this world. This wisdom, therefore, is written more clearly and perfectly in our hearts, if it has been revealed to us according to the revelation of the mystery, which was kept secret for long ages, but is now disclosed through the prophetic writings and through the appearing of our Lord and Savior Jesus Christ, to whom be glory forevermore. Amen (cf. Rom. 16:25–27; 2 Tim. 1:10; 1 Tim. 6:14).

CHAPTER TWO:
THAT MANY BY NOT UNDERSTANDING THE SCRIPTURES
SPIRITUALLY
AND BY BADLY UNDERSTANDING THEM FALL INTO HERESIES

1. Now that we have briefly discussed the inspiration of divine Scripture by the Holy Spirit, it seems necessary also to explain how certain people by failing to read or understand Scripture correctly have given themselves up to a great many errors, since the way one ought to approach the understanding of divine letters is unknown to a great many people. And so, the Jews, through the hardness of their heart and because they wish to seem wise in themselves, have not believed in our Lord and Savior. They suppose that what was prophesied of Him should be understood according to the letter, that is, that He ought to have "proclaimed release to the captives" (Is. 61:1; cf. Lk. 4:19) in a perceptible and visible way, and that He ought first to have built the city that they think is truly the city of God and at the same time to have "cut off the chariot from Ephraim and the war horse from Jerusalem" (Zech. 9:10; cf. Ezek. 48:15ff.; Ps. 46:4). He should have "eaten butter and honey before He knew how to refuse the evil and choose

the good" (Is. 7:15). And they suppose that the wolf, that four-footed animal, as was prophesied for the coming of Christ, ought to have "fed with the lambs, and the leopard lie down with the kids, and the calf and bull together feed with the lions and be led to pastures by a little child, and the ox and the bear lie down together in fields and their young be brought up in common, and the lions stand in the mangers with the oxen and eat straw" (Is. 11:6–7). Thus, since they see that none of these things that were prophesied of Him have happened according to the narrative meaning of Scripture,[59] and since they hold the belief that in them especially the signs of the coming of Christ were to be observed, they have been unwilling to accept the presence of our Lord Jesus Christ. On the contrary, against law and divine right, that is, against the faith of prophecy, they crucified Him as though He had taken the name of Christ for Himself.

Then, indeed, the heretics read what was written in the Law, "In my anger a fire is kindled" (Jer. 15:14) and "I am a jealous god, visiting the iniquity of the fathers upon the children to the third and the fourth generation" (Ex. 20:5) and "I repent that I have anointed Saul king" (1 Sam. 15:11) and "I am God, who make peace and create evil" (Is. 45:7) and again "Does evil befall a city, unless the Lord has done it?" (Amos 3:6) and "Evils have come down from the Lord upon the gates of Jerusalem" (Mic. 1:12) and "An evil spirit from God choked Saul" (1 Sam. 18:10) and many other passages in Scripture like these. When they read them, the heretics did not dare say that they were not the Scriptures of God, but they nevertheless suppose they are that Creator God's whom the Jews worshiped and who they think should be believed to be only just but not good. They think that the Savior came to proclaim to us a more perfect God, whom they deny to be the Creator of the world. But even about this very thing they disagree, holding various opinions, since those who once deserted belief in the Creator God, who is God of all, gave themselves up to various fictions and fables, devising falsehoods and saying that some things are visible and made by one God, while other things are invisible and created by another, just as the imagination and vanity of their soul suggested

---

59. Latin, *historia*. "Narrative meaning" will be adopted as the translation throughout.

to them. Moreover, some of the simpler people who seem to be included within the faith of the Church, while they do not think there is a God greater than the Creator God and in this preserve a right and sound opinion, nevertheless hold opinions about Him that should not be held concerning the most unjust and cruelest man.

2. Now the reason those we have just mentioned have a false understanding of these matters is quite simply that they understand Scripture not according to the spiritual meaning but according to the sound of the letter. For this reason, as far as our modest perception admits, we shall address those who believe the sacred Scriptures were not composed by any human words but were written by the inspiration of the Holy Spirit and were also delivered and entrusted to us by the will of God the Father through His Only Begotten Son Jesus Christ. And we shall try to make clear to them what seems to us the right way of understanding Scripture, observing that rule and discipline[60] which was delivered by Jesus Christ to the apostles and which they delivered in succession to their followers who teach the heavenly Church.

Now the fact that certain mysterious dispensations are disclosed by the holy Scriptures is something everyone, I think, even the more simple believers, will admit. But what they are or of what sort is something anyone of a right mind and who is not plagued with the vice of boasting will confess in the spirit of true religion he does not know. For if someone, for example, points out to us the stories of Lot's daughters and their apparently unlawful intercourse with their father, or of Abraham's two wives, or of the two sisters who married Jacob, or of the two maidservants who increased the number of his sons, what else can we answer than that these are certain mysteries and types of spiritual matters, but that we do not know of what sort they are? Moreover, when we read of the building of the tabernacle, we are, of course, certain that the things that have been described are types of certain obscure matters. But I think it is extremely difficult, I might almost say impossible, to fit them to their own measures and to uncover and describe each one of them. Nevertheless, as I have said, the fact that the description is

---

60. The Rule of Faith.

filled with mysteries does not escape even an ordinary understanding. Indeed, the entire narrative, which seems to be written about weddings or the births of sons or different battles or whatever other stories one wishes, what else must it be believed to be than the forms and types of hidden and sacred matters? But either because people bring too little zeal to the training of their minds or because they think they know before they have learned, it happens that they never begin to learn. On the other hand, if neither zeal nor a teacher is actually lacking and if these matters are sought after as divine and not as though they were human, that is religiously and piously and as matters we hope to be revealed in as many cases as possible through God's revelation, since they are, of course, extremely difficult and obscure for human perception, then perhaps the person who seeks this way will at last find what is right to find.

3. But perhaps this difficulty will be supposed present only in the prophetic words, since it is certainly clear to everyone that the prophetic style is always strewn with types and enigmas. What shall we say when we come to the Gospels? Does not an inner meaning, the Lord's meaning, also lie hidden there that is revealed only by that grace he received who said, "But we have the mind of Christ . . . that we might understand the gifts bestowed upon us by God. And we impart this in words not taught by human wisdom but taught by the Spirit" (1 Cor. 2:16, 12–13)? And if anyone reads the revelations made to John, how can he fail to be amazed at how great an obscurity of ineffable mysteries is present there? It is evident that even those who cannot understand what lies hidden in them nevertheless understand that something lies hidden. And indeed, the letters of the apostles, which do seem to some clearer, are they not so filled with profound ideas that through them, as through some small opening, the brightness of an immense light seems to be poured forth for those who can understand the meaning of divine wisdom? Since all this is the case and since there are many in error in this life, I do not think that anyone can without danger proclaim that he knows or understands those things that require "the key of knowledge" before they can be opened. This key the Savior said was with those skilled in the Law. At this point, granted it is something of a digression, I think the question should nonetheless be put to those who say that before the coming of the Savior

there was no truth with those acquainted with the Law, how it could be said by our Lord Jesus Christ that the "keys of knowledge" are with those who held in their hands the books of the Law and the prophets. For this is what the Lord said, "Woe to you, teachers of the Law, for you have taken away the key of knowledge; you did not enter yourselves, and you hindered those who wanted to enter" (Lk. 11:52).

4. Nevertheless, as we began to say, we think that the way that seems to us right for understanding the Scriptures and seeking their meaning is such that we are taught what sort of understanding we should have of it by no less than Scripture itself. We have found in Proverbs some such instruction for the examination of divine Scripture given by Solomon. He says, "For your part describe them to yourself threefold in admonition and knowledge, that you may answer words of truth to those who question you" (Prov. 22:20–21 LXX). Therefore, a person ought to describe threefold in his soul the meaning of divine letters, that is, so that the simple may be edified by, so to speak, the body of the Scriptures; for that is what we call the ordinary and narrative meaning. But if any have begun to make some progress and can contemplate something more fully, they should be edified by the soul of Scripture. And those who are perfect are like those concerning whom the Apostle says, "Yet among the perfect we do impart wisdom, although it is not a wisdom of this world or of the rulers of this world, who are doomed to pass away. But we impart a secret and hidden wisdom of God, which God decreed before the ages for our glorification" (1 Cor. 2:6–7). Such people should be edified by that spiritual Law (cf. Rom. 7:14) which has a shadow of the good things to come (cf. Heb. 10:1), edified as by the spirit of Scripture. Thus, just as a human being is said to be made up of body, soul, and spirit, so also is sacred Scripture, which has been granted by God's gracious dispensation for man's salvation.

We see this also indicated in the book of the Shepherd (which some apparently despise) when Hermas is ordered "to write two books," and afterwards he is himself to "announce to the presbyters of the Church" what he has learned from the Spirit. This is what it says, "And you shall write two books, and give one to Clement and one to Grapte. And Grapte shall admonish the widows and orphans; and Clement shall send the message to all the cities outside;

and you shall announce it to the presbyters of the Church" (Hermas, Vis. II.4.3). Grapte, then, who is commanded to admonish the orphans and widows, is the plain meaning of the letter itself by which are admonished childlike souls, who have not yet deserved to have God as their Father and for this reason are called "orphans." And the "widows" are those souls that have left that unjust husband to whom they had been joined against the Law, but remain "widows" because they have not yet made sufficient progress to be joined to the heavenly bridegroom (cf. Mt. 25:1ff.). But Clement is ordered to send what has been said to those who have already left the letter for those "cities which are outside," just as if it said, to those souls which have been edified by the letter and have begun to be outside concern for the body and outside the desires of the flesh. And Hermas himself is ordered to announce what he had learned from the Holy Spirit not by letters or a book but by his living voice to the presbyters of the churches of Christ, that is, to those who because of their capacity for spiritual teaching support the mature meaning of wisdom.

5. But, of course, we must not ignore the fact that there are certain passages in Scripture in which what we have called the body, that is a logically coherent narrative meaning, is not always to be found, as we shall show in what follows. And there are places where only what we have called the soul and the spirit may be understood. I think this is also indicated in the Gospels, when "six stone jars" are said to be "standing there, for the Jewish rites of purification, each holding two or three measures" (Jn. 2:6). As I have said, this verse in the Gospel seems to refer to those whom the Apostle calls "Jews inwardly" (Rom. 2:29), because they are purified by the word of Scripture, sometimes holding "two measures," that is, receiving the meanings of the soul and of the spirit, according to what we have just said, and sometimes holding "three measures," when a reading for edification can keep the bodily meaning, which is the narrative meaning. And "six stone jars" are mentioned because they bear a logical relation to those who are placed in this world to be purified. For we read that in six days (which is a perfect number[61]) this world and everything in it were finished.

---

61. Cf. Philo, *De op. mund.* 3. Six is perfect because it is the sum of its parts, $1 + 2 + 3$.

6. Now the whole multitude of believers, which believes quite faithfully and simply, is a witness to what great profit lies in the first meaning, which I have called narrative. Nor is much argument needed, since the point is perfectly clear to everyone. And the Apostle Paul has given us a great many examples of that meaning which we have called above the soul, as it were, of Scripture, first, for example, the passage in his letter to the Corinthians, "For it is written, 'You shall not muzzle an ox when it is treading out the grain' " (1 Cor. 9:9; Deut. 25:4). He goes on to explain how this commandment should be understood and says, "Is it for oxen that God is concerned? Does He not speak entirely for our sake? It was written for our sake, because the ploughman should plow in hope and the thresher thresh in hope of a share in the crop" (1 Cor. 9:9–10). Moreover, a great many other sayings like this one, which are interpreted from the Law in this way, bestow the greatest instruction upon those who hear them.

Then, the spiritual explanation refers, for example, to someone who can make clear the heavenly things of which those who are Jews according to the flesh served the copies and shadows (Heb. 8:5; Rom. 8:5) and the good things to come of which the Law has a shadow (Heb. 10:1), and any similar things found in the holy Scriptures. And the spiritual meaning is involved when it is asked what is that "secret and hidden wisdom of God, which God decreed before the ages for our glorification, which none of the rulers of this world understand" (1 Cor. 2:7–8), or in what the Apostle himself observes when he is using certain examples from Exodus or Numbers and says, "Now these things happened to them in a type, but they were written down for us, upon whom the ends of the ages have come" (1 Cor. 10:11). And he gives us an opportunity of understanding how we can direct our minds to the things of which their experiences were types by saying, "For they drank from the spiritual Rock which followed them, and the Rock was Christ" (1 Cor. 10:4).

Moreover, concerning the tabernacle he makes mention in another letter of the command that had been given to Moses, "You shall make everything according to the pattern which was shown you on the mountain" (Heb. 8:5; Ex. 25:40). And when he writes to the Galatians and rebukes those who are apparently reading the

Law for themselves but do not understand it, because they are unaware that there are allegories in the Scriptures, he says to them with a certain amount of chiding, "Tell me, you who desire to be under the Law, do you not hear the Law? For it is written that Abraham had two sons, one by a slave and one by a free woman. But the son of the slave was born according to the flesh, the son of the free woman through promise. Now this is an allegory: These women are two covenants, and the rest" (Gal. 4:21–24). In this passage we must also consider how carefully the Apostle said what he did, "You who desire to be under the Law"—and not "you who are under the Law"—"do you not hear the Law?" that is, "do you not understand?" or "do you not know?"

Further, in the letter to the Colossians, embracing and drawing together concisely the meaning of the Law as a whole, he says, "Therefore let no one pass judgment on you in questions of food and drink or with regard to a festival or a new moon or a sabbath. These are a shadow of what is to come" (Col. 2:16–17). And when he writes, as well, to the Hebrews and discusses those who are from the circumcision, he says, "They serve a copy and shadow of the heavenly things" (Heb. 8:5). Now those who accept the Apostle's writings as divinely spoken will probably not doubt this conclusion with respect to the five books of Moses because of the preceding examples. But about the rest of the Old Testament narrative they may ask whether what is included in it may also be said to have happened "in a type" (cf. 1 Cor. 10:11) to those about whom it is written. We have noticed that the point is addressed in the letter to the Romans, where Paul uses an example from 1 Kings and says, "I have kept for myself seven thousand men who have not bowed the knee to Baal" (Rom. 11:4; 1 Kings 19:18). Paul takes this as spoken in a type about those who are called Israelites "by election" (Rom. 11:5), in order to show that the coming of Christ brought help not only to the Gentiles but also to a great many of the nation of Israel, who were called to salvation.

7. Since these points have been established, we shall sketch out how we should understand divine Scripture in particular points by using as examples and models what we have been able to find. First, we shall repeat and demonstrate the point that the Holy Spirit, who enlightened the ministers of truth, the prophets and the

apostles, by the providence and will of God through the power of His Only Begotten Word, who was God in the beginning with God (cf. Jn. 1:1) [wished first to teach them how][62] to understand the mysteries of those events or purposes that happen among human beings or from human beings. By human beings I now mean souls placed in bodies. They portrayed those mysteries, known and revealed to them by the Spirit, by narrating them as human deeds or by handing down in a type certain legal observances and rules. They did this so that not anyone who wanted would have these mysteries laid bare and ready, so to speak, to be trodden underfoot, but so that the person who devoted himself to studies of this sort with all purity and continence and careful watching might be able in this way to inquire into the profoundly hidden meaning of God's Spirit that had been woven together with an ordinary narrative looking in another direction. And in this way they thought someone might become an ally of the Spirit's knowledge and a participant in the divine counsel. And this is because no soul can arrive at the perfection of knowledge in any other way than by becoming inspired by the truth of divine wisdom. Therefore, it is chiefly the doctrine of God, that is, the Father, Son, and Holy Spirit, that is described by those men filled with the divine Spirit. And then, as we have said, filled with the divine Spirit, they brought forth the mysteries of the Son of God, how the Word was made flesh (Jn. 1:14) and for what purpose He went so far as to take the form of a servant (Phil. 2:7). And then it necessarily followed that they taught the race of mortals with divine words about rational creatures, heavenly as well as earthly, the blessed and the lower, and also about the differences among souls and how these differences arose. And finally, it was necessary for us to learn from the divine words what this world is, why it was made, and why there is so much and such great evil on earth, and whether it is only on earth or also in other places.

8. Therefore, although it is the Holy Spirit's purpose to enlighten holy souls, which have dedicated themselves to the service of the truth, concerning such matters and others like them, He

---

62. Koetschau conjectures that these words must be added.

has in the second place an aim in regard to those who either cannot or will not give themselves to the effort and diligence by which they might deserve to be taught or to know matters so great and excellent. As we have already said, His aim is to envelop and hide secret mysteries in ordinary words under the pretext of a narrative of some kind and of an account of visible things. Therefore, the account of the visible creation is introduced and the making and fashioning of the first man; then his offspring follow in succession. Also some of the exploits done by certain righteous men are recounted, while along with them certain of their crimes as men are recorded; then some instances of the unchastity or wickedness of the impious are described. Moreover, an account of battles is related in order in a marvelous way; and the different fates, now of those who conquer and now of those who are conquered, are described, by which certain ineffable mysteries are revealed to those who know how to examine accounts of this kind. Moreover, in the legal passages of Scripture the law of truth is sown and prophesied by the amazing teaching of wisdom; each one by some divine art of wisdom is woven into a kind of garment and veil for the spiritual meanings. And this is what we have called the body of sacred Scripture—so that even by what we have called the garment of the letter itself, since it has been woven by the art of wisdom, a great many can be edified and make progress who otherwise would be unable to do so.

9. But if in all the parts of this garment, that is, the narrative, the logical coherence of the Law had been kept and its order preserved, because we should have a continuous way of understanding, we should not believe that there was anything shut up within the sacred Scriptures in addition to what is disclosed on the first appearance. For this reason the divine wisdom[63] has arranged for there to be certain stumbling blocks or interruptions of the narrative meaning, by inserting in its midst certain impossibilities and contradictions, so that the very interruption of the narrative might oppose the reader, as it were, with certain obstacles thrown in the way. By them wisdom denies a way and an access to the common

---

63. The *Philocalia* has "the Word of God" throughout the discussion.

understanding; and when we are shut out and hurled back, it calls us back to the beginning of another way, so that by gaining a higher and loftier road through entering a narrow footpath it may open for us the immense breadth of divine knowledge.

Moreover, we should also know that since the chief aim of the Holy Spirit was to keep the logical order of the spiritual meaning either in what is bound to happen or in what has already taken place, if anywhere He found that what happened according to the narrative could be fitted to the spiritual meaning, He composed something woven out of both kinds in a single verbal account, always hiding the secret meaning more deeply. But where the narrative of events could not be coherent with the spiritual logic, He sometimes interspersed either events less likely or absolutely impossible to have happened and sometimes events that could have happened but in fact did not. Sometimes He did this with a few words that seem unable to preserve the truth according to the bodily meaning, sometimes by interspersing many words.

This is found with special frequency in the Law, where there are many commandments that are obviously useful in their bodily form, but where there are a good many in which no straightforward useful purpose is evident; and sometimes impossibilities may even be discerned. All these things, as we have said, the Holy Spirit arranged so that from them, since what first appears cannot be true or useful, we might be called back to examine the truth to be sought more deeply and to be investigated more diligently, and might seek a meaning worthy of God in the Scriptures, which we believe were inspired by God. And not only did the Holy Spirit arrange this for what had been written up to the coming of Christ, but since He is one and the same Spirit and proceeds from the one God, He likewise did the same thing also in the Gospels and the writings of the apostles. For even those accounts He inspired through them He did not weave together apart from the art of His wisdom, whose character we have already explained. Thus, even in these writings He mingled not a few things by which the order of the narrative account is interrupted or cut up so that by the impossibility He might turn and call back the mind of the reader to the examination of the inner meaning.

Chapter Three:
Examples from the Scriptures
of How Scripture Should Be Understood

1. So that what we say may be understood quite concretely, let us now bring the argument to bear upon actual passages in Scripture. To what person of intelligence, I ask, will the account seem logically consistent that says there was a "first day" and a "second" and "third," in which also "evening" and "morning" are named, without a sun, without a moon, and without stars, and even in the case of the first day without a heaven[64] (Gen. 1:5–13)? And who will be found simple enough to believe that like some farmer "God planted trees in the garden of Eden, in the east" and that He planted "the tree of life" in it, that is a visible tree that could be touched, so that someone could eat of this tree with corporeal teeth and gain life, and, further, could eat of another tree and receive knowledge "of good and evil" (Gen. 2:8–9)? Moreover, we find that God is said to stroll in the garden in the afternoon and Adam to hide under a tree (cf. Gen. 3:8). Surely, I think no one doubts that these statements are made by Scripture in the form of a type by which they point toward certain mysteries. Also Cain's going away "from the face of God" (Gen. 4:16) obviously stirs the wise reader to ask what "the face of God" is and how any one could "go away" from it. But there is no need for us to enlarge the discussion too much beyond what we have in hand, since it is quite easy for everyone who wishes to collect from the holy Scriptures things that are written as though they were really done, but cannot be believed to have happened appropriately and reasonably according to the narrative meaning. And this form of Scripture also finds abundant and copious expression in the Gospels, when, for example, the devil is said to have placed Jesus on "a very high mountain" to show Him from there "all the kingdoms of the world and the glory of them" (Mt. 4:8). How could it possibly happen according to the letter either that the devil led Jesus to a very high mountain or that to His fleshly eyes he "showed," as though they were below and

---

64. Koetschau compares this sentence with fragment 29, Justinian's Letter to Mennas (Mansi IX.533).

next to that one mountain, "all the kingdoms of the world," that is, the kingdoms of the Persians, the Scythians, the Indians, and how their kings are glorified by men? Moreover, whoever reads with special care will find a great many other passages like this in the Gospels. In this way he will notice that into these accounts that seem to have been described according to the letter there have been sown in and woven together things that the narrative meaning will not admit but that preserve the spiritual meaning.

2. Moreover, similar passages may be found in contexts where commandments are given.[65] In the Law of Moses it is commanded that "every male who was not circumcised on the eighth day shall be destroyed" (Gen. 17:14 LXX). This is completely contradictory, since if the Law was handed down to be obeyed according to the narrative meaning, it ought to have ordered that parents or those who bring up the children should be punished if they did not circumcise their children. But as it is, Scripture says, "The uncircumcised male," that is, "who was not circumcised on the eighth day . . . shall be destroyed from his people" (Gen. 17:14 LXX).

But if we must ask also about impossible laws, we find an animal called the "goat-stag," which does not even exist, listed among the clean animals Moses orders to be eaten; and the lawgiver prohibits eating the "griffin," which no one has ever mentioned or heard of being able to fall into human hands (cf. Deut. 14:5; Lev. 11:13 LXX). Moreover, concerning the quite well-known observance of the sabbath, it says, "You shall sit, each one of you, in your houses; no one shall move from his place on the seventh day" (Ex. 16:29). It is impossible to observe this commandment according to the letter, for no human being can sit for a whole day so as not to move from the place where he is sitting.

In regard to these points of detail even those who are of the circumcision and who are unwilling that anything in the holy Scriptures should be understood beyond what is made clear by the letter do not believe that the laws about the goat-stag, the griffin, and the vulture need to be examined; but concerning the sabbath they bring to mind idle and frivolous tales, and arguing from I know not what traditions say that one person's "place" is to be

---

65. The *Philocalia* gives as the first example the prohibition of eating vultures, to which Rufinus alludes in his summary list in the last paragraph on this page.

reckoned within two thousand cubits (cf. Num. 35:5). But others, among whom is the Samaritan Dositheus,[66] find fault with interpretations of this sort, but order something still more absurd, that everyone should remain until evening in the posture, the place, and the position he happened to be in on the sabbath day, that is, if he was sitting, he must sit the whole day, or if he was lying down, he must lie down the whole day.

Moreover, the commandment "Do not bear a burden on the sabbath day" (cf. Jer. 17:21) seems to me impossible. For by these words the Jewish teachers have fallen into "endless fables," as the holy Apostle says (1 Tim. 1:4), by saying that it is not reckoned a "burden" if someone has shoes without nails, but that it is a "burden" if someone has Gallic shoes with nails. And if someone carries something on one shoulder, they judge it a "burden," but if he carries it on both shoulders, they will deny it is a burden.

3. And now if we look for similar examples from the Gospels, how will it fail to seem ridiculous if we understand according to the letter the statement "Salute no one on the road" (Lk. 10:4)? For certain of the simpler believers think that our Savior gave the apostles this order. Moreover, how will it be possible, especially in those places where an extremely harsh winter is rough with icy frosts (cf. Vergil, *Geor.* II.263), to observe the commandment that no one should have "two tunics or sandals"[67] (Mt. 10:10)? And what about the commandment that the person struck on the right cheek should offer also the left one, since anyone who struck with the right hand would hit the left cheek (cf. Mt. 5:39; Lk. 6:29)? Also to be considered one of the impossibilities is the verse in the Gospel "If your right eye has offended, let it be plucked out" (cf. Mt. 5:29, 18:9). For even if we refer the saying to fleshly eyes, how will it appear logical that the blame for the offense is referred to one eye, the right one, when a person sees with both eyes? Or who would be considered innocent of a great crime if he laid hands on himself?[68]

Perhaps the letters of the Apostle Paul will appear free from these difficulties. But consider what he says, "Was any one at the time of his call already circumcised? Let him not seek uncircumci-

---

66. Founder of an ascetic sect. Cf. *Contra Celsum* VI.11.
67. This sentence is not found in the *Philocalia*.
68. The *Philocalia* also cites Mt. 5:28.

sion" (1 Cor. 7:18). In the first place, if one examines the passage carefully, it will not appear addressed to the subjects that are being discussed in the context. For Paul's discussion concerns instructions for marriage and chastity, and the verse that has been cited will appear beside the point in such matters. Second, what would be the objection if someone could return to uncircumcision in order to escape the disfigurement that comes from circumcision? Third, this certainly cannot be done by any manner of means.[69]

4. Now we have brought all these examples in order to show that the aim of the Holy Spirit, who thought it right to give us the divine Scriptures, is not that we might be able to be edified by the letter alone or in all cases, since we often discover that the letter is impossible or insufficient in itself because by it sometimes not only irrationalities but even impossibilities are described. But the aim of the Holy Spirit is that we should understand that there have been woven into the visible narrative truths that, if pondered and understood inwardly, bring forth a law useful to men and worthy of God.

But someone might suspect us of the opinion that no narrative in Scripture actually happened, since we believe that some of them did not happen, or that no commandment of the Law can be established according to the letter, since we have said that some cannot be observed according to the letter because either reason or the possibility of the matter does not allow it, or that what is written of the Savior should not be thought fulfilled in a way also perceived by the senses, or that His commandments ought not be preserved according to the letter. Our response, therefore, must be that we judge it evident that in a great many cases the truth of the narrative meaning both can and ought to be preserved. For who could deny that Abraham was buried in the double cave in Hebron, as were Isaac and Jacob and one wife of each of them? Or who would doubt that Shechem was given in Joseph's portion?[70] or that Jerusalem is the chief city of Judea and that the temple of God was built in it by Solomon? Countless other examples could be given. For the passages that can be established according to the narrative meaning are far more numerous than those that contain only the spiritual mean-

---

69. The *Philocalia* does not include the third reason.
70. The *Philocalia* does not include this example.

ing. Then, too, who would not affirm the commandment that orders "Honor your father and your mother, that it may be well for you" (Ex. 20:12) and say that it is sufficient without any spiritual meaning and must necessarily be observed? This is especially so since Paul, as well, repeated the commandment in the same words and confirmed it (cf. Eph. 6:2–3). And what should be said about the verses "You shall not commit adultery, you shall not kill or steal, you shall not bear false witness, and the rest" (Ex. 20:13–16)? Or what about the commandments given in the Gospel, can anyone doubt that most of them must be observed according to the letter? For example,[71] when He says, "But I say to you, do not swear at all" (Mt. 5:34); and when He says, "Everyone who looks at a woman lustfully has already committed adultery with her in his heart" (Mt. 5:28). And we may add the instructions of Paul the Apostle, "Admonish the idlers, encourage the faint-hearted, help the weak, be patient with them all" (1 Thess. 5:14), and a great many others.[72]

5. Nevertheless, if someone reads with great care, I do not doubt that in a great many cases he will hesitate whether this narrative or that should be thought true according to the letter or less true, and whether this or that commandment should be observed according to the letter or not.[73] For this reason we must rely on great zeal and effort so that each reader may with all reverence understand that he is pondering words that are divine and not human and that have been sown into the holy books. Therefore, the understanding that we consider should be observed rightly and

---

71. The *Philocalia* gives Mt. 5:22 as the first example.
72. The *Philocalia* completes the sentence: ". . . even if with the more zealous each one of them can be kept without rejecting that commandment according to the phrase 'the depths of the wisdom of God' " (Rom. 11:33; 1 Cor. 2:10).
73. The *Philocalia* completes section 5 as follows: "Therefore, the person who reads accurately, observing the commandment of the Savior to 'search the Scriptures' (Jn. 5:39), must carefully test where the meaning according to the letter is true and where it is impossible, and must, so far as he is able, track down from similar expressions scattered everywhere through Scripture the meaning of what is impossible according to the letter. Therefore, as will be clear to the readers, when the entire passage is impossible according to the letter, but its chief point is not impossible or even true, every effort must be made to grasp the meaning as a whole, linking together intellectually the account of what is impossible according to the letter with what is not only not impossible but even true in the narrative, treating it allegorically in common with what did not happen according to the letter. For we are disposed to think concerning all of divine Scripture that everything has a spiritual meaning, but not everything a bodily meaning. For often the bodily meaning is proved to be impossible."

logically in interpreting the holy Scriptures is, we think, of this kind.

6. The divine writings proclaim that a certain nation on earth was elected by God. And they give this nation a number of different names, for sometimes the entire nation is called Israel, sometimes Jacob; and in particular, when the nation was itself divided by Jeroboam the son of Nebat into two parts (cf. 1 Kings 12:2ff.), the ten tribes constituted under him were called Israel, while the other two, with which was also the tribe of Levi and which included the tribe from which the royal family of David descended, were named Judah. Moreover, all those places which that nation held and which it had received from God were called Judea, in which Jerusalem was the metropolis; it is called a metropolis as a kind of mother of a great many cities. You will find the names of these cities mentioned frequently in passages scattered in the other divine books, but they are included woven together in one place in the book of Joshua, son of Nun. Therefore, although all these facts are the case, the holy Apostle, wishing us to lift our understanding and raise it somehow from earth, says in one place, "Consider Israel according to the flesh" (1 Cor. 10:18). By this he means that there is another Israel, which is not according to the flesh, but according to the Spirit.[74] And in another place he says, "For not all who are from Israel are Israel" (Rom. 9:6).

8. Therefore, since we have been taught by Paul that there is

---

74. Rufinus's translation resumes with section 8. At this point the *Philocalia* has the following lengthy passage: "And elsewhere he says, 'It is not the children of the flesh who are the children of God' (Rom. 9:8), 'for not all who are from Israel are Israel' (Rom. 9:6). Moreover, neither 'is he a real Jew who is one outwardly, nor is true circumcision something external and in the flesh. He is a Jew who is one in secret, and real circumcision is a matter of the heart, spiritual and not literal' (Rom. 2:28–29). Now if the distinguishing mark of the Jew is taken from the phrase 'in secret,' it must be understood that just as there is a nation of bodily Jews, so also there is a nation of Jews 'in secret,' since the soul has acquired this noble birth by certain ineffable words. Moreover, many prophecies are found concerning Israel and Judah, describing what would happen to them. Surely, do not such promises written for them, so far as they are lowly according to the letter and show nothing lofty or worthy of God's promise, require a mystical interpretation? And if the promises proclaimed through what can be perceived by the senses are spiritual, so those to whom the promises were made are not bodily. 7. But lest we should dwell upon the subject of the Jew 'in secret' and the Israelite of 'the inner man' (cf. Rom. 7:22), since these questions are obvious to those who are not dull minded, we shall return to the previous topic. Now we say that Jacob was the father of the twelve patriarchs, and they of the rulers of the people, and they of the Israelites who came later. Therefore, the bodily Israelites trace their ancestry to the rulers of the people,

one Israel according to the flesh and another according to the Spirit, when the Savior says, "I was sent only to the lost sheep of the house of Israel" (Mt. 15:24), we do not understand Him as do they who have an earthly wisdom, that is, the Ebionites, who are also called by their name itself "the poor" (for poor is translated *ebion* by the Hebrews).[75] Rather, we understand that there is a nation of souls named Israel. Even the meaning of the name itself suggests this, since Israel is translated "the mind seeing God" or "man seeing God."

Moreover, the Apostle makes such revelations about Jerusalem as "The Jerusalem above is free, and she is our mother" (Gal. 4:26). And in another of his letters he says, "But you have come to Mount Zion and to the city of the living God, the heavenly Jerusalem, and to innumerable angels in festal gathering, and to the Church of the firstborn who are enrolled in heaven" (Heb. 12:22–23). If, therefore, there are certain souls in this world that are called Israel, and in heaven a certain city that is named Jerusalem, it follows that those cities that are said to belong to the nation of Israel have as their metropolis the heavenly Jerusalem. And we understand all of Judea in this way. We also think that the prophets spoke about it in certain mysterious accounts when they prophesied something about Judea or about Jerusalem or if the sacred narrative proclaims that different sorts of invasions happened to Judea or Jerusalem.[76] Therefore, whatever is either told or prophesied about Jerusalem, if we hear the words of Paul as of Christ speaking in him (cf. 2 Cor. 13:3), we should understand according to his opinion to have been

---

and the rulers of the people to the patriarchs, and the patriarchs to Jacob and to those still earlier. So, the spiritual Israelites of whom the bodily were a type, are they not from the peoples, the peoples having come from the tribes, and the tribes from one person who had not a bodily birth like the rest, but a better one, since he was born of Isaac, and Isaac descended from Abraham, and all traced their ancestry to Adam, who the Apostle says is Christ (cf. 1 Cor. 15:45)? For the entire beginning of the families that are with the God of all traces its origin down from Christ, who after the God and Father of all is the Father of every soul, just as Adam is the father of all men. And if Eve has been interpreted by Paul to refer to the Church, it is not surprising, since Cain was born of Eve and everyone thereafter traced their ancestry to Eve, that they should be types of the Church, since everyone is born from the Church in a higher sense." The main point of the passage is to elaborate the allegorical meaning of "Jew" by use of the Adam-Christ typology, but an allusion may also exist, as Butterworth suggests, to the two genealogies of Christ.

75. The *Philocalia* does not include the phrase in parenthesis.
76. The *Philocalia* does not include this sentence.

spoken of that city which he calls the heavenly Jerusalem and of all those places or cities that are said to be cities of the holy land of which Jerusalem is the metropolis. We must also suppose that the Savior, wishing to call us forth to a higher understanding, promises some of these cities to those who have made good use of the money entrusted to them by Him, telling them to have authority "over ten cities" or "over five cities" (cf. Lk. 19:17–19).

9. Therefore, if the prophecies made about Judea, Jerusalem, Israel, Judah, and Jacob, so long as they are not understood by us in a fleshly way, point to certain divine mysteries, it follows that also those prophecies given about Egypt and the Egyptians or about Babylon and the Babylonians, Sidon and the Sidonians, should not be understood as prophecies about the Egypt or Babylon or Tyre or Sidon that is on earth (cf. Ezek. 26ff.). Certainly, the prophecies Ezekiel the prophet made concerning Pharaoh, the king of Egypt, are quite impossible to apply to any human being who appears to have ruled in Egypt, as the passage itself taken as a whole makes perfectly clear. Likewise, what is said about the Prince of Tyre cannot be understood of any human being or king of Tyre. As well, how can we possibly suppose that what is said in many places by Scripture, especially in Isaiah, about Nebuchadnezzar are said about a human being? For no human being is said to have "fallen from heaven" or to have been "Lucifer" or the one who "arose every morning" (Is. 14:12). No less do we find a similar problem with what is said in Ezekiel about Egypt, for example, that it is to be made desolate for "forty years" so that "no foot of man" will be found in it, that it will be so taken by assault that through the entire land human blood will rise up to the knees (cf. Ezek. 29:11–12; 30:7, 10–12; 32:5–6, 12–13, 15). I do not know how anyone with sense could apply all this to that earthly Egypt which borders on Ethiopia.[77]

But we must see whether it is not possible to find a more worthy interpretation for these passages. Now just as there is a heavenly Jerusalem and Judea and, doubtless, a nation that dwells in it that is called Israel, so it is possible that near them there are certain places apparently called Egypt, Babylon, Tyre, or Sidon,

---

77. The rest of section 9 is not included in the *Philocalia*.

and that the princes and souls of these places, if any live in them, are called Egyptians, Babylonians, Tyrians, and Sidonians. And in the case of some of these souls, in accordance with that way of life they have there, some sort of captivity seems to have taken place, by which they are said to have descended from Judea into Babylon or into Egypt from better and higher places or to have been scattered among certain other nations.

10. For perhaps, just as those who leave this world by that death common to all are ordered according to their acts and to what they deserve, in proportion to which their worth has been judged, and are assigned, some to the place that is called "the lowerworld," others to "Abraham's bosom," and others to different places or homes,[78] so also they die, so to speak, there and from those places they descend from higher things to this lower world.[79] For I believe that it is to make this distinction that the lowerworld to which the souls of the dead are led from here is called by Scripture "the lower lowerworld," as it says in Psalms, "And you have delivered my soul from the lower lowerworld" (Ps. 85:13 LXX, reading *eks hadou katōterou* instead of *katōtatou*—Ps. 86:13). Therefore, each one of those descending to earth is ordered in accordance with what it deserves or with its place that it had held there, and is born in this world in different places, nations, ways of life, or weaknesses and is the offspring either of devout or much less religious parents, with the result that sometimes it happens that an Israelite descends among the Scythians and a poor man from Egypt is led up to Judea. Nevertheless, our Savior came to gather the lost sheep of the house of Israel (Mt. 11:23; Lk. 16:22), and since a great many of the Israelites did not accept His teaching, those who were from the Gentiles were called.[80]

And so it will appear to follow logically that the prophecies made concerning the different nations ought rather to be applied to souls and to their different homes in heaven. Moreover, as to the narratives of events that are said to have happened to the nation of Israel, to Jerusalem, or to Judea, when they were at war with

---

78. The *Philocalia* does not include "others to 'Abraham's . . . homes."
79. The *Philocalia* does not include the next sentence or the part of the following sentence ending with "or weaknesses."
80. The *Philocalia* does not include the rest of section 10.

different nations, we must thoroughly examine and question how, since in a great many cases the bodily deeds did not happen, they may rather be applied to those nations of souls that dwelt or must be thought to dwell in that heaven which is said to pass away[81] (cf. Mt. 24:35).

Because we have compared the souls going down from this world to the lower world to those souls that have died in a sense and come down from the higher heaven to our dwelling places, we must search out with wise questioning whether we can say the same thing in regard to the birth of individuals. This would imply that just as the souls born on this earth of ours either come back from the lower world to higher places by their desire of better things and so take a human body or descend as far as to us from better places, so also those places that are above in the firmament are inhabited by some souls that have progressed from our abodes to better things, and also by other souls that have fallen from heavenly places as far as to the firmament but have not sinned so greatly as to be thrust down to the lower places that we inhabit. . . . The firmament is a lower world by comparison with the higher heaven, and this earth that we inhabit is called a lower world by comparison with the firmament, and further, by comparison with the lower world that is under us, we are said to be heaven, so that what to some is the lower world is to others heaven.

11. But if someone asks of us plain and completely clear proofs of these conclusions from the holy Scriptures, we must answer that it was the Holy Spirit's purpose to hide these things more completely and to bury them more deeply in what appear to be narratives of events in which people are said to go down to Egypt or to be taken captive into Babylon, where some were greatly humiliated and put in the service of masters, while others were considered so famous and noble in the very places of their captivity that they held authority and office and were placed over the people to rule them.[82] Now all these truths, as we have said, are concealed hidden and buried in the narratives of holy Scripture, because "the kingdom of heaven is like treasure hidden in a field, which a man found and

---

81. The following paragraph is added by Koetschau, who takes it from Jerome's Letter to Avitus, Ep. 11, PL 22.1069f.

82. The *Philocalia* does not include this sentence.

covered up; then in his joy he goes and sells all that he has and buys that field" (Mt. 13:44). Consider very carefully whether this passage does not point to the fact that the soil and surface, so to speak, of Scripture, that is, the meaning according to the letter, is the "field" filled and flowering with plants of all kinds, while the deeper and more profound spiritual meaning is "the treasures of wisdom and knowledge" (Col. 2:3), which the Holy Spirit through Isaiah calls "obscure, invisible, and hidden treasures" (cf. Is. 45:2–3).

To be able to find them we need the help of God, who alone can "break in pieces the doors of bronze" by which they are shut up and hidden and who "cuts asunder the bars of iron" (Is. 45:2) and the bolts by which access was prohibited for attaining all the truths that were written and hidden in Genesis: concerning the different kinds of souls, concerning the seeds and generations that either pertain directly to Israel or are separated much further from his offspring, and what that "descent of seventy souls into Egypt" is, where the seventy souls became "as the stars of heaven for multitude" (cf. Deut. 10:22; Gen. 46:27; Ex. 1:5). But because not all who were from them are the light of this world (cf. Mt. 5:14)—for not all who are from Israel are Israel (cf. Rom. 9:6)—some who came from those seventy souls became "as the innumerable grains of sand by the seashore"[83] (cf. Heb. 11:12; Gen. 15:5, 22:17).

12. This descent of the holy fathers into Egypt, that is into this world, can be regarded to have been permitted by God's providence for the enlightening of others and for the instruction of the human race, so that through them other souls might be helped and enlightened. For, to begin with, they are entrusted with the oracles of God (Rom. 3:2), since it is only that nation that is said "to see God"; this is what the name *Israel* means when it is translated. And so it follows that this is how we ought to apply and interpret the stories of Egypt's being chastised with ten plagues to allow the people of God to leave (cf. Ex. 7:14–12:36), or of what happened to the people in the wilderness (cf. Ex. 19ff.), or of the building of the tabernacle from what was collected from all the people (cf. Ex. 25ff.), or of the making of the priestly robe (cf. Ex. 28), or of what is

---

83. The parallel text from the *Philocalia* stops at this point.

told about the vessels of the temple service (cf. Ex. 30:17ff.), because they truly contain in themselves, as it is written, "the shadow" and type "of heavenly things." For Paul clearly says of them that "they serve a shadow and copy of heavenly things" (Heb. 8:5). In this same Law there are no less included the laws and customs by which they were to live in the holy land. Moreover, threats are placed against those who transgress the Law; as well, various kinds of purifications for those who need purification are handed down (cf. Lev. 12–15) as though for people who would be quite often polluted, so that through them they might come to that one purification after which no further pollution is permitted (cf. Heb. 9 and 6:6).

Moreover, the people itself is enumerated, though not entirely (cf. Num. 1–4, 26). For childlike souls do not yet have enough time to be numbered by the divine command, and not even those souls that cannot become the head of someone else but are themselves subjected to others as their head, which Scripture calls "women," are included in the numbering ordered by God (cf. Num. 1:2, 4; 1 Cor. 11:3). Only those are numbered who are called "men," so as to show that the others could not be numbered on their own, but could be included with those who are called "men."

Of special prominence among those who came to the holy number are those prepared to march to the wars of Israel, who are able to fight against those enemies and foes whom the Father subjects to the Son sitting at His right hand that He may destroy every principality and power (cf. Eph. 1:20, 22; 1 Cor. 15:27, 24). God's purpose is that through those numbered as His soldiers, who as soldiers on service to God do not get entangled in worldly pursuits (2 Tim. 2:4), He may overturn the kingdoms of the Adversary.[84] By them the shields of faith are carried and the weapons of wisdom brandished; on them the helmet, the hope of salvation, gleams; and the breastplate of love protects their breast filled with God (cf. Eph. 6:16; 1 Thess. 5:8). This is what I think is meant by the soldiers, and these are the kinds of wars for which those are prepared who are commanded in the divine books by the order of God to be numbered.

---

84. Cf. Jerome's Letter to Avitus 11.

But singled out as much more distinguished and perfect than these are those "the hairs of whose head" are said to be numbered (cf. Mt. 10:30). On the other hand, those who were punished for their sins, whose bodies fell in the wilderness, appear to resemble those who have made not a little progress, but have been unable to arrive at the goal of perfection for various reasons—because they are said to have murmured or worshiped idols or committed fornication or considered any sin that should not even be entertained by the mind (cf. Num. 11, 14, 16, 21, 25; Ex. 32; 1 Cor. 10:5–10; Heb. 3:17).

And I think that not even that passage is empty of all mystery in which some who had much cattle and much other livestock go before and take ahead of time a place suitable for grazing and feeding cattle, which the right hand of Israel defended in war the first of all (cf. Num. 32). By asking Moses for this place, they were separated beyond the Jordan river and cut off from possession of the holy land. This Jordan can be seen when taken as a type of heavenly things (cf. Heb. 8:5) to moisten and to flood the thirsty souls and minds next to it. And it will not even seem useless that Moses hears from God the laws described in Leviticus, but in Deuteronomy the people becomes a hearer of Moses and learns from him what it could not hear from God (cf. Lev. 1:1, etc.; Deut. 1:1, 5:1). For that reason Deuteronomy is called, as it were, a second Law. To some this fact will appear to mean that when the first Law, which was given through Moses, came to an end (cf. Jn. 1:17), there was apparently a second Law formed that was handed down in a special way from Moses to Joshua, his successor (cf. Deut. 31). And Joshua is believed to preserve the type of our Savior, by whose second Law, that is, the commandments of the Gospel, everything is led to perfection.

13. But we must see whether it may not further appear to show that just as in Deuteronomy the Law is declared more plainly and openly than in the books that were written first, so also from the coming He fulfilled in humility, when He took the form of a servant (Phil. 2:7), an indication is found of the second clearer and more glorious coming of the Savior in the glory of His Father (Mt. 16:27). And by it the type of Deuteronomy is fulfilled, when in the kingdom of heaven all the saints will live by the laws of that "eternal

Gospel" (cf. Rev. 14:6).[85] And just as by coming now He fulfills the Law that has a shadow of the good things to come (Heb. 10:1), so also through His glorious coming the shadow of this coming will be fulfilled and brought to perfection. For so the prophet spoke of Him, "The Spirit of our countenance is Christ the Lord, of whom we said that under His shadow we shall live among the Gentiles" (Lam. 4:20). The fulfillment will come when He rightly transfers all the saints from the temporal Gospel to the "eternal Gospel," according to what John in Revelation describes with respect to "the eternal Gospel" (Rev. 14:6).[86]

14. But in all these speculations let our understanding have sufficient coherence with the rule of piety, and let us think of the Holy Spirit's words not as something that shines as a speech fashioned by frail human eloquence, but, as it is written, "All the king's glory is within" (Ps. 44:14 LXX–45:13) and the treasure of divine meanings is confined, shut up within the frail vessel of the common letter (cf. 2 Cor. 4:7). Then if someone seeks in a more speculative way an explanation of individual points, let him come and let him hear together with us how Paul the Apostle by the Holy Spirit, who searches out even the depths of God (1 Cor. 2:10) and examines the depth of divine wisdom and knowledge (cf. Rom. 11:33), is yet not strong enough to attain the end and, so to speak, intimate knowledge; he proclaims and says in hopelessness and amazement, "Oh the depth of the riches of the wisdom and knowledge of God" (Rom. 11:33). And with what hopelessness of perfect understanding he proclaims this, hear him say, "How unsearchable are the judgments of God and how inscrutable His ways" (Rom. 11:33). For he did not say it was difficult to search out the judgments of God, but that it was altogether impossible. Nor did he say that it was difficult to investigate His ways, but that they could not be investigated. For no matter how far a person advances in his investigation and makes progress by a keener zeal, even if the grace of

---

85. Cf. Jerome's Letter to Avitus 12.
86. Koetschau inserts here fragment 30: Justinian's Letter to Mennas (Mansi IX.532) = Jerome's Letter to Avitus 12. The fragment speaks of a repetition of Christ's crucifixion in the heavenly places and in succeeding ages. Cf. Theophilus Alex. Ep. synod. 4 (Jerome Ep. 92) and Ep. pasch. I. 10–11 (Jerome Ep. 96).

God is within him and enlightens his mind (cf. Eph. 1:18), he cannot arrive at the perfect end of the truths he seeks. No mind that is created has the ability to understand completely by any manner of means, but as it finds some small part of the answers that are sought, it sees other questions to be asked. And if it arrives at those answers, it will again see beyond them to many more questions that they imply must be asked. This is why that wisest Solomon in his contemplation of nature by wisdom said, "I said, 'I will be wise,' but wisdom itself was far from me, further than it was. Who will find its profound depth?" (Eccles. 7:24–25 LXX). Moreover, Isaiah knew that the first principles of the universe cannot be found by mortal nature and not even by those natures that are somehow more divine than human nature but are nonetheless themselves made or created. Thus, he knew that by none of them can either the beginning or the end be described; and he said, "Tell us the former things, what they are, and we shall know that you are gods. Or proclaim the last things that are, and then we shall see that you are gods" (Is. 41:22–23 LXX).

As well, my Hebrew teacher used to impart the following tradition. With regard to the fact that neither the beginning nor the end of all things can be understood by anyone, unless only by the Lord Jesus Christ and by the Holy Spirit, he used to say that Isaiah by the type of his vision had spoken of two seraphim alone who with two wings cover the face of God, with two wings His feet, and with two wings fly, crying to one another and saying, "Holy, holy, holy is the Lord of Sabaoth, the whole earth is full of your glory" (Is. 6:2–3). Thus, because the two seraphim alone have their wings over God's face and His feet, we must dare to say that not even the army of the holy angels (cf. Lk. 2:13) nor the holy thrones, dominations, principalities, and powers (cf. Col. 1:16) can correctly know the beginning of everything and the ends of the universe. But we must understand that those holy beings whom we have listed are spirits and powers near to the first principles themselves and touch upon them to a degree the others are not strong enough to attain. Nevertheless, whatever those powers say by the revelation of the Son of God and the Holy Spirit, and however many truths they have been able to overtake, the higher much more than the powers below them, it is still impossible for them to understand everything, since it is written, "Most of God's works are concealed" (Sir. 16:21).

Therefore, it is desirable that everyone always should, so far as his powers allow, strain forward to what lies ahead, forgetting what lies behind (Phil. 3:14), striving both for better deeds and for a purer understanding and knowledge through Jesus Christ our Savior, to whom be glory forever (cf. Tit. 3:6, 8; Rom. 16:27).

15. Therefore, everyone who is concerned with truth should be little concerned with names and words (cf. 1 Tim. 1:4), because different nations have different customs about words. And he should pay more attention to what is meant than to how it is expressed in words, especially in the case of such great and difficult matters. For example, suppose we ask whether there is any substance in which neither color nor shape nor touch nor size may be understood, which is perceptible to the mind alone, and which a person can call by whatever name he wishes. The Greeks call it *asōmaton*, that is, "incorporeal"; but the divine Scriptures use the word "invisible," since the Apostle proclaims that God is "invisible" and says that Christ is "the image of the invisible God." Moreover, he says further that through Christ "all things, visible and invisible, were created" (Col. 1:15–16). By this it is made clear that even among creatures there are some that are "invisible" substances by their own properties. But although they are not corporeal, they nevertheless make use of bodies, though they are themselves better than corporeal substances. But the substance of the Trinity, which is the first principle and cause of everything, from which are all things and through which are all things and in which are all things (Rom. 11:36), must not be believed to be a body or to exist in a body, but to be completely incorporeal.

Even though we have digressed, let what we have been obliged to say briefly as an implication of the main argument suffice to show that there are some things the meaning of which cannot in any way rightly be explained by any words of a human language (cf. 1 Cor. 2:4), but are made plain by a purer intellectual apprehension rather than by any properties words have. As well, the understanding of divine letters must be kept to that rule by which what is said is judged not according to the common character of the word but according to the divinity of the Holy Spirit, who inspired their writing.

CHAPTER FOUR
A SUMMARY CONCERNING THE FATHER, THE SON, AND THE HOLY SPIRIT AND OTHER MATTERS PREVIOUSLY DISCUSSED

1. The time has now come in our discussion to sum up one by one, so far as we are able, the subjects we have treated and that we have discussed in a scattered way, and first of all to repeat what we have said about the Father, the Son, and the Holy Spirit. Since God the Father is invisible and inseparable from the Son, the Son is not generated by a production from Him, as some think. For if the Son is a production of the Father and *production* is defined as the sort of generation by which the offspring of animals or of men are accustomed to come into existence, then necessarily both He who produces and He who is produced will be bodies.[87] For we do not say, as the heretics suppose, that any part of God's substance has been turned into the Son or that the Son has been generated from the Father from no substance at all, that is, outside His own substance, so that there would be a time when He was not. But we remove all notion of corporeality and say that the Word and Wisdom is generated from the invisible and incorporeal God apart from any corporeal passion, as will proceeds from mind. Nor will it seem absurd if it is thought of by the analogy of will, since He is said to be "the Son of love" (Col. 1:13).[88] Moreover, John points out that "God is light" (1 John 1:5), and Paul points out that the Son is "the splendor of eternal light" (cf. Heb. 1:3). Therefore, just as light can never exist without splendor, so neither can the Son, who is said to

---

87. Koetschau places here fragment 31: Marcellus apud Eusebius's Contra Marcellum II.4. The content of the fragment is substantially the same as Rufinus's translation.

88. Koetschau inserts here three fragments: fragment 32: Justinian's Letter to Mennas (Mansi IX.525), citing Col. 1:15, Heb. 1:3, Prov. 8:22; fragment 33: Athanasius, Ep. de decret. Nic. Syn. 27 (PG 25.465), citing Col. 1:15, 1 John 1:5, Heb. 1:3; and fragment 34:ibid. The content of these fragments insists on the distinct identity of the Word, but agrees substantially with Rufinus's translation, even to the extent of refuting what resemble the slogans of the later Arians.

be "the express stamp of His substance" (Heb. 1:3) and His Word and Wisdom, ever be understood without the Father. Therefore, how can it be said that there was a time when the Son was not? For that would be no different from saying that there was a time when truth was not, when wisdom was not, when life was not, since it should be judged that the substance of God the Father involves all of these things. They cannot be separated from Him, nor can they ever be cut off from His substance. And what are said to be many by intellectual apprehension, nevertheless are one in fact and in substance; and in them there exists the fulness of Godhead (cf. Col. 2:9).

But what we have said, that there never was a time when He was not, must be taken with a qualification. For the very words "when" and "never" bear a meaning implying the notion of time. But what is said about the Father, the Son, and the Holy Spirit must be understood above all time, above all ages, and above all eternity. For that only is the Trinity which surpasses every sense of our understanding, not only temporal but also eternal. It is other things that are outside the Trinity that must be measured in ages and times. Therefore, as to this Son of God, because He is the Word who is God and who was in the beginning with God (Jn. 1:1–2), no one will rightly think that He is contained in any place, nor will he draw that conclusion because He is wisdom or because He is truth or because He is life or righteousness or sanctification or redemption. None of these things require a place to be able to do something or to act, but they must be understood individually, when they refer to those who partake of the Word's power and operation.

2. But perhaps someone will say that through those who are participants (cf. Heb. 3:14) in God's Word or His Wisdom or truth or life the Word and Wisdom appears Himself to be in a place. The answer must be given that there is no doubt that Christ insofar as He is Word and Wisdom and all the rest was in Paul, because of which he said, "Or do you desire proof that Christ is speaking in me?" (2 Cor. 13:3). And again, "But it is no longer I who live, but Christ who lives in me" (Gal. 2:20). Then, therefore, since He was in Paul, who will doubt that He was likewise in Peter, in John, and in each one of the saints, and not only in those on earth but also in

those in the heavens? For it is absurd to say that Christ was in Peter and in Paul, but not in Michael the Archangel and in Gabriel. From this it is clearly discovered that the divinity of the Son of God was not confined to any place, since He was not so much in one as not to be in another. Rather, since He is not confined in any place because of the majesty of His incorporeal nature, He is further understood not to be absent from any place.

But this one difference must be understood, that although He is present in diverse beings, as we have said He is in Peter or Paul or Michael or Gabriel, nevertheless He is not present in a similar way in every one. And He is present more fully and more clearly and, if I may put it this way, more openly in the archangels than in holy men. This is evident from the fact that when the saints arrive at the highest perfection, they are said to be made "like angels" or "equal" to angels according to the view of the Gospel (cf. Mt. 22:30; Lk. 20:36) It follows that Christ is made present in different ones to the degree that the reckoning of what they deserve permits.

3. Now that we have briefly repeated our account of the Trinity, we must go on in the same way to remind the reader that through the Son "all things" are said to be "created, in heaven and on earth, visible and invisible, whether thrones or dominions or principalities or powers—all things were created through Him and in Him. He is before all things; in Him who is the head all things hold together" (Col. 1:16–18). John in his Gospel also agrees with this and says that "all things were made through Him, and without Him was not anything made" (Jn. 1:3). And David points out the mystery of the entire Trinity in the creation of everything when he says, "By the Word of the Lord the heavens were made, and all their power by the Spirit of His mouth" (Ps. 33:6).

Next we shall properly call to mind the corporeal coming and incarnation of the Only Begotten Son of God. In it we must not take the view that the entire majesty of His divinity was shut up in the confines of one small body so that the entire Word of God and His Wisdom and substantial truth and life was cut off from the Father or forced within the small compass of that body and contained by it, and He should be thought active in no other way than this. Rather, the confession of our religion ought to beware of two extremes, so that neither should any lack in the divinity of Christ be believed, nor should any division be supposed to have taken place from within the Father's substance, which is everywhere. And John the Baptist points to some such conclusion when in Jesus' corporeal absence he said to the crowds, "Among you stands one whom you do not know, even He who comes after me, the thong of whose sandals I am not worthy to untie" (Jn. 1:26–27). John could not have said He stood in the midst of those among whom He was not corporeally present about Him who was absent so far as His corporeal presence was concerned. Thus, it is clear that the Son of God was both wholly present in the body and wholly present everywhere.

4. No one should think that we are maintaining by this the view that one part of the divinity of the Son of God was in Christ, but the remaining part somewhere else or everywhere. Those who can hold this opinion are ignorant of the nature of an incorporeal and invisible substance. For it is impossible to talk about part of something incorporeal or that any division could take place in it. Rather, it exists in all and through all and above all (cf. Eph. 1:22–23) in the same way we spoke of earlier, the way wisdom or word or life or truth is understood. And by this understanding any idea of confinement in a place is beyond doubt excluded. Therefore, when the Son of God wished to appear to men and live among men for the salvation of the human race, He took not only a human body, as some suppose, but also a soul, and one like our souls in its nature, but like Himself in purpose and power, and such as could fulfill without turning all the wishes and dispensations of the Word and Wisdom.[89]

Moreover, that He had a soul the Savior points out with perfect clarity Himself in the Gospels by saying, "No one takes my soul from me, but I lay it down of my own accord. I have power to lay it down, and I have power to take it again" (Jn. 10:18). And again, "My soul is very sorrowful, even to death" (Mt. 26:38). And again, "Now is my soul troubled" (Jn. 12:27).[90] For the Word of God must not be understood as a "sorrowful" or "troubled" soul,

---

89. Koetschau suspects a lacuna and inserts fragment 35: Justinian's Letter to Mennas (Mansi IX.506D), which refers to Origen's belief in the preexistence of Jesus' soul.

90. Koetschau places here fragment 36: Theophilus Alex. Ep. pasch. II.16 = Jerome Ep. 98 (PL 22.804f.), Theodoret, Dial. II.4 (PG 83.197).

because He says on the authority of His divinity, "I have power to lay down my soul" (Jn. 10:18). Nevertheless, we do not say that the Son of God was in that soul the way He was in the soul of Paul or of Peter or of the other saints in whom Christ is believed to speak just as in Paul (cf. 2 Cor. 13:3). In the case of all of them we must hold the opinion of Scripture that "no one is clean of defilement, not even if his life lasts only one day" (Job 14:4–5 LXX). But that soul which was in Jesus chose good before it knew evil (cf. Is. 7:15–16). And because it "loved righteousness and hated wickedness, therefore God anointed it with the oil of gladness above its fellows" (Ps. 45:7). Thus, it is "anointed with the oil of gladness" when it was joined with the Word of God in a pure bond, and by this it was the only one of all the souls incapable of sin, because it was capable of holding the Son of God well and fully.[91] Consequently, it is one with Him, named by His titles, and called Jesus Christ, through whom all things are said to have been made (cf. Jn. 1:3; Col. 1:16).

It is concerning this soul, since it had received in itself the whole of God's Wisdom and truth and life, that I think the Apostle spoke when he said, "Your life is hid with Christ in God. When Christ who is our life appears then you also will appear with Him in glory" (Col. 3:3–4). For what other Christ must be understood here, who is said to be "hid in God" and afterwards to "appear," unless the reference is to the one anointed "with the oil of gladness," that is, filled in a substantial way with God, in whom he is now said to be "hid." And that is why Christ is set forth as an example to all believers, because just as he always "chose good" even before "he knew evil" and "loved righteousness and hated wickedness, and therefore God anointed him with the oil of gladness," so also each person either after a fall or after an error cleanses himself from stains by the example set forth; and since he has a leader for the journey, he enters upon the difficult road of virtue. The aim for which we hope is that so far as it can happen we may be made participants in the divine nature by imitating him, as it is written, "He who says he believes in Christ ought to walk in the same way in which he walked" (cf. 1 John 2:6). Therefore, this

---

91. Koetschau here places fragment 37: Theophilus Alex. Ep. pasch. II.16 = Theodoret, Dial. II.4 (PG 83.197).

Word and this Wisdom, through whose imitation we are said to be wise or rational, "becomes all things to all that He might gain all"; He became weak to the weak that He might gain the weak (1 Cor. 9:22). And because He was made weak, it is said of Him, "Although He was crucified in weakness, yet He lives by the power of God" (2 Cor. 13:4). And for the Corinthians, who were weak, Paul "decided to know nothing among them except Christ Jesus and Him crucified" (1 Cor. 2:2).

5. Moreover, there are some who wish what the Apostle says to be referred to that soul when it first assumed a body from Mary, "who though he was in the form of God, did not think equality with God a thing to be grasped, but emptied himself, taking the form of a servant" (Phil. 2:6–7). By this, I suppose, it restored the form of a servant to the form of God by better examples and customs, and it called it back to that fulness from which it had emptied itself.

But just as a person receives the adoption of sons by participation in the Son of God and is made wise by participation in God's Wisdom, so also he is made holy and spiritual by participation in the Holy Spirit. For it is one and the same thing to receive participation in the Holy Spirit as to receive it in the Father and the Son, since, of course, the nature of the Trinity is one and incorporeal. And what we have said about the participation of the soul must be understood to apply to angels and heavenly powers, just as it does to souls, since every rational creature requires participation in the Trinity.

Moreover, the question arises as to the meaning of this visible world, since a great deal of investigation customarily takes place about how it is constituted. And we have discussed the matter so far as we could in the earlier books for those who are accustomed to search out a reason also for believing in our faith and for those who stir up heretical strife against us and are accustomed to toss about with great frequency the name of matter, which they have not even been able to understand themselves by any clear definition of what it is. And so I think it necessary to call the subject to mind briefly now.

6. Now first it must be known that the term *matter*, referring to that substance which is said to underlie bodies, is a word we have

never found up to the present in the canonical Scriptures. For what Isaiah says, "And He will consume the *hylē*, that is, the matter, like straw" (Is. 10:17 LXX) refers to those appointed for punishments, and he uses the word matter to stand for *sins*. Moreover, wherever else the word matter may be written, it never, I think, will be found to have the meaning into which we are now inquiring, unless possibly in Wisdom, which was written by Solomon and is not considered an authoritative book by everyone. What he says is, "For your all-powerful hand, which created the world out of formless matter, did not lack the means to send upon them a multitude of bears, or bold lions" (Wis. 11:17). A great many people with reason suppose that it is that matter from which things are made that Moses writes about at the beginning of Genesis, "In the beginning God created the heavens and the earth. The earth was invisible and unfashioned" (Gen. 1:1 LXX). For Moses appears to mean nothing other than unformed matter by the words "invisible and unfashioned earth." But if this is, in truth, matter, then the implication is established that the first beginnings of bodies are not unchangeable.

For those who posit atoms, either those that cannot be divided into parts or those that can be divided into equal parts, or those who posit each one of the elements as the first principles of corporeal things could not establish the term matter, that is in its principal definition, among the first principles. And even if they place matter as a substance underlying every body, in every way changeable or mutable or divisible, they will not regard it as an underlying substance according to its own properties apart from qualities. And we are in agreement with them, because we deny in every way that matter should be called ungenerated or uncreated. This is what we demonstrated so far as we were able in the earlier books, when we proved that from water and earth, air or heat, different fruits are produced by different kinds of trees, or when we taught that fire, air, water, and earth are changed into one another in turn and each is resolved into another by a certain mutual affinity, and, as well, when we proved that from the foods of men or animals the substance of flesh comes into existence or that the moisture of the natural seed is changed into solid flesh and bones. All these arguments are proof that corporeal substance is completely mutable and passes in every case from one quality to another.

7. Nevertheless, it is right to know that since a substance never exists without quality, matter is what underlies bodies and receives quality, but is discerned only by the mind. Thus, those who are willing to examine these matters more deeply have dared to say that corporeal nature is nothing else but qualities. For if hardness and softness, heat and cold, moistness and dryness, are qualities, and if when they or other things like them are taken away nothing else is understood to be underlying, then the qualities will apparently be all there is. Consequently, those who hold this view have ventured the opinion that since all who say that matter is uncreated agree that qualities have been created by God, it may be found in this way that even according to their opinion matter is not uncreated, if indeed all things are qualities, which no one denies have been made by God.

But those who wish to show that qualities are added from without to a certain underlying matter use examples of the following sort. For example, Paul undoubtedly is either silent or speaks, either is awake or sleeps, or is found in a certain bodily posture, for he either sits or stands or lies. Now all these things are accidental for men, and they are almost never found without them. Nevertheless, our mind clearly does not define *man* by any of them, but we understand or think of him by them in such a way that we do not grasp in a general way the rational account of his circumstances, but think of him either awake or asleep or as speaking or silent or as anything else that necessarily happens to men. Therefore, just as someone might consider *Paul* to be what is without all these accidents that come to him, so also someone can understand what is without qualities to be the underlying substance. When, therefore, our mind by removing intellectually every quality regards the point, so to speak, of the underlying substance by itself and clings to that, paying no attention at all to the hardness, softness, heat, cold, moistness, or dryness of the substance, then by some sort of mental representation it will apparently look upon matter bare of all qualities.

8. But perhaps someone may ask whether we can find some basis for this understanding in the Scriptures. Something like it seems to me meant in the Psalms, when it is said by the prophet, "My eyes beheld your unfinished" (Ps. 138:16 LXX–139:16). The

mind of the prophet, inquiring into the beginning of things with very clear contemplation and separating matter from its qualities by understanding and reason alone, apparently perceived the "unfinished" of God, which is understood to be completed by the addition of qualities. Moreover, in the book of Enoch it says, "I walked as far as to the unfinished" (En. 21:1). And I think this can be understood in a similar way, namely, that the mind of the prophet "walked" by examining and discussing different individual points concerning visible things until he arrived at that beginning in which he saw through to "unfinished" matter without qualities. For it is written in the same book, Enoch himself speaking, "I have seen every kind of matter" (Slav. En. 40:1, 12). The meaning is that I have seen all the classes of matter, which are different kinds divided from one into each sort, that is of man or animals or heaven or the sun or all that is in this world.

Next after all these subjects we proved so far as we were able in the earlier books that existing things were created by God and that there is nothing uncreated except the nature of the Father, Son, and Holy Spirit and that God, who is good by nature, wishing to have those whom He might benefit and who might enjoy the benefits received from Him, made creatures worthy of Himself, that is, who could receive Him worthily, of whom He said, "I have begotten sons" (Is. 1:2). And He made everything by number and measure, for to God nothing is without end or without measure.[92] And He included everything by His own power, but He was not Himself comprehended by the mind of any creature.[93] For that nature is known only to itself. Only the Father knows the Son, and only the Son knows the Father, and only the Holy Spirit searches even the depths of God (1 Cor. 2:10).

Therefore, every creature is distinguished by God within a certain number or measure, that is, either number for rational beings or measure for corporeal matter. And since it was necessary for the intellectual nature to use bodies and since by the very condition

---

92. Koetschau places here fragment 38: Justinian's Letter to Mennas (Mansi IX.525). The fragment speaks of God's power being limited.

93. Koetschau places here fragment 39: Justinian's Letter to Mennas (Mansi IX.525). Cf. Jerome's Letter to Avitus 13. The fragment speaks of limitations placed upon the Son's knowledge of the Father.

that it is created it is discerned to be mutable and changeable (for what was not and began to be is by that very fact defined as having a mutable nature, and so it possesses virtue or vice not as its substance but as its accident)—since, therefore, as we have said, the rational nature was mutable and changeable, so that it would use a different bodily garment of this or that quality depending on its deserts, just as God necessarily knew beforehand the future diversities either of souls or of spiritual powers, so also He made corporeal nature so as to change by the will of the Creator and by the permutation of qualities into everything that circumstances required. And it was necessary for it to last as long as souls who need a corporeal garment last. Now there will always be rational natures that need a corporeal garment, and so there will always be a corporeal nature, the garments of which rational creatures must use—unless someone supposes he can show by any proofs that a rational nature can live apart from a body of any kind. We have demonstrated in the detailed discussion of our earlier books that this is difficult or almost impossible for us to understand.[94]

9. Now I think it not apparently against our purpose if we repeat as briefly as possible also what concerns the immortality of rational natures. Everyone who participates in something is doubtless of one substance and one nature with one who participates in the same thing. For example, all eyes participate in light, and so all eyes that participate in light are of one nature. But granted that every eye participates in light, nonetheless, since one sees more sharply and another more dully, not every eye participates equally in the light. Again, all hearing receives a voice or a sound, and so all hearing is of one nature. But according to its quality of purity and clearness different hearings hear more or less quickly. But let us pass from these examples taken from perceptibles to the consideration of intelligibles.

Every mind that participates in the intelligible light ought undoubtedly to be of one nature with every other mind that in a similar fashion participates in the intelligible light. If, therefore, the heavenly powers by the fact that they participate in wisdom and

---

94. Koetschau places here fragment 40: Justinian's Letter to Mennas (Mansi IX.532). The fragment says that bodies were created because of the fall, that they will finally disappear, and that the cycle will continue forever.

sanctification receive participation in the intelligible light, that is, the divine nature, and if the human soul receives participation in the same light and wisdom, they and it will be of one nature and of one substance with one another. Moreover, the heavenly powers are incorruptible and immortal; so, doubtless, the substance of the human soul will be incorruptible and immortal. Not only this, but since the nature of the Father, Son, and Holy Spirit, from whose intelligible light alone the entire creation draws participation, is itself incorruptible and eternal, it certainly both follows and is necessary that every substance that draws participation from that eternal nature also endures itself forever both incorruptible and eternal, so that the eternity of the divine goodness may be understood by the fact that those who receive His benefits are also eternal. But just as in our examples the diversity of perceiving the light is retained, since the vision of the person seeing is described as duller or sharper, so also in the case of participation in the Father, Son, and Holy Spirit diversity is retained in proportion to the attention of the understanding and the capacity of the mind.

But from another point of view let us consider whether it does not appear impious that the mind that can receive God should suffer the destruction of its substance, as though the very fact that it can understand and perceive God were not able to afford it continual duration. This is especially so since, even if the mind falls through negligence so that it cannot receive God into itself purely and entirely, it nonetheless always retains in itself, as it were, certain seeds of restoration and of being recalled to a better understanding, when the "inner man" (cf. Rom. 7:22), which is also called the rational man, is called back to the image and likeness (cf. Gen. 1:26) of God, who created him. For this reason the prophet says, "All the ends of the earth shall remember and be turned to the Lord, and all the families of the nations shall worship before Him" (Ps. 22:27).

10. But if anyone dares to attribute corruption of substance to what was made according to the image and likeness of God, in my opinion he extends the charge of impiety also to the Son of God Himself, since He is also called in Scripture "the image of God" (cf. Col. 1:15; 2 Cor. 4:4). At least the one who holds the opinion will certainly find fault with the authority of Scripture, which says that

man was made after the image of God. And the traces of the divine image are clearly recognized not through the likeness of the body, which undergoes corruption, but through the intelligence of the soul, its righteousness, temperance, courage, wisdom, discipline, and through the entire chorus of virtues that are present in God by substance, and can be in man through effort and the imitation of God, as also the Lord points out in the Gospel when He says, "Be merciful, even as your Father is merciful" (Lk. 6:36) and "Be perfect, as your Father is perfect" (Mt. 5:48). Consequently, it is quite clear that in God all these virtues can never enter or leave, but they are acquired by men little by little and one by one.

It follows that human beings appear to have some affinity with God for this reason. And although God knows everything and nothing related to intelligible things escapes His notice (for only God the Father with His Only Begotten Son and the Holy Spirit holds knowledge not only of what He created but also of Himself), nevertheless, even the rational mind can by progressing from small things to greater and from visible to invisible (cf. Col. 1:16) arrive at a more perfect understanding. For it is placed in a body and necessarily progresses from perceptible things, which are corporeal, to imperceptible, which are incorporeal and intelligible. But lest it appear to anyone unbecoming to say that intelligible things are imperceptible, let us use the example of Solomon's opinion, when he says, "You will also find the divine perception" (Prov. 2:5). By this he makes it plain that things that are intelligible must be sought not by corporeal perception but by some other one which he calls "divine."

Moreover, by this perception a person must consider one by one the things we have called rational, and by this perception he must listen to what we say and consider what we write. For the divine nature knows even what we silently consider within ourselves. And this opinion must be held, according to the principles we have just explained, about what we have said and about the other things that are implied by them.

THE PROLOGUE TO
THE COMMENTARY ON
THE SONG OF SONGS

This book seems to me an epithalamium, that is, a wedding song, written by Solomon in the form of a play, which he recited in the character of a bride who was being married and burned with a heavenly love for her bridegroom, who is the Word of God. For whether she is the soul made after His image or the Church, she has fallen deeply in love with Him. Moreover, this book of Scripture instructs us in the words this marvelous and perfect bridegroom uses toward the soul or the Church that has been united with Him. As well, from the same book, which is entitled Song of Songs, we come to know what the young girls appointed as the bride's companions said, and also what the friends and companions of the bridegroom said. And the friends of the bridegroom were given the ability of saying some things, so far as they could, that they had heard from the bridegroom Himself, since they were rejoicing at His union with the bride. Moreover, the bride addresses not only the bridegroom but also the young girls, and further the bridegroom not only addresses the bride but also turns to the friends of the bridegroom. And this is what we meant a moment ago by saying that it is a wedding song written in the form of a play. For a play is defined as a story, usually acted on the stage, where different characters are introduced, and where with some characters entering and others making their exits the structure of the narrative is completed by different speeches addressed to different characters. Each of these elements the book of Scripture includes by its own order, and its whole body is fashioned together through fine and mysterious words.

But first we must understand that just as children are not

moved to the passion of love, so neither is the age of the inner man, if it is that of a little one and an infant, allowed to grasp these words. I am referring to those who are nourished in Christ by milk and not by solid food (cf. Heb. 5:12) and who now for the first time long for the milk that is spiritual and without deceit (cf. 1 Pet. 2:2). Indeed, in the words of Song of Songs may be found that food of which the Apostle says, "But solid food is for the perfect" and requires such people as listeners who "have their faculties trained by practice to distinguish good from evil" (Heb. 5:14). Thus, if those we have called "little ones" come to these places in Scripture, it can happen that they receive no profit at all from this book or even that they are badly injured either by reading what has been written or by examining what has been said to interpret it. But if any one approaches who is a grown man according to the flesh, no little risk and danger arises for such a person from this book of Scripture. For if he does not know how to listen to the names of love purely and with chaste ears, he may twist everything he has heard from the inner man to the outer and fleshly man and be turned away from the Spirit to the flesh. Then he will nourish in himself fleshly desires, and it will seem because of the divine Scriptures that he is impelled and moved to the lusts of the flesh. For this reason I give warning and advice to everyone who is not yet free of the vexations of flesh and blood and who has not withdrawn from the desire for corporeal nature that he completely abstain from reading this book and what is said about it. Indeed, they say that the Hebrews observe the rule that unless some one has attained a perfect and mature age, he is not even permitted to hold this book in his hands. Moreover, we also accept the observance of the following rule from them—it is their custom that all the Scriptures should be given to children by the teachers and the wise, and that at the same time those passages which they call *deuteroseis* should be held back to the last.[95] There are four of them: the beginning of Genesis in which the creation of the world is described, the first chapters of Ezekiel the prophet in which mention is made of the

---

95. The Greek word presumably translates "mishnah." The context, however, indicates that the term applies to the four sections of Scripture prohibited from ordinary reading by the rabbis because they were the basis of mystical speculation.

cherubim, the end of Ezekiel, which includes the building of the Temple, and this book, Song of Songs.

With all this in mind it seems to me necessary before we begin our discussion of what is written in this book to discuss briefly, first, love itself, which is the chief subject of the book and, next, the order of Solomon's books, among which this book is apparently put in third place. Then we shall also discuss the title of the book itself and why it is called "Song of Songs." Finally, we shall also speak of how it is apparently composed in the form of a play and as a story that is customarily acted on the stage by the interchange of the characters.

Among the Greeks a good many learned men, wishing to inquire into the investigation of truth, have published many different books about the nature of love, some of them even written in a dialogue style. They have tried to show that the power of love is no other than the power that leads the soul from earth to the lofty heights of heaven and that we cannot arrive at the highest blessedness unless the ardent desire of love impels us. Moreover, questions about love are brought up for discussion, as it were, in banquets among those, I think, who were holding a banquet not of food but of words. Others, as well, have left us certain books of "arts" by which this love is apparently capable of being born or increased in the soul. But fleshly people have carried off these arts to vicious desires and to the mysteries of a faulty love. It is, therefore, no wonder if also with us, where the simple and, consequently, the ignorant seem to be in the majority, we have called the consideration of the nature of love difficult and dangerous. For among the Greeks who were reputed wise and learned there were nevertheless some who did not take these books in the sense in which they were written; but pleading the authority of what had been written about love, they fell headlong into the sins of the flesh and the precipitous paths of lewdness, either by taking suggestions and inducements from the writings we have already mentioned or by presenting the writings of those of old as a veil for their incontinence.

Therefore, lest we also should in any way offend against what was written well and spiritually by those of old through twisting it in a vicious or fleshly sense, let us stretch forth the hands of our soul as of our body to God, that the Lord, who gave His Word to the preachers with great power (Ps. 67:12 LXX—Ps. 68:11), may also give us the Word with His power, by whom we may be enabled to make clear from our treatise a sound understanding of the name and nature of love and one suitable for building up chastity.

At the beginning of Moses' words, where he describes the creation of the world, we find reference to two men that were created, the first made after the image and likeness of God (cf. Gen. 1:26) and the second formed from the dust of the ground (cf. Gen. 2:7). Paul the Apostle well knew this and possessed a clear understanding of these matters. In his letters he wrote more openly and clearly that every person is two different men. This is what he said, "Though our outer man is wasting away, our inner man is being renewed every day" (2 Cor. 4:16) and further, "For I delight in the law of God in my inner man" (Rom. 7:22). And he wrote a good many passages like these. On this basis I think that no one ought now to doubt that Moses at the beginning of Genesis wrote about the making or forming of two men, when he sees Paul, who understood better than we do what was written by Moses, saying that every person is two different men. He mentions that one of them, that is, the inner man, is renewed every day; but he asserts that the other, the outer man, in the saints and in people like Paul, is wasting away and growing weak. But if there will appear to be any doubt in the matter, it will be better explained in the proper places. Now, however, that we have made mention of the inner and the outer man, we shall go on.

What we wish to show on this basis is that in the divine Scriptures by synonyms, that is, by similar designations and sometimes by the same words, both the members of the outer man and the parts and desires of the inner man are designated and that they are to be compared with one another not only with respect to the designations but also with respect to the realities themselves. For example, someone can be in age a child according to the inner man; and it is possible for him to grow and to attain the age of youth and from there by succeeding growth to arrive at mature manhood (cf. Eph. 4:13) and become a father. Moreover, we have tried to use these names so that we may employ designations in agreement with the divine Scripture, specifically with what John wrote when he said, "I write to you, children, because you know the Father. I write to you, fathers, because you know Him who is from the beginning. I write to you, young men, because you are strong, and the Word of God abides in you, and you have overcome the Evil One" (1 John 2:13–14). It is so clear that I think no one can doubt that John here uses the terms *children*, *youths* or *young men*, and *fathers* according to the age of the soul and not of the body.

Moreover, Paul says in one place, "I could not address you as spiritual men, but as men of the flesh, as babes in Christ. I fed you with milk, not solid food" (1 Cor. 3:1–2). And he uses the expression "babe in Christ" undoubtedly according to the age of the soul and not according to that of the flesh. And then the same Paul says in another place, "When I was a child, I spoke like a child, I thought like a child, I reasoned like a child; when I became a man, I gave up childish ways" (1 Cor. 13:11). And, further, he says at another time, "Until we all attain . . . to mature manhood, to the measure of the stature of the fullness of Christ" (Eph. 4:13). For he knows that all who believe will attain to mature manhood, to the measure of the stature of the fullness of Christ. Thus, just as the names of ages we have spoken of are applied with the same designations both to the outer and to the inner man, so you will also find that the names of the members of the body are applied to the members of the soul, or rather they are said of the power and desire of the soul. Thus, it is said in Ecclesiastes, "The wise man has his eyes in his head" (Eccles. 2:14). And in the Gospel, "He who has ears to hear, let him hear" (Mk. 4:9). Also in the prophets, "The word of the Lord which was written by the hand of Jeremiah the prophet"—or of whatever other prophet (cf. Jer. 50:1; Is. 20:2). The verse is similar that says, "And your foot will not stumble" (Prov. 3:23). And further, "But as for me, my feet had almost stumbled" (Ps. 73:2). It is also, obviously, the womb of the soul that is indicated, when it says, "O Lord, we have conceived in the womb by fear of you" (Is. 26:18 LXX). How can anyone doubt the point, when it says, "Their throat is an open sepulchre" (Ps. 5:9)? And further, "Destroy, O Lord, and divide their tongues" (Ps.

55:9)? Moreover it is written, "You have broken the teeth of sinners" (Ps. 3:7). And further, "Break the arm of the sinner and evildoer" (Ps. 10:15). What need is there for me to list further examples, since the divine Scriptures are filled with more than an abundance of witnesses?

On the basis of the evidence we have cited it is clearly demonstrated that these names for members can by no means be applied to the visible body, but must be referred to the parts and powers of the invisible soul. The reason is that both carry similar designations, but the examples given obviously and without any ambiguity bear meanings that apply not to the outer man but to the inner man. Therefore, this material man, who is also called the outer man, has food and drink related to his nature, specifically corporeal and earthly. And in a similar way, the spiritual man, who is called the inner man, also has his own food, that living bread which came down from heaven (cf. Jn. 6:33, 41). And his drink is from that water which Jesus promised when He said, "Whoever drinks of the water that I shall give him will never thirst" (Jn. 4:14). And so through everything a similarity of designations is applied according to each of the men; but the special properties of what each of them is are distinguished from one another and kept separate. Corruptible things are granted to the corruptible man, but incorruptible things are set forth for the incorruptible man. Because of this it happens that certain of the simpler Christians, since they do not know how to distinguish and to keep separate what in the divine Scriptures must be allotted to the inner man and what to the outer man, misled by the similarities in the designations, have turned themselves to certain foolish stories and vain fictions, so that even after the resurrection they believe that corporeal foods must be used and drink taken not only from that true Vine which lives forever, but also from vines and fruits of wood (cf. Jn. 15:1). But we shall turn our attention to them another time.

Now, therefore, as we have noted in our earlier observations, there is one person according to the inner man without children and "barren," but another abounding in "children." In this regard we have noticed the verse "The barren has borne seven, and she who has many children is deprived of strength" (1 Sam. 2:5). And as it is said among the blessings, "No one among you shall be without children and barren" (cf. Ex. 23:26). Thus, if these conclusions are sound, just as there is said to be a fleshly love, which the poets also call Love,[96] according to which the person who loves sows in the flesh, so also there is a spiritual love according to which the inner man when he loves sows in the Spirit (cf. Gal. 6:8). And to speak more plainly, if there is someone who still bears the image of the earthly according to the outer man, he is led by an earthly desire and love. But the person who bears the image of the heavenly according to the inner man is led by a heavenly desire and love (cf. 1 Cor. 15:49). Indeed, the soul is led by a heavenly love and desire when once the beauty and glory of the Word of God has been perceived, he falls in love with His splendor and by this receives from Him some dart and wound of love. For this Word is the image and brightness of the invisible God, the First Born of all creation, in whom all things were created, in heaven and on earth, visible and invisible (cf. Col. 1:15f.; Heb. 1:3). Therefore, if anyone has been able to hold in the breadth of his mind and to consider the glory and splendor of all those things created in Him, he will be struck by their very beauty and transfixed by the magnificence of their brilliance or, as the prophet says, "by the chosen arrow" (Is. 49:2). And he will receive from Him the saving wound and will burn with the blessed fire of His love.

We should also realize that just as illicit and unlawful love can come upon the outer man, for example, that he should love not his bride or wife but a harlot or adulteress, so also there can come upon the inner man, that is, the soul, a love not for its legitimate bridegroom, who we have said is the Word of God, but for some adulterer and seducer. Ezekiel the prophet makes this quite clear, using the same figure, when he brings forward "Oholah" and "Oholibah" to appear for Samaria and Jerusalem depraved by adulterous love (cf. Ezek. 23:4ff.). The Scriptural passage in the prophet clearly shows this to those who wish to know more about it. And so the spiritual love of the soul blazes up, as we have taught, sometimes toward certain spirits of wickedness, but sometimes toward the Holy Spirit and the Word of God, who is called the faithful bridegroom and husband of the well-trained soul. And the soul, especially in this

---

96. I.e., *Amor* or *Eros*.

book of Scripture we have in hand, is called the Word's bride, as we shall show more fully with the Lord's help when we begin to explain the words of the book itself.

Nevertheless, it seems to me that divine Scripture wishes to warn us, lest the word *love* should provide an occasion of falling for the readers; and so for those who are rather weak Scripture uses the words *loving affection* or *affectionate love* as more honorable terms for what is called by the wise of this world *desire* or *love*.[97] For example, Scripture says of Isaac, "And he took Rebekah, and she became his wife; and he affectionately loved her" (Gen. 24:67). Further, Scripture speaks in a similar way of Jacob and Rachel: "But Rachel had beautiful eyes and a lovely face; and Jacob affectionately loved Rachel, and said, 'I will serve you seven years for your younger daughter Rachel' " (Gen. 29:17–18). But the unchanged sense of this term appears more clearly in the story of Amnon, who fell in love with his sister Tamar; for it is written, "And it came to pass after this that Absalom, David's son, had a very beautiful sister, whose name was Tamar; and Amnon, David's son, affectionately loved her" (2 Sam. 13:1). The text has "affectionately loved" instead of "fell in love." And it says, "And Amnon was so tormented that he made himself ill because of his sister Tamar; for she was a virgin, and it seemed difficult to Amnon to do anything to her" (2 Sam. 13:2). And a little further on Scripture speaks of the violence that Amnon inflicted on Tamar his sister as follows, "And Amnon was unwilling to listen to her appeal, but he was stronger than she, and he forced her down and slept with her. Then Amnon hated her with very great hatred; so that the hatred with which he hated her was greater than the affectionate love with which he had affectionately loved her" (2 Sam. 13:14–15).

Thus, in these and a great many other places you will find that divine Scripture has avoided the term *love* and has put down "affectionate love" and "loving affection." Nevertheless, sometimes, granted it is rare, Scripture calls love by its own term and summons and impels souls to it. For example, in Proverbs it says of Wisdom, "Fall in love with her, and she will keep you . . . put her around

---

97. The words in the translation stand for the Latin and the presumed Greek words as follows: loving affection = *caritas* = *agapē*; affectionate love = *dilectio*, *diligo* = agapē; desire = *cupido* = *epithumia*; love = *amor* = *erōs*.

you, and she will exalt you; honor her that she may embrace you" (cf. Prov. 4:6, 8). Moreover, in the book called the Wisdom of Solomon this is what is written about the same Wisdom, "I became a lover of her beauty" (Wis. 8:2). Now I think that where there is no apparent opportunity for error, Scripture in these cases introduces the word love. For what can any one find passible or shameful in the love of Wisdom or in the person who professes himself a "lover" of Wisdom? But if it had said that Isaac fell in love with Rebekah or Jacob with Rachel, passion as something certainly shameful could have been understood through these words by the holy people of God, especially among those who do not know how to ascend from the letter to the Spirit.

Quite obviously, as well, in the book we have in hand the term love has been changed into the designation "loving affection" in the passage where it says, "I adjure you, O daughters of Jerusalem, if you find my beloved, that you tell Him I am wounded with loving affection" (Song of Songs 5:8). This certainly stands for what might be said, "I have been struck by the dart of His love." Thus, there is no difference in the divine Scriptures whether "love" is used or "loving affection" or "affectionate love," save insofar as the term "loving affection" is given a higher place, because God Himself is also called "loving Affection." For example, John says, "Beloved, let us affectionately love one another, for loving affection is from God, and he who affectionately loves is born of God and knows God. He who does not affectionately love does not know God; for God is loving Affection" (1 John 4:7–8). And although there may be another opportunity to say something about the verses we have used as an example from John's letter, nonetheless it does not seem foolish to touch briefly upon some other points made by his letter. He says, "Let us affectionately love one another, for loving affection is from God" and a little further on, "God is loving Affection." Here he shows both that God is Himself loving Affection and that loving Affection is from God. Who, then, is "from God" save He who said, "I came from God and have come into this world" (cf. Jn. 16:28)? But if God the Father is loving Affection and the Son is loving Affection, and if "loving affection" and "loving affection" are one and the same and differ in no respect, it follows that the Father and the Son are one and the same and differ in no respect.

Moreover, Christ is quite suitably called loving Affection, just as He is called Wisdom and power and righteousness and Word and truth (cf. 1 Cor. 1:24, 30; Jn. 1:1, 14:6). And so Scripture says that "if loving affection remains in us, God remains in us" (cf. 1 John 4:12). And "God," that is, the Father and the Son, "come to him" who is perfected in loving affection according to the word of our Lord and Savior, who says, "I and my Father will come to him and make our home with him" (cf. 1 John 4:18; Jn. 14:23).

Therefore, we must know that this loving affection, which is God and takes its existence in Him, affectionately loves nothing earthly, nothing material, nothing corruptible. For it is against its nature to love anything corruptible affectionately, since it is itself the source of incorruption. And it alone has immortality, if indeed God is loving Affection, who alone has immortality and dwells in unapproachable light (1 John 4:8; 1 Tim. 6:16). And what else is immortality but the eternal life that God promises He will give to those who believe in Him the only true God and in Jesus Christ, His Son, whom He has sent (cf. Jn. 17:3)? Furthermore, then, first of all and before all else this is said to be worthy of God's love and good pleasure, that a person should "affectionately love the Lord his God with all his heart and with all his soul and with all his strength" (cf. Lk. 10:27). And because God is loving Affection and the Son, who is from God, is loving Affection, He demands something like Himself from us, so that through that loving affection which is in Christ Jesus we may be brought into fellowship with God, who is loving Affection, as by a relationship made kindred by the term loving affection.

Thus it is that he who was already united with Him said, "Who shall separate us from the loving affection of God which is in Christ Jesus our Lord?" (cf. Rom. 8:35, 39). And this loving affection makes every one a neighbor. It was because of this that the Savior confounded a man who thought that a righteous soul should not observe the rights of friendship toward a soul fallen among wicked deeds. And for this reason He told in a secret way the parable that says that a certain man fell among robbers while he was going down from Jerusalem to Jericho. And He finds fault with the priest and the Levite, who saw him half dead and passed by. But He cherishes the Samaritan, who had compassion. And He asserted in His answer that he was the neighbor of the man who had raised the question, and He told him, "Go and do likewise" (Lk. 10:29ff.). Indeed, by nature we are all neighbors of one another; but by deeds of loving affection that person becomes a neighbor who can do good to the one who has no power. That is why our Savior was also made our neighbor, and He did not pass us by when we were lying half dead from the wounds inflicted by the robbers. Therefore, we must know that loving affection for God always strives toward God from whom it took its origin, and it has regard for the neighbor with whom it shows participation, since he was similarly created in incorruption.

So, therefore, whatever has been written about loving affection you must understand as though it were said of love, paying no attention to the different words; for the same meaning is indicated by both. But if someone should say that we speak of affectionately loving money, a harlot, and other equally evil things and that the verb is apparently derived from *loving affection*, let him know that in these instances the word loving affection is not used in its proper sense but inexactly. The same thing is true, for example, in regard to the word *God*. It chiefly refers to the One from whom are all things, through whom are all things, and in whom are all things, which, of course, openly proclaims the power and nature of the Trinity (cf. 1 Cor. 8:6). But in second place and, so to speak, inexactly Scripture uses the word god of those "to whom the Word of God came," as the Savior confirms in the Gospels (cf. Jn. 10:35). Moreover, the celestial powers are apparently called by this name when it is said, "God has taken His place in the assembly of gods, and in the midst He judges the gods" (Ps. 82:1). But in the third place, not inexactly but falsely, demons are called the gods of the nations when Scripture says, "All the gods of the nations are demons" (Ps. 96:5).

In the same way, then, the word loving affection refers in the first instance to God, and this is why we are commanded to love God with all our heart and with all our soul and with all our strength so that, of course, we may be able to love affectionately Him from whom we have this very power. And in this command there is undoubtedly included the one that we should love affectionately wisdom and righteousness and piety and truth and all the virtues alike; for to love God affectionately is one and the same thing as to love good things affectionately. In the second place, as though in an inexact and derived sense of the term, we are commanded to love our neighbor as ourselves (cf. Lk. 10:27). But the third, which is designated falsely by the term loving affection, is loving affectionately money or pleasure or anything that is related to corruption and error. There is, therefore, no difference whether God is said to be loved or to be affectionately loved, nor do I think any one can be blamed if he calls God "love," just as John called Him "loving affection." And besides, I remember that one of the saints named Ignatius said of Christ, "But my love has been crucified" (Ignatius, Rom. 7:2), nor do I judge him deserving of rebuke for this. Nevertheless, we must know that every one who affectionately loves either money or what is of corruptible matter in the world brings down the meaning of loving affection, which is from God, to earthly and perishable things and misapplies the things of God to things He does not wish. For God did not give them to men to be loved affectionately but to be used.

We have discussed these questions at some length, since we wished to distinguish quite clearly and carefully the nature of loving affection from that of love, lest perhaps because Scripture says God is loving Affection, everything that is affectionately loved, even if it is corruptible, should be thought from God because of the terms loving affection and affectionate love. But the fact appears that while loving affection is God's and His gift, nevertheless it is not always received by men to use for what belongs to God and what He wills. Moreover, it should be known that it is impossible for human nature not always to love something. For everyone who comes to what they call the age of puberty loves something, whether less than rightly when he loves what he should not, or rightly and beneficially when he loves what he should. But some either draw away this emotion of love, which has been implanted in the rational soul by the favor of the Creator, to the love of money and the pursuit of covetousness, or to the winning of fame and become desirous of vainglory or to the pursuit of harlots and are found slaves of shamelessness and lust, or they pour away the power of so great a good as love upon other similar pursuits.

Moreover, when this love is placed among the different arts

that are conducted by physical prowess or among pursuits necessary only for this life, for example, by being compared to the art of wrestling or the exercises of racing or even to geometry, music, or arithmetic, or to any other disciplines of this kind, then it does not seem to me it has been used commendably. But if what is good is also commendable and if what is good is not properly understood in relation to corporeal uses but in God first and in the powers of the mind, the conclusion follows that only that love is commendable which is joined to God and to the powers of the mind. And that this is the case is shown by the Savior's own definition, when He was asked by someone what was the greatest commandment of all and the first in the Law and answered, "You shall love the Lord your God with all your heart, and with all your soul, and with all your strength; and a second is like it, You shall love your neighbor as yourself." And He added, "On these two commandments hang all the Law and the prophets," showing that righteous and lawful love consists of these two commandments and that the whole Law and the prophets depend on them (Mt. 22:35f.). Moreover, the commandments "You shall not commit adultery, you shall not kill, you shall not steal, you shall not bear false witness" and any other commandment are summed up in the saying "You shall love your neighbor as yourself" (cf. Mt. 19:18; Rom. 13:9).

The point will be more easily explained as follows. Suppose, for example, a woman burns with love for a certain man and desires to be taken as his wife. Will she not do everything and rule all her emotions in such a way that she may learn how to please the one she affectionately loves, lest perhaps if she acts in anything against his will, that excellent man might refuse her as his wife and scorn her? Could that woman, who burns with her love of that man with all her heart, all her soul, and all her strength, commit either adultery when she knew he loved chastity, or murder when she knew he was gentle, or theft when she knew that generosity pleased him, or desire anything else when she had all her desires bound up with her love of that man? This, then, is how in the perfection of loving affection every commandment is said to be summed up and the meaning of the Law and the prophets to depend upon it.

Because of that good thing, loving affection or love, the saints are neither crushed in affliction nor driven to despair in perplexity nor destroyed when struck down, but their present light momentary affliction is preparing for them an eternal weight of glory beyond all comparison (2 Cor. 4:8–9, 17). For it is not to all, but to Paul and those like him, that this present affliction is said to be momentary and light, because they have the perfect loving affection of God in Christ Jesus through the Holy Spirit poured into their hearts (cf. Rom. 5:5). So, in addition, love of Rachel did not allow the patriarch Jacob, who was obliged to work for seven years in a row, to feel any burning of daily heat and nightly cold. So I hear Paul himself kindled by the force of love saying, "Loving affection bears all things, believes all things, hopes all things, endures all things. Loving affection never falls" (1 Cor. 13:7–8). Thus, there is nothing the one who loves affectionately with perfection does not endure. But we do not endure many things; so it is certain because of this that we do not have loving affection that endures all things. And if we do not bear some things patiently, it is because we lack loving affection, which is patient in all things. Then, too, we often fall in the struggle we have against the devil; undoubtedly it is because that loving affection which never falls is not in us. The present book of Scripture, then, speaks of this love with which the blessed soul burns and is on fire in regard to the Word of God. And she sings this wedding song through the Spirit, by which the Church is joined and united with its heavenly bridegroom Christ, desiring to be mingled with Him through the Word so that she may conceive from Him and be enabled to be saved through this chaste bearing of children (cf. 1 Tim. 2:15). And this will happen when the children continue in faith and holiness with modesty as they were conceived of the seed of the Word of God and brought forth and born either by the spotless Church or by the soul that seeks nothing corporeal, nothing material, but is on fire with love only for the Word of God.

For the time being these are the thoughts that have been able to come our way concerning love or loving affection, which is the theme of this epithalamium, the Song of Songs. But we must know how much ought to be said about this loving affection and how much about God, if He is indeed loving Affection. For just as no one knows the Father except the Son and anyone to whom the Son chooses to reveal Him (Mt. 11:27), so no one knows loving affection except the Son. And likewise no one knows the Son, since He is also loving Affection, except the Father. And according to what is called loving affection it is only the Holy Spirit, who proceeds from the Father who, therefore, comprehends the thoughts of God as the spirit of a man knows a man's thoughts (cf. Jn. 15:26; 1 Cor. 2:11). Thus, this Paraclete, the Spirit of truth, who proceeds from the Father, goes about seeking if He may find any worthy and fit souls to whom He may reveal the excellence of that loving affection which is from God. Now, therefore, by calling upon God the Father, who is loving Affection, through that loving Affection which is from Him, let us turn to the other subjects for discussion.

First, let us examine why it is, since the churches of God acknowledge three books written by Solomon, that of them the book of Proverbs is put first, the one called Ecclesiastes second, and the book Song of Songs has third place. The following ideas have been able to come our way about this subject. There are three general disciplines by which one attains knowledge of the universe. The Greeks call them ethics, physics, and enoptics; and we can give them the terms moral, natural, and contemplative. Some among the Greeks, of course, also add logic as a fourth, which we can call reasoning. Others say that it is not a separate discipline, but is intertwined and bound up throughout the entire body with the three disciplines we have mentioned. For this "logic," or, as we have said, reasoning, which apparently includes the rules for words and speech, is instruction in proper and improper meanings, general and particular terms, and the inflections of the different sorts of words. For this reason it is suitable that this discipline should not so much be separated from the others as bound in with them and hidden. Then the moral discipline is defined as the one by which an honorable manner of life is equipped and habits conducive to virtue are prepared. The natural discipline is defined as the consideration of the nature of each individual thing, according to which nothing in life happens contrary to nature, but each individual thing is assigned those uses for which it has been brought forth by the Creator. The contemplative discipline is defined as that by which we transcend visible things and contemplate something of divine and heavenly things and gaze at them with the mind alone, since they transcend corporeal appearance.

Now it seems to me that certain wise men of the Greeks took

these ideas from Solomon, since it was long before them in age and
time that he first gave these teachings through the Spirit of God.
The Greeks have brought them forth as their own discoveries, and
they have also included them in their books of instructions and left
them to be handed down to their successors. But, as we have said,
Solomon discovered them before all the rest and taught them
through the wisdom he received from God, as it is written, "And
God gave Solomon understanding and wisdom beyond measure,
and largeness of heart like the sand on the seashore. And his wisdom was made greater than that of all the ancient sons of men and
all the wise men of Egypt" (1 Kings 4:29–30). Thus, Solomon,
since he wished to distinguish from one another and to separate
what we have called earlier the three general disciplines, that is,
moral, natural, and contemplative, set them forth in three books,
each one in its own logical order.

Thus, he first taught in Proverbs the subject of morals, setting
regulations for life together, as was fitting, in concise and brief
maxims. And he included the second subject, which is called the
natural discipline, in Ecclesiastes, in which he discusses many natural things. And by distinguishing them as empty and vain from
what is useful and necessary, he warns that vanity must be abandoned and what is useful and right must be pursued. He also
handed down the subject of contemplation in the book we have in
hand, that is, Song of Songs, in which he urges upon the soul the
love of the heavenly and the divine under the figure of the bride and
the bridegroom, teaching us that we must attain fellowship with
God by the paths of loving affection and of love. Indeed, he was not
unaware that he was laying the foundations of the true philosophy
and founding the order of its disciplines and principles, nor was the
subject of reasoning rejected by him. He demonstrates this clearly
at the very beginning of his Proverbs, first of all, because he entitles
this very book of his "Proverbs." That word means something that
is said openly, but points to something deep within. Even the
ordinary use of proverbs teaches this, and John in his Gospel writes
that the Savior said this, "I have spoken to you in proverbs; the
hour will come when I shall no longer speak to you in proverbs but
tell you plainly of the Father" (Jn. 16:25). So much for the title of
the book itself.

But in what immediately follows he adds some distinctions of words and divides "knowledge" from "wisdom" and "instruction" from "knowledge"; and he posits "the understanding of words" as one thing, and says that prudence lies in being able to draw out "the subtlety of words." For he distinguishes "true righteousness" from "wise dealing." Moreover, he also names a certain "sagacity" as necessary for those whom he instructs, that sagacity, I believe, by which the subtlety of fallacies can be understood and avoided. And so he says that through wisdom "sagacity" is given to "the innocent," doubtless lest they be deceived in the Word of God by any sophistical deceit (cf. Prov. 1:2ff.). Moreover, here he seems to me mindful of the reasoning discipline, by which instruction about words and the meanings of speech are discerned and a fixed proper use of each word is marked by reason. It is especially suitable for children to be trained in this. Solomon urges this when he says, "Let him give the young child perception and deliberation" (Prov. 1:4). And because the person who is instructed in these matters necessarily governs himself rationally by what he learns and balances his life with moderation, he consequently says, "And the man of understanding will acquire governance" (Prov. 1:5). Next, he understands that in the divine words, by which a rule for living has been handed down to the human race through the prophets, there are different forms of speech and various figures of speaking; and he knows that among them is found one figure called a "parable" and another called "obscure speech," and that there are others designated "enigmas" and others called "words of the wise." For this reason he writes, "You will also understand the parable and the obscure speech and the words of the wise and the enigmas" (cf. Prov. 1:6).

Thus, by these distinct terms he obviously and clearly explains the subject of reasoning; and after the custom of the men of old he sets forth great and perfect ideas in concise and brief maxims. And if there is someone who meditates on the Law of the Lord day and night (Ps. 1:2) and someone who is like the mouth of the righteous that meditates on wisdom (Ps. 37:30), he will be able to inquire more carefully and to find, provided he seeks rightly and in seeking knocks on the door of wisdom to ask God that it may be opened to him and he be worthy to receive through the Holy Spirit the word of wisdom and the word of knowledge and to become a fellow of Solomon's wisdom that said, "I stretched out my words and you did not hear" (Prov. 1:24; cf. Col. 4:3). And he rightly says that He stretched out words in his heart, because, as we said a moment ago, God gave him largeness of heart (1 Kings 4:29). For that person's heart is enlarged who can explain what is briefly said in mysteries by a broader teaching with assertions taken from the divine books. Thus, it is necessary according to the same teaching of that wisest Solomon for the person who longs to know wisdom to begin with moral training and to understand what is written, "You have desired wisdom; keep the commandments, and the Lord will give her to you" (Sir. 1:26).

Therefore, for this reason the teacher who first taught men the divine philosophy puts the book of Proverbs as the introduction to his work. In it, as we have said, the subject of morals is handed down so that, when anyone has made progress in understanding and morals, he may come also to the discipline of natural knowledge and there by distinguishing the causes and the natures of things learn that "vanity of vanities" must be abandoned and he must hasten to what is eternal and everlasting. And so after Proverbs he comes to Ecclesiastes, which teaches, as we have said, that everything visible and corporeal is transitory and weak. And when the person who is eager for wisdom discovers that this is so, he will doubtless despise those things; and by renouncing, so to speak, the whole world, he will press on to the invisible and eternal teachings that are given to the spiritual senses in Song of Songs through certain veiled figures of loves. So indeed, this book occupies the last place, so that a person may come to it when he has been purged in morals and has learned the knowledge and distinction of corruptible and incorruptible things. By this preparation he is enabled to receive no harm from those figures by which the love of the bride for her heavenly bridegroom, that is, of the perfect soul for the Word of God, is described and fashioned. For with these preliminaries accomplished by which the soul is purified through its acts and habits and conducted to the discernment of natural things, the soul comes suitably to doctrines and mysteries, and is led up to the contemplation of the Godhead by a genuine and spiritual love.

Then, too, I think this triple form of the divine philosophy was indicated beforehand in those holy and blessed men on behalf of whom the highest God in the holiest instructions wanted to be called "the God of Abraham, the God of Isaac, the God of Jacob" (cf. Ex. 3:6). Now Abraham expounds moral philosophy through obedience; for so great was his obedience and so great his keeping of the commandments that when he heard, "Go out from your country and your kindred and your father's house" (Gen. 12:1), he did not delay, but did so at once. Moreover, he did something much greater than this. When he heard he was to sacrifice his son, not even then did he waver; but he submitted to the order. In order to give an example to posterity of obedience, which is moral philosophy, he did not withold his only begotten son (cf. Gen. 22:16). As well, Isaac holds the place of natural philosophy, since he dug wells and explored the depths of things. Moreover, Jacob receives the subject of contemplation, since he was named Israel because of the contemplation of divine things and since he saw the encampments of heaven and gazed at the house of God and the paths of the angels, the ladders that stretched from earth to heaven (cf. Gen. 28:12, 17, 32:2). That is why we find that those three blessed men were worthy of building altars for God, that is, of dedicating their progress to His philosophy, by which they taught that it was to be attributed not to human skills but to the grace of God (cf. Gen. 22:5, 26:25, 33:20, 35:7). Moreover, they dwelt in tents (cf. Heb. 11:9), so that through this they might make it clear that whoever is eager for the divine philosophy must not have any place of his own on earth and must always move on, not so much from place to place as from the knowledge of lower things to the knowledge of perfect things. And you will find many other details in the divine Scriptures that indicate in the same fashion that order which we said was contained in the books of Solomon; but the subject is too extensive for us to pursue, since we have something else in hand.

Therefore, if a person completes the first subject by freeing his habits from faults and keeping the commandments—which is indicated by Proverbs—and if after this, when the vanity of the world has been discovered and the weakness of its perishable things seen clearly, he comes to the point of renouncing the world and everything in the world, then he will come quite suitably also to contemplate and to long for the things that are unseen and are eternal (2 Cor. 4:18). But in order to be able to attain them we shall need the divine mercy, if we are indeed to be strong enough, when we have gazed upon the beauty of the Word of God, to be kindled with a saving love for Him, so that He too may think it right to love affectionately a soul that He has seen longing for Him.

Next, the order of our discussion obliges us to speak also about the title of Song of Songs. Indeed, it resembles what is called in the tent of testimony the "Holy of Holies" (cf. Ex. 30:29), what is mentioned in the book of Numbers as the "works of works" (cf. Num. 4:47), and what in Paul is called the "ages of ages" (cf., e.g., Rom. 16:27). But we have discussed, so far as we were able, in our commentaries what the difference is between holies and holy of holies in Exodus and between works and works of works in the book of Numbers (cf. *Hom. Num.* 5:2). Moreover, we have not passed over ages of ages in the places where it occurs; and lest we say the same thing again, let this be enough (cf. *In Ep. ad Rom. comm.* 10:23). But now let us ask first what the songs are of which this is said to be the Song of Songs. I think, then, that they are those that were sung of old by the prophets or by the angels. For the Law is said to have been "ordained by angels by the hand of an intermediary" (Gal. 3:19). Thus, all the proclamations made by them were songs that went before, sung by the friends of the bridegroom; but this is the one song that was to be sung in the form of an epithalamium to the bridegroom when He is about to take His bride. In it the bride does not want the song sung to her by the friends of the bridegroom right away, but she longs to hear the words of the bridegroom now present. She says, "Let Him kiss me with the kisses of His mouth" (Song 1:2). This is why it deserves to be placed before all the other songs. For apparently the other songs, which the Law and the prophets sang, were recited for the bride when she was still a little girl and had not yet crossed the threshold of a mature age; but this song is recited for her when she is grown up, quite strong, and now able to receive manly power and perfect mystery. In accord with this it is said of her that "one is perfect, the dove" (cf. Song 6:8). Thus, as the perfect bride of the perfect husband she received the words of the perfect teaching.

COMMENTARY ON THE SONG OF SONGS

Now the first song is the one Moses and the children of Israel sang to God when they saw the Egyptians dead upon the seashore and when they saw the mighty hand and the stretched-out arm of the Lord and believed in God and in His servant Moses (Ex. 14:30f., 6:6). Then they sang saying, "We will sing to the Lord, for He has triumphed gloriously" (Ex. 15:1). Now I think that no one can attain that perfect and mystical song and that perfection of the bride who is found in this book of Scripture unless he first walks on dry ground in the midst of the sea, the waters being a wall to him on the right hand and on the left, and thus escapes from the hands of the Egyptians so as to see them dead upon the seashore and unless, seeing the strong hand of the Lord, which He brought against the Egyptians, he believes in the Lord and in His servant Moses (Ex. 14:29–31). And by Moses I mean the Law and the Gospels and all the divine Scriptures; for then he will deservedly sing and say, "Let us sing to the Lord, for He has triumphed gloriously" (Ex. 15:1). But the person will sing the song we are talking about now when he has first been delivered from bondage to the Egyptians.

And after that, when he has passed through all the events described in Exodus and in Leviticus and has come to the point when he is taken up into the divine Numbers, then he will sing the second song. This is when he goes out of the Valley of Zered, which is translated "a foreign descent," and comes to the well about which it is written, "And the Lord said to Moses, 'Gather the people together, and I will give them water to drink from the well' " (Num. 21:16). For there he will sing and say, "Consecrate the well. The princes dug it; the kings of the nations prepared it in their reign, when they held dominion over them" (Num. 21:17–18 LXX). But more is said about these verses in our book on Numbers, according to what the Lord has given us (cf. *Hom. Num.* 12:2). Thus, it is necessary to come to the well that was dug by the princes and prepared by the kings. In this work no common person works, but all are princes, all are kings, that is, royal and princely souls, which reach into the depth of the well that holds living water.

After this song he comes to the song of Deuteronomy, about which the Lord said, "And now write for yourselves the words of this song, and teach it to the children of Israel; put it in their mouths, that this song may be a witness for me against the children of Israel" (Deut. 31:19). And see how great and important this song is. The earth is not enough to hear it, but heaven is also summoned. For it says, " Give ear, O heaven, and I will speak; and let the earth hear the words of my mouth" (Deut. 32:1). See how great, how immense are the words that are spoken. It says, "Let my speech be awaited as rain, and let it descend as dew upon the grass, and as snow upon the hay, because I have called upon the name of the Lord, and the rest" (Deut. 32:2–3).

The fourth song is in the book of Judges. Concerning it there is written, "And Deborah and Barak the son of Abinoam sang on that day, saying, 'That the princes took the lead in Israel, that the people offered themselves willingly, bless the Lord! Hear, O kings, give ear, O governors!' and the rest" (Judg. 5:1–3). And the person who sings this ought to be a bee, whose product is used by kings and ordinary people for their health. For "Deborah," who sings this song, means "bee." Moreover, Barak is with her; and his name means "flashing." And this song is sung after a victory, because no one can sing of what is perfect unless he has conquered his adversaries. Furthermore, it is said in this song, "Awake, awake, Deborah! Stir up the thousands of the people. Awake, awake, utter a song! Awake, Barak!" (Judg. 5:12 LXX). But you will find these matters more fully discussed in the homilies we have given on the book of Judges.

Next, the fifth song is in Second Samuel, when "David spoke to the Lord the words of this song on the day when the Lord delivered him from the hand of all his enemies and from the hand of Saul. He said, 'The Lord is my rock, and my fortress, and my deliverer; my God will be my protector' " (2 Sam. 22:1–2). If, then, you prove able to examine who are the "enemies" David defeats and overthrows in First and Second Samuel and how he was made worthy of deserving the Lord's help and of being delivered from enemies of this kind, then you will be able to sing this fifth song yourself.

The sixth song is in First Chronicles where David first established Asaph and his brothers for praising the Lord. The beginning of the song is as follows, "Praise the Lord, give thanks to Him, and call upon His name; make known His purposes among the peoples! Sing to Him, sing praises to Him, tell of all His wonderful works, which the Lord has done, and so forth" (1 Chron. 16:8–9). It should, however, be known that the song in Second Samuel is very much like Psalm 18. Furthermore, the first part of the text in First Chronicles, up to the place where it says "and do my prophets no harm" (1 Chron. 16:22), is like Psalm 105. And the latter part of it, following the verse just mentioned, bears a likeness to the first part of Psalm 96, where it says, "Sing to the Lord, all the earth" up to the place where it says, "for He comes to judge the earth" (Ps. 96:1, 13).

If, therefore, the number of songs should be brought to a close with these, then this book, Song of Songs, must evidently be put in seventh place. But someone may th ink that the song of Isaiah should be listed with the rest (Is. 5; cf. *Hom. Song of Songs* 1:1). Of course, it would not appear fully suitable to think that the song of Isaiah preceded this one, because Isaiah wrote at a much later time than Solomon. Nevertheless, if someone thinks that the prophetic writings must be interpreted not by reference to time but by their meaning, he will also add Isaiah's song and will say that Solomon's is not only the song of the songs that were before it but also of the ones that appear to have been sung after it. And if someone thinks that passages from the book of Psalms should also be included, if anywhere in it either a song is written or whole psalms are songs, then he will assemble a great number of songs to go before Song of Songs. For he will join to the others the fifteen songs of ascents (Ps. 120–134), and by examining the excellences of each of the songs he will acquire from them steps for the soul in its progress, and by a spiritual understanding will bring together the order and coherence of these matters. Then he will be able to make clear with what noble steps the bride walks through all these and arrives at the wedding chamber of the bridegroom. She departs into the place of the marvelous tabernacle, to the house of God, with glad shouts and songs of thanksgiving and the sound of banqueting (Ps. 41:5 LXX–Ps. 42:4); and she arrives, as we have said, at the wedding chamber of the bridegroom, so that she may hear and speak all that is included in Song of Songs.

Furthermore, before we come to the main body of the book,

we can also examine why Solomon, who apparently served the will of the Holy Spirit in these three books, is called in Proverbs "Solomon, son of David, who ruled in Israel" (Prov. 1:1), but in the second book "Solomon" is not written. Instead, it says, "The words of Ecclesiastes, the son of David, the king of Israel in Jerusalem" (Eccles. 1:1). He writes that he is the son of David and the king of Israel, just as he did in the first book. But there he put down "Proverbs"; here, "words." And there he called himself Solomon; but here, Ecclesiastes. And whereas there he put down only the nation in which he ruled, here he both puts the nation and indicates the place of his rule as Jerusalem. But in Song of Songs he writes neither the name of the nation nor the place where he rules, and he omits altogether the fact that he is king and has David as his father. Rather, it says simply, "The Song of Songs, which is Solomon's" (Song 1:1).

And although it seems to me difficult either to examine and be able to draw conclusions with respect to these different points or to explain the conclusions of an investigation clearly and entrust them to paper, nevertheless, so far as our understanding and the hearing of our readers can reach, we shall try to explain a few of the points. I do not think it can be doubted that in a great many respects Solomon bears a type of Christ, either because he is called "peaceful" or because "the queen of the south came from the ends of the earth to hear the wisdom of Solomon." (Mt. 12:42). Thus, Christ also rules in Israel because He is called Son of David and because He rules over those kings in respect to whom He is called king of kings (cf. 1 Tim. 6:15). Furthermore, the true "Ecclesiastes" is the one who, though He was in the form of God, emptied Himself, taking the form of a servant (Phil. 2:6–7) in order to assemble the Church; for "Ecclesiastes" is derived from "to assemble the Church." Then, indeed, who is so much "Solomon," that is, peaceful, as our Lord Jesus Christ, whom God made our wisdom and righteousness and peace (cf. 1 Cor. 1:30). Therefore, in the first book, Proverbs, when He establishes us by moral instructions, He is said to be "king in Israel," but not yet in Jerusalem, because although we are called Israel because of faith, that does not yet mark an attainment by which we should appear to have arrived at the heavenly Jerusalem. But when we have made enough progress for it to come to pass that we are brought into fellowship with the Church of the firstborn, which is in heaven, and know by previous careful consideration and by natural reasons that the heavenly Jerusalem is our mother, then Christ is made for us, as well, Ecclesiastes and is said to rule not only in Israel but also in Jerusalem (cf. Heb. 12:22–23; Gal. 4:26). And when the time has indeed come for the perfection of all things and the bride, as no less than the entire rational creation, has been perfected and is ready to be joined to Him, because He has brought peace by His own blood not only to earthly things but also to heavenly (cf. Col. 1:20), then He is called only "Solomon," since "He delivers the kingdom to God the Father after destroying every rule and every authority. For He must reign until He has put all His enemies under His feet. The last enemy to be destroyed is death" (1 Cor. 15:24–26). And so, when everything has been made peaceful and subject to the Father, God will be "all in all." Then He will be called merely Solomon, that is, only "peaceful."

Therefore, it is appropriate that in this book, which was to be written about the love of the bridegroom and the bride, there should for this reason be written neither Son of David nor king nor anything else that could be related to a corporeal meaning. And so, the bride now made perfect may worthily say of Him, "Even though we once regarded Christ according to the flesh, we know Him thus no longer" (2 Cor. 5:16). She says this lest anyone should think she loves anything corporeal or placed in the flesh, and she be thought not to have fallen in love with Him spotlessly. That is why, then, it is "the Song of Songs, which is" merely "Solomon's" (Song 1:1) and not the Son of David's or the king of Israel's; absolutely no meaning that might come from a fleshly name is mingled with the themes of the book. And you should not be surprised that although our Lord and Savior is one and the same, we speak of Him first as less in Proverbs, then as increasing in Ecclesiastes, and after that as more perfect in Song of Songs, when you see this also written in the Gospels, where He is said to increase for us and among us. For it is reported that "Jesus increased in age and in wisdom with God and men" (cf. Lk. 2:52). I think, then, that for all these reasons neither Son of David nor king of Israel is written, and that it is also because in Song of Songs the bride has now made such great progress that she has attained something greater than the rule of Jerusalem. For the Apostle says there is a heavenly Jerusalem and mentions those who believe they have come to it. Indeed, the same Paul, when he calls the bridegroom to which the bride now hastens the "High Priest," writes about Him as though He were not in heaven, but had entered and passed through all the heavens (cf. Heb. 12:22, 4:14). His perfect bride will also follow Him there; cleaving entirely to Him and united with Him, she will climb up there, for she has been made one spirit with Him (cf. 1 Cor. 6:17). It seems to me this is also why to Peter, who was unable to follow Him at first when He said "Where I am going you cannot come now," He said, "But you shall follow afterward" (Jn. 13:36).

Moreover, we deduce that there is something greater and apart from Israel from the fact that in the book of Numbers all of Israel is numbered and allotted by fixed number to the twelve tribes of Israel, but the tribe of Levi, because its excellence surpasses the others, is considered above this number and is by no means counted in the number of Israel (cf. Num. 2:32f.). For this is what it says, "This is the inspection by which the children of Israel were numbered by the houses of their families. The entire inspection of them amounted to six hundred and three thousand five hundred and fifty. But the Levites were not numbered among them, as the Lord commanded Moses" (Num. 2:32–33). You see how the Levites are separated from the children of Israel as more excellent and are not included in their number. Furthermore, the priests are described as more excellent than the Levites; for in the same book of Scripture is included the statement, "And the Lord said to Moses, 'Take the highest part of the Levites, and you shall set them in the sight of Aaron the priest, and they shall minister to him" (Num. 3:5–6). Do you see by this how it designates the priests superior to the Levites and, further, places the Levites as more excellent than the children of Israel?

We decided to discuss these matters with some care, since we wanted to show by them, as well, the reason why Solomon was obliged to use different titles for his books, and why he distinguished by their very titles the books of Proverbs, Ecclesiastes, and Song of Songs as three different things. Furthermore, because in Song of Songs, where perfection is revealed, neither Son of David nor king is written, it can also be said that when the servant is made like his teacher, the servant appears no longer to be a servant, since he has been made like his Lord, nor the disciple to be a disciple, because he has been made like his teacher. Rather, he who was once a disciple is now indeed like a teacher; and he who was once a servant is now indeed like a Lord (cf. Mt. 10:24; Lk. 6:40). Thus, a similar reasoning can evidently be applied to "king" and to those over whom He rules, when the kingdom will be delivered to God the Father (cf. 1 Cor. 15:24). Moreover, it has not escaped our attention that some write the title of this book "Songs of Songs." This is incorrect; for it should not be in the plural, but in the singular, "Song of Songs." This is what we have to say by way of preface concerning the superscription or title of the book.

Now with our Lord's help we approach the opening sections of the book itself. Yet, so that we may leave nothing out, we must examine the question some raise about the title and superscription of the book, which reads "The Song of Songs, which is Solomon's." Those who have raised the question understand the verse as though it said this is one of Solomon's songs, so that he designates this as one of his many songs. But how shall we accept an interpretation of this kind, when neither the Church of God has accepted any other songs written by Solomon save this one nor is any other book of Solomon's but the three we also have included in their canon by the Hebrews, by whom the noble words of God have evidently been handed down to us? Nevertheless, those who hold the opinion we are discussing wish to prove their opinion by the fact that in 1 Kings it is written that there were many songs of Solomon, so that they may prove this to be one of many. There, indeed, it is reported, "And God gave Solomon understanding and wisdom beyond measure, and largeness of heart like the sand on the seashore. And Solomon was made wiser, surpassing the wisdom of all those of old and all the wise men of Egypt, surpassing Ethan the Ezrahite, and Heman, Calcol, and Darda. And Solomon uttered three thousand proverbs; and his songs were five thousand" (1 Kings 4:29–32). Thus, they wish this song that we have in hand to be known as one of these five thousand songs. But when or where the other songs were sung has failed to come not only to the custom of the churches of God but even to their knowledge.

It would be too large a task and too far from our present undertaking if we should wish now to examine how many books are mentioned in the divine Scriptures, the text of which has not been handed down to us in any way. Moreover, we have found among the Jews no use made of texts of this kind, either because it pleased the Holy Spirit they should be taken away since they contained matters beyond human understanding or because the elders decided no acceptance should be given to those writings which are called "apocryphal," since in them is found much that is corrupt and contrary to the true faith, and that they should not be admitted as authoritative. It exceeds our competence to make pronouncements concerning such matters. It is, however, obvious that many examples exist of passages, taken by the apostles or by the evangelists and put into the New Testament, which we never read among those Scriptures we hold to be canonical, but which are found in the apocryphal writings and may be clearly demonstrated to have been taken from them. But not even this must be thought to argue for acceptance of the apocryphal writings, for "the ancient landmarks which our fathers have set must not be removed" (Prov. 22:28). It could have happened that the apostles or evangelists, filled with the Holy Spirit, knew what ought to be taken from those writings and what ought to be refused. But for us, who do not have such a great fulness of the Spirit, it is not without danger to attempt such a discrimination. Consequently, with respect to the verse under consideration we hold to the view we explained earlier, especially when the clear distinction is made in the text itself, when it says, "The Song of Songs, which is Solomon's." For if it had wished us to understand that this is one of Solomon's songs, it would have said, "The Song of Songs which are Solomon's" or "A Song from the Songs of Solomon." As it is, however, since it says "which *is* Solomon's," it makes clear that this song, which we have in hand and which had been sung for him, is Solomon's and that it preserves the title he gave it. So, let us now look at what follows.

HOMILY XXVII ON NUMBERS

1. When God established the world, He created numberless different kinds of foods in accordance, of course, with the differences of human desire or of the nature of animals. That is why when a person sees the food of animals, he knows it was created not for him but for the animals. Not only is this the case, but even the animals themselves know their own food; and, for example, the lion uses some; the deer, others; the cow, others; birds, others. Moreover, among men there are some differences in the food that is sought. One person who is quite healthy and has a strong bodily constitution needs strong food and has the conviction and confidence he can eat everything, like the strongest of athletes (cf. Rom. 14:2). But if someone perceives he is weaker and feeble, he is pleased with vegetables and does not accept strong food because of the weakness of his body. And if someone is a child, although he cannot put what he wants into words, still he seeks no other nourishment than that of milk. So it is that each individual, whether in accordance with his age or his strength or the health of his body, looks for food suitable for himself and fit for his strength.

If you have considered sufficiently this illustration from corporeal things, let us now turn from them to an understanding of spiritual things. Every rational nature needs to be nourished by foods of its own and suitable for it. Now the true food of a rational nature is the Word of God. But just as in the nourishment of the body we have a moment ago granted many differences, so also in the case of a rational nature, which feeds, as we have said, on reason and the Word of God, not every one is nourished by one and the same Word. That is why, as in the corporeal example, the food

245

some have in the Word of God is milk, that is, the more obvious and simpler teachings, as may usually be found in moral instructions and which is customarily given to those who are taking their first steps in divine studies and receiving the abc's of rational instruction. Thus, when they are read some passage from the divine books in which there is nothing apparently obscure, they gladly receive it, for example, the book of Esther or of Judith, or even of Tobit, or the precepts of Wisdom. But if they are read the book of Leviticus, their mind is constantly offended and refuses it as not its own food. For since such a mind comes to learn how to worship God and to accept His commandments of righteousness and true religion, if he hears instead orders given about sacrifices and rites of immolation taught, how could he avoid constantly being inattentive and refusing the food as not suitable for him?

Moreover, when the Gospels or the Apostle or the Psalms are read, another person joyfully receives them, gladly embraces them, and rejoices in assembling from them, as it were, remedies for his weakness. But if the book of Numbers is read to him, and especially those passages we have now in hand, he will judge that there is nothing helpful, nothing as a remedy for his weakness or a benefit for the salvation of his soul. He will constantly reject and spit them out as heavy and burdensome food, because they do not agree with his sick and weak soul. But, for example—to come back to examples from corporeal things—if understanding were given to a lion, he would not constantly blame the abundance of grasses that has been created simply because he feeds himself on raw meat, nor would he say that they have been produced by the Creator unnecessarily because he does not use them as food. Neither should a human being, because he uses bread and other food suitable for him as nourishment, blame God for making snakes, which apparently supply food for deer. Nor should the sheep or the cow, for example, find fault with the fact it has been given to other animals to feed on meat, while grasses alone are enough for them to eat. Now it is just the same way in the case of rational food, I mean the divine books. You should not constantly either blame or reject Scripture when it appears too difficult or too obscure to understand or when it contains what either the beginner and child or the weaker and feebler in his general understanding cannot use and does not think will bring him anything useful or saving. Rather, you should bear in mind that the snake and the sheep, the cow and the human being, and straw are all creatures of God; and their very diversity points to the praise and glory of their Creator, because they either supply or take food suitably and timely for each of those for whom they were created. In just the same way each individual insofar as he perceives himself healthy or weak takes all the passages that are words of God and in which there is different food according to the capacity of the souls.

Moreover, if we examine as carefully as possible, for example, the reading of the Gospel or the apostolic teaching in which you apparently delight and in which you reckon to find the food most suitable and agreeable to you, how many are the points that have escaped your notice, if you investigate and inquire carefully into the commandments of the Lord? But if what seems obscure and difficult is constantly shunned and avoided, you will find even in the passages about which you are confident so many obscure and difficult points that if you persist in your opinion, you will be forced to give it up. Nevertheless, there are a great many passages in them that are spoken openly and simply enough to edify the hearer of limited understanding.

Now we have made all these points first by way of a preface so as to stir up your minds, since the passage we have in hand is one that is hard to understand and seems unnecessary to read. But we cannot say of the Holy Spirit's writings that there is anything useless or unnecessary in them, however much they appear obscure to some. What we ought rather to do is to turn the eyes of our mind toward Him who ordered this to be written and to ask of Him their meaning. We must do this so that if there is weakness in our soul, He who heals all its infirmities (Ps. 103:3) may heal us, or so that if we are children in understanding, the Lord may be with us guarding His children and may nourish us and add to the measure of our age (cf. Eph. 4:13). For it is in our power to be able to attain both health from weakness and manhood from childhood. It is, then, our part to ask this of God. And it is God's to give to those who ask and to open to those who knock (cf. Mt. 7:7). Let this be enough by way of introduction.

2. Now let us turn to the beginning of the passage that has

been read so that with God's help we may be able to summarize the
main points and explain their meaning, even though we may not
expect total clarity. This is what it says, "These are the stages of the
children of Israel, when they went forth out of the land of Egypt
with their power by the hand of Moses and Aaron. And Moses
wrote down their starting places and stages by the Word of the
Lord, and so forth" (Num. 33:1–2). You have heard that Moses
wrote this down by the Word of the Lord. Why did the Lord want
him to write it down? Was it so that this passage in Scripture about
the stages the children of Israel made might benefit us in some way
or that it should bring us no benefit? Who would dare to say that
what is written "by the Word of God" is of no use and makes no
contribution to salvation, but is merely a narrative of what happened and was over and done a long time ago, but pertains in no
way to us when it is told? These opinions are irreligious and foreign
to the Catholic faith; they belong only to those who deny that the
God and Father of our Lord Jesus Christ (cf. Rom. 15:6) is the one
and only wise God of the Law and the Gospels. We shall try, then,
in a summary fashion so far as time allows, to investigate what a
faithful understanding ought to think about these stages.

Now the previous homily gave us the opportunity of speaking
about the departure of the children of Israel from Egypt, and we
said that in a spiritual sense there can be seen a double exodus from
Egypt, either when we leave our life as Gentiles and come to the
knowledge of the divine Law or when the soul leaves its dwelling
place in the body. Therefore, these stages, which Moses now writes
down "by the Word of the Lord," point toward both. Indeed, it is
concerning those stages in which souls divested of their bodies or
again clothed with bodies will dwell that the Lord made His proclamation in the Gospel by saying, "With my Father are many
stages; if it were not so, would I have told you that I go to prepare a
stage for you?" (Jn. 14:2). Thus, there are many stages that lead to
the Father. And in the case of each of them what purpose, what
sojourn of use to the soul, or what instruction or enlightenment a
person may receive is something only the Father of the age to come
knows (cf. Is. 9:6). He says of Himself, "I am the door . . . no one
comes to the Father but by me" (Jn. 10:9, 14:6). He will probably
become in each of the different stages the door for each soul, so that

it may go in through Him and go out through Him and find pasture (cf. Jn. 10:9), and again so that it may go into another and from there to another stage until it attains to the Father Himself.

But we have nearly forgotten our preface and have suddenly raised your hearing to lofty heights. Let us then, by all means, return to what happens among us and in us. When the children of Israel were in Egypt, they were afflicted with mortar and brick (Ex. 1:14) for the works of Pharaoh the king until they cried out in their groaning to the Lord (cf. Ex. 2:23). And He heard their cry and sent His Word to them by Moses and led them out of Egypt. We, then, when we were also in Egypt, I mean in the errors of this world and in the darkness of ignorance, did the works of the devil in lusts and desires of the flesh. But the Lord had pity on our affliction and sent the Word, His Only Begotten Son, to deliver us from ignorance of our error and to lead us to the light of the divine Law.

3. But first of all contemplate the reckoning up of the mystery. If one examines as carefully as possible, he will find in the Scriptures that there are forty-two stages in the departure of the children of Israel from Egypt; and, further, the coming of our Lord and Savior into this world is traced through forty-two generations. This is what Matthew the Evangelist points out when he says, "From Abraham to David the king, fourteen generations. And from David to the Babylonian Exile, fourteen generations. And from the Babylonian Exile to Christ, fourteen generations" (Mt. 1:17). Therefore, in descending to the Egypt of this world Christ passed those forty-two generations as stages; and those who ascend from Egypt pass by the same number, forty-two stages. And Moses made the point with great perception when he said, "The children of Israel went up with their power" (Num. 33:1). What is their "power" unless it is Christ Himself, who is the power of God (1 Cor. 1:24)? And so, the person who ascends, ascends with Him who descended from there to us, so that he may arrive at the place from which He descended not by necessity but because He deemed it right. This demonstrates the truth of what is said in the verse "He who descended is He who also ascended" (Eph. 4:10). Therefore, the children of Israel by forty-two stages attained the beginning of taking their inheritance. And the beginning of taking the inheritance was when Reuben, Gad, and the half tribe of Manasseh

received the land of Gilead (Josh. 17:6). And so the number is fixed for Christ's descent, when He came down to us through forty-two ancestors according to the flesh as through forty-two stages. And the ascent of the children of Israel to the beginning of the promised inheritance was through the same number of stages.

If you have understood how great a mystery that number of the descent and the ascent contains, then come and let us begin to ascend through the stages by which Christ descended, and make that the first stage which He passed last of all, namely, when He was born of the Virgin. Let this be the first stage for us who wish to go out of Egypt. In it we left the adoration of idols and the worship of demons—not gods—and believed that Christ was born of the Virgin and from the Holy Spirit and that the Word made flesh (Jn. 1:14) came into this world. After this let us strive to go forward and to ascend one by one each of the steps of faith and the virtues. If we persist in them until we come to perfection, we shall be said to have made a stage at each of the steps of the virtues until, when we attain the height of our instruction and the summit of our progress, the promised inheritance is fulfilled.

4. Moreover, when the soul sets out from the Egypt of this life to go to the promised land, it necessarily goes by certain roads and, as we have said, observes certain stages that were made ready with the Father from the beginning. I think the prophet was mindful of this when he said, "I remembered these things, and I poured out my soul upon me: how I went into the place of the marvelous tabernacle, to the house of God" (Ps. 42:4). Those stages and that tabernacle are what he speaks of in another place, "How lovely are your tabernacles, O Lord of hosts! My soul longs, yea, faints for the courts of the Lord" (Ps. 84:1–2). For that reason the same prophet says in another place, "My soul has long been on pilgrimage" (Ps. 119:6 LXX–Ps. 120:6). Understand, then, if you can, what the pilgrimages of the soul are in which it laments with groaning and grief that it has been on pilgrimage so long. We understand these pilgrimages only dully and darkly so long as the pilgrimage still lasts. But when the soul has returned to its rest, that is, to the fatherland in paradise, it will be taught more truly and will understand more truly what the meaning of its pilgrimage was. The prophet contemplated this in the form of a mystery and said, "Re-

turn, O my soul, to your rest; for the Lord has dealt bountifully with you" (Ps. 116:7). But for the time being the soul is on pilgrimage; it journeys on and makes stages, doubtless because God has ordained them in His promises for the sake of some kind of profit. This is what is said in one passage, "I have afflicted you and fed you with manna in the wilderness, which your fathers did not know, so that what is in your heart might be made known" (Deut. 8:2–3 LXX). Therefore, the stages are those by which the soul journeys from earth to heaven.

Who will be found worthy and so understanding of the divine mysteries that he can describe the stages of that journey and ascent of the soul and explain either the toils or the rest of each different place? For how will he explain that after the first and second stages Pharaoh is still in pursuit; the Egyptians are in pursuit? And while they do not catch them, they keep on pursuing; while they have been drowned, they still pursue. How will he interpret the fact that the people of God who had been saved only after a few stages first sang the song, saying, "Let us sing to the Lord, for He has triumphed gloriously. The horse and his rider has He thrown into the sea" (Ex. 15:1)? But, as I have said, I do not know who would dare to explain the stages one by one and also to guess at the special properties of the stages by contemplating their names. I am uncertain whether the understanding of the preacher would be sufficient for such weighty mysteries or the hearing of the listeners capable of understanding. How will he explain the wars encountered with the Amalekites or the different temptations? How will he explain those whose limbs fell in the wilderness (cf. Heb. 3:17; 1 Cor. 10:5) and that it was not at all the children of Israel but the children's children of Israel that were able to enter the holy land? For all that ancient people whose life and dwelling had been with the Egyptians fell; and only a new people that did not know the Egyptians arrived at the kingdom, the priests and the Levites excepted. For if anyone could find a place in the order of priests and Levites, if anyone could have no portion in the lands but the Lord Himself, then he would not fall in the wilderness, but would attain the promised land. That is why if you do not wish to fall in the wilderness but to attain the promised land of the fathers, you should have no portion in the land nor should you have anything in common with earth.

Let your portion be only with the Lord, and you will never fall. Therefore, the ascent from Egypt to the promised land is something by which, as I have said, we are taught in mysterious descriptions the ascent of the soul to heaven and the mystery of the resurrection from the dead.

5. Moreover, names are given to the stages. For it did not seem suitable that every place under heaven, mountains, hills, or fields, should have names, but that the ascent of the soul to the kingdom of God should lack names for its stages. The ascent does have for its stages names fitted to mysteries; and it has as its guide not Moses—for he did not know where to go himself—but the pillar of fire and the cloud, that is, the Son of God and the Holy Spirit. This is what the prophet says in another place, "The Lord Himself led them" (Ps. 78:14). Such, then, will be the ascent of the blessed soul, when all the Egyptians have been drowned, and the Amalekites and all who fought against it. And by passing through each of the different stages, that is, those "many stages" that are said to be with the Father (Jn. 14:2), it will be increasingly enlightened as it passes from one to the other. It will always gain an increase of enlightenment until it grows accustomed to the true Light Himself, who lightens every man (Jn. 1:9), and can endure looking upon Him and bear the splendor of His marvelous majesty.

But if we return to the second line of interpretation we mentioned earlier and understand the stages to teach about the progress of the soul when placed in this life, then after its conversion from Gentile life it follows not Moses so much as the Law of God and not Aaron but that Priest who remains forever (cf. Heb. 6:20). Before it arrives at perfection, it dwells in the wilderness, where, of course, it is trained in the commandments of the Lord and where its faith is tested by temptations. And when it conquers one temptation and its faith has been proved in it, it comes to another one; and it passes, as it were, from one stage to another. So, when it proceeds through the different temptations of life and faith one by one, it is said to have stages in which increases in virtues are sought one by one. In this way there is fulfilled what is written, "They will go from virtue to virtue" (Ps. 84:7) until the soul arrives at its goal, namely the highest summit of virtues, and crosses the river of God and receives the heritage promised it.

6. Thus, employing a double line of interpretation, we must examine the entire order of stages as it is narrated, so that our soul may make progress by both interpretations, when we learn from them either how we ought to live the life that turns from error and follows the Law of God or how great an expectation we have of the future hope that is promised on the basis of the resurrection. For in this way I think that an understanding worthy of the laws of the Holy Spirit may be taught in regard to what we read. For suppose we knew the place in the wilderness, for example, said to be where the children of Israel camped as they were passing through. What use would that be to me, or what progress could it afford to those who read and meditate on the Law of God day and night (cf. Ps. 1:2)? The point is especially clear when we see what great care the Lord took in describing those stages so that their description would be introduced in a second place. For those names are recounted, granted with some differences, at the point when the children of Israel are said to have left each different place and to have camped at it. And now again the Word of God orders Moses to describe them. Moreover, because of the very fact that the description is repeated a second time, it seems to me we have a detail in harmony with the mystery of the interpretation we have suggested. The stages are repeated twice in order to show two journeys for the soul. One is the means of training the soul in virtues through the Law of God when it is placed in flesh; and by ascending through certain steps it makes progress, as we have said, from virtue to virtue, and uses these progressions as stages. And the other journey is the one by which the soul, in gradually ascending to the heavens after the resurrection, does not reach the highest point unseasonably, but is led through many stages. In them it is enlightened stage by stage; it always receives an increase of splendor, illumined at each stage by the light of Wisdom, until it arrives at the Father of lights Himself (cf. Jas. 1:17).

"The children of Israel went forth with their power" (Num. 33:1). That power was with them that had said, "I will go down with you to Egypt" (Gen. 46:4). And it is because that power was with them that the prophet says, "And there was none in their tribes who was weak" (Ps. 105:37). And they went forth "by the hand of Moses and Aaron." The one hand of Moses was not enough for going forth from Egypt, and the hand of Aaron was also needed. Moses stands for knowledge of the Law; Aaron, for skill in making sacrifices and immolations to God. It is, therefore, necessary for us when we come forth from Egypt to have not only the knowledge of the Law and of faith, but also the fruits of works well pleasing to God. For the hand of Moses and Aaron is mentioned so that you may understand "hand" to mean works. If when I leave Egypt and turn to God I cast away pride, then I have sacrificed a bull to God by the hand of Aaron. If I have destroyed wantonness and lust, I believe I have killed a goat for the Lord by the hand of Aaron. If I have conquered desire, a calf; if folly, I will seem to have sacrificed a sheep. In this way when the vices of the soul are purged, the hand of Aaron works in us. And the hand of Moses is with us when we are enlightened by the Law to understand these very things. And so, each hand is necessary for those coming forth from Egypt so that there may be found in them not only the perfection of faith and knowledge, but also that of deeds and works. Nevertheless, these are not two hands, but one. For "by the hand of Moses and Aaron" the Lord led them forth, and not by the "hands" of Moses and Aaron. There is a single work for each hand and a single fulfillment of perfection.

7. "And Moses wrote down their starting places and their stages by the Word of the Lord" (Num. 33:2). He wrote them down, then, "by the Word of the Lord" so that when we read them and see how many starting places lie ahead of us on the journey that leads to the kingdom, we may prepare ourselves for this way of life and, considering the journey that lies ahead of us, may not allow the time of our life to be ruined by sloth and neglect. The danger is that while we linger in the vanities of the world and delight in each of the sensations that come to our sight or hearing or even to our touch, smell, and taste, days may slip by, time may pass on, and we shall not find any opportunity for completing the journey that lies ahead. Then we give up halfway there, and there will happen to us what is reported of those who could not complete the journey but whose limbs fell in the wilderness (cf. Heb. 3:17; 1 Cor. 10:5). Thus, we are on a journey; and we have come into this world that we may pass from virtue to virtue (cf. Ps. 84:7), not to remain on earth for earthly things like the man who said "I will pull down my

barns, and build larger ones . . . and I will say to my soul, Soul, you have ample goods laid up for many years; eat, drink, be merry." We must take care that the Lord not say to us as He said to him, "Fool! This night your soul will be taken from you" (Lk. 12:18–20). He did not say "this day," but "this night." He was destroyed at night like the firstborn of the Egyptians (cf. Ex. 12:29), because he loved the world and its darkness and was a fellow of the rulers of the darkness of this world (cf. Eph. 6:14). For this world is called darkness and night because of those who live in ignorance and do not accept the light of truth. Those who are like this do not set out from Ramesse, nor do they pass on to Sochoth[98] (Num. 33:3, 5; Rameses, Succoth).

8. But let us see when the children of Israel first set out from Ramesse. It says, "In the first month, on the fifteenth day of the month" (Num. 33:3). On the fourteenth day of the month by the commandment of the Lord they keep the Passover in Egypt, killing a lamb the day before they set out; and they who were still in Egypt perform a kind of beginning of the feast. Then on the following day, which is the first day of unleavened bread, the fifteenth day of the first month, they set out from Ramesse and come to Sochoth to celebrate the day of the feast of unleavened bread there. "Who is wise and will understand these things? or discerning and he will know them?" (Hos. 14:10). Indeed, who is there that even understands them in part, as the Apostle says, "For we know in part, and we prophesy in part" (1 Cor. 13:9)? Who understands how we may keep the feast days "in part" so that no one will pass judgment on us for part of a feast or a new moon or a sabbath (cf. Col. 2:16)? For every feast day that is celebrated on earth by human beings is celebrated in part, not completely or with the perfect title of a feast. But when you come forth from that Egypt, then you will have a perfect feast; then you will keep the unleavened bread of sincerity and truth (1 Cor. 5:8) to perfection; then you will celebrate the day of Pentecost in the wilderness; and then you will first receive the strong and heavenly food of manna and will keep each of the different feasts about which we spoke earlier so far as we were able

---

98. The translation gives the place names as found in the Septuagint, the text Origen used. The more familiar names from the Hebrew text will be given in parentheses with the citation.

(*Hom. Num.* 23, 24). But know that after the Passover that happened in Egypt we found one Passover kept in the wilderness when the Law was given, another as we have noticed in Numbers, but none ever celebrated afterwards except in the promised land.

Therefore, "on the fifteenth day of the first month," the day after Passover, which is the first day of unleavened bread, the children of Israel set out from Ramesse "with a high hand in the sight of all the Egyptians" (Num. 33:3). What is the high hand? Indeed, it says in another place, "Let your hands be lifted up" (Ps. 10:12). Where there is no human or earthly work but a divine one, there the expression "a high hand" is used. For by "hand," work is quite often to be understood. Thus, with a high hand in the sight of all the Egyptians they set out.

And it says, "The Egyptians were burying their dead" (Num. 33:4). But the living were following the Lord their God. After this it is said that "upon their gods also the Lord executed punishment" (Num. 33:4). Moreover, in Exodus it says, "And on all the gods of the Egyptians the Lord will execute punishment" (Ex. 12:12). Now here it says that the Lord executed punishment upon them. And the Apostle says, "There are those called gods in heaven or on earth" (1 Cor. 8:5). Moreover, in the Psalms it is said, "All the gods of the Gentiles are demons" (Ps. 96:5). Thus, it calls not the images but the demons who dwell in the images gods upon whom the Lord executed punishment. But I should want to ask how God may execute punishment on the demons, when the day of punishment and of judgment has not yet come. Now I think that this punishment happens to demons when a person who had been deceived by them to worship idols is converted by the Word of the Lord and worships the Lord. And from the work of conversion itself punishment is given to him who had deceived. In just the same way, if someone who had been deceived by demons to commit fornication is converted to chastity, loves purity, and weeps for his error, the demon burns and is on fire because of the tears of his penitence, and so punishment is given to the author of deception. Again in the same way, if someone returns from pride to humility or from prodigality to thrift, by these acts each one whips and tortures the different demons who had deceived them. With what torments do you think they are driven if they see the man who according to the Lord's word sells everything he possessed, gives to the poor, and takes up his cross and follows Christ (cf. Mt. 19:21, 16:24)? But worse than any other sorts of torments for them and worse than any other punishment is if they see someone giving his attention to the Word of God by seeking out the mysteries of the Scriptures with attentive exertions. This sets them all ablaze; and in that fire they are burned up, since they had darkened human minds with the darkness of ignorance and had gained their object that God might be unknown and the zealous pursuits of divine worship might be transferred to them. What a punishment do you think is given them? What a blazing fire of torments is brought upon them when they see the darkness opened by the light of truth and the clouds of their deceit dispersed by knowledge of the divine Law? For they possess all who live in ignorance. They rush upon not only those still in ignorance but also those who have known God, and they try to make them work again the deeds of ignorance. There is not a sin accomplished without them. For when someone commits adultery, it is not without a demon; or when he is seized by excessive anger, or when he plunders someone else's goods, or the one who sits against his neighbor and slanders him (cf. Ps. 101:5), and the one who puts a stumbling block in the way of his mother's son (cf. Rom. 14:13)—it is not without a demon. And so we must be active in every way lest we stir up against us once more the firstborn of the Egyptians or their gods whom the Lord struck down and destroyed, by giving them an opportunity to work in us what God hates. But if we keep ourselves from all of them in the way we have already explained, then "God has executed punishment upon all the gods of the Egyptians," and the demons receive torments from our amendment and conversion.

9. So, the children of Israel went forth from Egypt, and setting out from Ramesse, they came to Sochoth. The order of setting out and the distinction of the stages are quite necessary and must be observed by those who follow God and set their minds on progress in the virtues. With respect to this order I remember that already in other places where we have spoken for edification we have pursued the points that the Lord thought right to give us. But we shall now remind you of them again briefly, since you ask it.

Now the first starting place was from Ramesse; and whether

the soul starts out from this world and comes to the future age or is converted from the errors of life to the way of virtue and knowledge, it starts out from Ramesse. For in our language Ramesse means "confused agitation" or "agitation of the worm." By this it is made clear that everything in this world is set in agitation and disorder, and also in corruption; for this is what the worm means. The soul should not remain in them, but should set out and come to Sochoth.

Sochoth is interpreted "tents." Thus, the first progress of the soul is to be taken away from earthly agitation and to learn that it must dwell in tents like a wanderer, so that it can be, as it were, ready for battle and meet those who lie in wait for it unhindered and free.

Then when the soul thinks it is ready, it sets out from Sochoth and camps at Buthan (Num. 33:6; Etham). Buthan means "valley." Now we have said that the stages refer to progress in the virtues. And a virtue is not acquired without training and hard work, nor is it tested as much in prosperity as in adversity. So the soul comes to a valley. For in valleys and in low places the struggle against the devil and the opposing powers takes place. Thus, in the valley the battle must be fought. Then, too, Abraham fought against the barbarian kings in the Valley of Siddim (Gen. 14:8), and there he gained the victory. Therefore, this wanderer of ours descends to those who are in deep and low places, not to linger there, but to gain the victory there.

"Then they set out from Buthan and camped at the mouth of Iroth" (Num. 33:7; Pi-ha-hiroth). Iroth means "villages." For the soul has not yet come to the city; nor is what is perfect already held; but first and for the moment some small places are taken. For progress consists in coming to great things from small ones. So the soul comes to Iroth, that is to the first entrance of a village, which is the beginning of conversion and of a moderate self-control. For full and immoderate self-control is dangerous at the beginning. Now Iroth is situated opposite Beelsephon and opposite Magdalum (Num. 33:7; Baal-zephon, Migdol). Beelsephon means "the ascent of the watchtower or citadel." So, the soul ascends from small things to great and is not yet placed in that watchtower, but opposite the watchtower, that is, in sight of the watchtower. For it begins to watch and to look for the future hope and to contemplate the height of the progresses; little by little it grows, while it is more nourished by hope than worn out by toils. This camp or stage is opposite Magdalum, but not yet in Magdalum itself. For Magdalum means "grandeur." Thus, since it has in view both the ascent of watching and the grandeur of the things to come, the soul, as we have said, is fed and nourished by great hopes. It is now situated in starting places and not in perfection.

10. Next, they set out from Iroth and pass through the midst of the Red Sea, and camp at the Bitter Waters (Num. 33:8; Marah). We have said that the time of starting places is a time of dangers. How hard a temptation it is to pass through the midst of the sea, to see the waves rise piled up, to hear the noise and rumbling of the raging waters! But if you follow Moses, that is, the Law of God, the waters will become for you walls on the right and left, and you will find a path on dry ground in the midst of the sea (cf. Ex. 14:22). Moreover, it can happen that the heavenly journey that we say the soul takes may hold peril of waters; waves may be found there. For one part of the waters is above the heavens and another part under heaven (cf. Gen. 1:7). For the time being we endure the waves and billows of the waters under heaven. And God will see whether they can be quiet and calm and not stirred up by any winds blowing upon them. But meanwhile, when we come to the crossing of the sea, although we see Pharaoh and the Egyptians in pursuit, we shall in no way be alarmed, shall have no fear of them, no terror. Let us simply believe in the only true God and His Son Jesus Christ, whom He sent (cf. Jn. 17:3). And if it is said that the people believed in God and in His servant Moses, we also believe in this way in Moses, that is, the Law of God and the prophets. Therefore, stand fast and in a little while you will see the Egyptians lying on the seashore (Ex. 14:30). And when you see them lying there, rise up and sing songs to the Lord, and praise Him who sank the horse and his rider in the Red Sea (cf. Ex. 15:1ff.).

And so they camped at the Bitter Waters. Do not be terrified or afraid when you hear of Bitter Waters. "For the moment all discipline seems bitter rather than pleasant; later it yields the sweetest and most peaceful fruit of righteousness to those who have been trained by it," as the Apostle teaches (Heb. 12:11). Then, too, the unleavened bread is commanded to be eaten with bitter herbs (Ex. 12:8); nor is it possible to attain the promised land unless we pass through bitterness. For just as physicians put bitter substances in medicines with a view to the health and healing of the infirm, so also the Physician of our souls with a view to our salvation has wished us to suffer the bitterness of this life in various temptations, knowing that the end of this bitterness gains the sweetness of salvation for our soul, just as, on the contrary, the end of the sweetness found in corporeal pleasure, as the example of that rich man teaches (cf. Lk. 16:19ff.), brings a bitter end of torments in hell. You, then, who enter the path of virtue, should not turn back from camping at the Bitter Waters. For you will set out from there just as the children of Israel did.

11. It says, "They set out from the Bitter Waters and came to Helim" (Num. 33:9; Elim). Helim is where there are twelve springs of water and seventy-two palm trees. You see after bitterness, after the hardships of temptations, what pleasant places receive you! You would not have come to the palm trees unless you had endured the bitterness of temptations. Nor would you have come to the sweetness of the springs unless you had first overcome what was sad and harsh. The end of the journey and the perfection of all things does not, however, lie in these delights. But God, who orders souls, has on this journey put some places of refreshment into the midst of toils so that the soul may be refreshed and restored by them and may more readily return to the toils that remain.

And Helim means rams; rams are the leaders of flocks. Thus, who are the leaders of Christ's flock but the Apostles, who are also the twelve springs? But since our Lord and Savior chose not only those twelve but also seventy-two others, there are not only twelve springs but also seventy-two palm trees mentioned in Scripture. They, too, are called apostles, as Paul himself says when he is explaining the resurrection of the Savior. He says that He appeared to the Eleven and then to all the apostles (1 Cor. 15:7). By this he makes it clear that there are other apostles besides those Eleven. Therefore, this pleasantness will receive you after bitterness, this rest after toil, this grace after temptations.

It says, "They set out from Helim and camped by the Red Sea" (Num. 33:10). Notice that they do not enter the Red Sea, since entering it once was enough. Now they camp next to the sea, so that they look at the sea and regard its waves, but in no way fear its motions and assaults.

"And they set out from the Red Sea and camped in the wilderness of Sin" (Num. 33:11). Sin means "bramble bush" or "temptation." Thus, the hope of good things now begins to smile upon you. What is the hope of good things? The Lord appeared from the bush and answered Moses; and this became the beginning of the Lord's coming to the children of Israel (cf. Ex. 3:2ff.). But it is not insignificant that Sin also means temptation. For visions usually involve temptation. Sometimes an angel of wickedness disguises himself as an angel of light (cf. 2 Cor. 11:4). And so you must beware and exercise great care in order to discern with knowledge the kinds of visions, just as Joshua the son of Nun, when he saw a vision and knew there was temptation in it, immediately asked the one who appeared to him and said, "Are you for us, or for our adversaries?" (Josh. 5:14). So, then, the soul progresses when it comes to the place where it begins to distinguish between visions; and it is proved to be spiritual if it knows how to discern them all (cf. 1 Cor. 2:15). That is why, as well, one of the spiritual gifts, given by the Holy Spirit, is mentioned as "the ability to distinguish between spirits" (1 Cor. 12:10).

12. "And they set out from the wilderness of Sin and came to Raphaca" (Num. 33:12; Dophkah). Raphaca means "health." You see the order of the progresses, how when the soul is once made spiritual and begins to have the discernment of heavenly visions, it arrives at health. The point is rightly put by the verse, "Bless the Lord, O my soul, and all that is within me, bless His holy name!" What Lord? The one "who heals all your infirmities, who redeems your life from destruction" (Ps. 103:1–4). For the soul has many infirmities. Avarice is one of the worst of its infirmities; pride, anger, boasting, fear, inconstancy, timidity, and the like. When, Lord Jesus, will you cure me of all these infirmities? When will you heal me so that I may say, "Bless the Lord, O my soul, who heals all your infirmities" so that I may be able to make a stage at Raphaca, which is healing?

It would be a long task if we wanted to go through each of the stages and explain one by one what is suggested by contemplating their names. Nevertheless, let us go through them in a summary and brief fashion, not so we may give you a full interpretation, since time does not allow, but so you may have some opportunity to understand them.

Thus, they set out from Raphaca and come to Halus (Num. 33:13; Alush). Halus means "toils." Nor should you be surprised if toils follow health. For the soul acquires health from the Lord in order to accept toils with delight and not unwillingly. It is said, "You shall eat the toils of your fruits; you shall be blessed, and it shall be well with you" (Ps. 128:2).

Next they come to Raphidin (Num. 33:14; Rephidim). Now Raphidin means "praise of judgment." Praise most justly follows toils, but what is the praise of? Judgment, it says. Therefore, the soul becomes worthy of praise when it judges rightly, discerns rightly, that is, when it judges all things spiritually and is itself judged by no one (1 Cor. 2:15).

Next it arrives at the wilderness of Sina (Num. 33:15; Sinai). Sina itself is a place in the wilderness that was earlier mentioned as Sin. But this place is, rather, the name of the mountain that is in that wilderness; it is called Sina after the name of the wilderness. Therefore, after the soul has been made praiseworthy in judgment and begins to have a right judgment, then it is given the Law by God, since it has begun to be capable of receiving divine mysteries and heavenly visions.

From there they come to the Tombs of Lust (Num. 33:16; Kibroth-hattavah). What are the Tombs of Lust? Doubtless it is where lusts are buried and covered over, where all desire is quenched and the flesh no longer lusts against the spirit, since it has been put to death by the death of Christ (cf. Gal. 5:17; Rom. 7:4).

Next they come to Aseroth (Num. 33:17; Hazeroth). This means "perfect halls" or "blessedness." Consider quite carefully, each of you wanderers, what the order of progresses is. After you have been buried and have handed over the lusts of the flesh to death, you will come to the spacious dignity of halls, you will come to blessedness. For blessed is the soul that is no longer driven by any vices of the flesh.

From there they come to Rathma or Pharam (Num. 13:18; Rithmah). Rathma means "completed vision," but Pharam means "visible face." Why? Unless because the soul so grows that when it has ceased being driven by the troubles of the flesh, it has completed visions and gains perfect understanding of things, since it has a fuller and higher knowledge of the reasons for the Incarnation of the Word of God and the purposes of His dispensations.

From there they come to Remonphares (Num. 33:19; Rimmonperez), which in our language means "a high cutting through," that is, where the separation and distinction of great and heavenly things from earthly and lowly things takes place. For as the understanding of the soul grows, it is also furnished with an acquaintance with high things and is given judgment by which to cut what is eternal away from what is temporal and to distinguish what is perishable from what is everlasting.

Next they come to Lebna (Num. 33:20; Libnah), which means "whitewashing." I know that in some respects whitewashing has a pejorative connotation, as when we speak of a "whitewashed wall" (Acts 23:3) and "whitewashed tombs" (Mt. 23:27). But this whitewashing is that concerning which the prophet says, "You will wash me and I shall be whiter than snow" (Ps. 51:7). And again Isaiah says, "Though your sins are like scarlet, I will whiten them like snow and will make them white like wool" (Is. 1:18). Again in the psalm, "They were whitened with snow in Zalmon" (Ps. 68:14). And the hair of the Ancient of Days is said to be dazzling white, that is, white like wool (Dan. 7:9). So then, this whitewashing must be understood to come from the radiance of the true light and to descend from the brightness of heavenly visions.

The next stage takes place in Ressa (Num. 33:21; Rissah), which could be put into our words as "visible or praiseworthy temptation." Why is it that however great the progresses made by the soul nonetheless temptations are not taken away from it? Here it becomes clear that temptations are brought to it as a kind of protection and defense. For just as meat, if it is not sprinkled with salt, no matter how great and special it is, becomes rotten, so also the soul, unless it is somehow salted with constant temptations, immediately becomes feeble and soft. For this reason the saying is established that every sacrifice shall be salted with salt (Lev. 2:13). Then, too, that is why even Paul said, "And to keep me from being too elated by the abundance of revelations, a thorn was given me in the flesh, a messenger of Satan, to harass me" (2 Cor. 12:7). This, therefore, is the visible or praiseworthy temptation.

From it they come to Macelath, which is "sovereignty" or "staff" (Num. 33:22; Kehelathah). Power seems to be meant by both and that the soul has progressed so far as to rule over the body and to obtain by that the staff of power. Indeed, it is power not only over the body but over the whole world that Paul means, when he says, "By the cross the world has been crucified to me, and I to the world" (Gal. 6:14).

From there they come to Mount Sephar, which has the meaning "sound of trumpets" (Num. 33:23; Shepher). The trumpet is a sign of war. Therefore, when the soul perceives itself armed with so many and such important virtues, it necessarily goes forth to the war it has against principalities and powers and against the world rulers (cf. Eph. 6:12). Or, of course, the trumpet sounds in the Word of God, that is, in preaching and teaching, to give a distinct sound by the trumpet so that the person who hears it can prepare himself for war (1 Cor. 14:8).

Next they arrive at Charadath, which in our language signifies "made competent" (Num. 33:24; Haradah). Indeed, this is just what Paul says, "He has made us competent to be ministers of a new covenant" (2 Cor. 3:6).

From there a stage is made at Maceloth, which means "from the beginning" (Num. 33:25; Makheloth). For the person who strives for contemplation contemplates the beginning of things, or rather he refers everything to Him who was in the beginning, nor is there any time when he abandons that beginning.

Next a stage is made at Cataath, which is "encouragement" or "endurance" (Num. 33:26; Tabath). For it is necessary for someone who wants to be of use to others to suffer many things and to bear them all patiently, as it is said of Paul, "For I will show him how much he must suffer for the sake of my name" (Acts 9:16).

From there they come to Thara, which may be understood in our words as "contemplation of amazement" (Num. 33:27; Terah). (We cannot express the Greek word *ekstasis* with a single word in Latin; *ekstasis* refers to the mind's amazement when it admires some great thing.) Thus, the contemplation of amazement means a time when the mind is struck with amazement by the knowledge of great and marvelous things.

Next they come to Matheca, which means "new death" (Num. 33:28; Mithkah). What is the new death? When we die with Christ so that we may also live with Him (cf. 2 Tim. 2:11).

From there they come to Asenna, which is said to mean "bone" or "bones" (Num. 33:29; Hashmonah). By this it is doubtless strength and the firmness of endurance that is revealed.

Now from here a stage is made at Mesoroth, which is thought to mean "shutting out" (Num. 33:30; Moseroth). What do they shut out? Doubtless the wicked suggestions of the opposing spirit from their thoughts. For this is what the Wisdom of God says, "If the spirit of one having power rises against you, you will not leave your place" (Eccles. 10:4). Thus, the place must be held, and the adversary must be shut out lest he should find a place in our heart, as the Apostle says, "Give no place to the devil" (Eph. 4:27).

Next they come to Banaim, which means "springs" or "filterings," that is where one draws water from the springs of divine words until one filters them by drinking (Num. 33:31; Benejaakon). (The word "filter," *excolare*, comes from *colare*, to strain, and not from *colere*, to cultivate.) Thus, a person filters the word of God when he does not omit even the least commandment, indeed when he gains the understanding that not even one iota or one dot in the word of God is insignificant (cf. Mt. 5:18, 23:24).

Next they come to Galgad, which means "temptation" or "dense crowd" (Num. 33:32; Hor-haggidgad). Temptation, as I think, is a kind of strength and defense for the soul. For temptation is so mingled with virtues that no virtue appears to be seemly or complete without them. Then, too, for those making progress toward virtue various and "dense" stages in temptations are made.

When you pass through them, you will camp at Tabatha (Num. 33:33; Jotbathah). Tabatha means "good things." Thus, they do not come to good things except after the trials of temptations.

From there, it says, they camped at Ebrona, which is "passage" (Num. 33:34; Abronah). For everything must be passed through. Even if you have come to good things, you must pass through them to better things until you come to that good thing in which you should always remain.

Next they come to Gasiongaber, which means "the purposes of a man" (Num. 33:35; Ezion-geber). If someone ceases to be a child in understanding, he arrives at the purposes of a man, just as Paul, who said, "When I became a man, I gave up childish ways" (1 Cor. 13:11). Thus, the purposes of a man are great, as it says, "The purpose in a man's heart is like deep water" (Prov. 20:5).

From here they come again to Sin (Num. 33:36; Zin). And again Sin is "temptation." For we said that there is no other way of furthering our embarking upon this journey. It is just as though, for example, some goldsmith wishes to make a useful vessel. He brings it often to the fire; he strikes it often with his hammer; he burnishes it often, so that it may become more purified and brought to the shape and the beauty intended by the artisan.

Next they camp at Pharancades, which is "holy fruitfulness" (Num. 33:36; Kadish). You see where they come from; you see that holy fruitfulness follows the ploughed furrows of temptations.

Then they camp at Mount Or, which means "mountainous" (Num. 33:37; Mount Hor). For one comes to the mount of God so that he may himself become a fruitful mountain and a massive mountain (cf. Ps. 68:15) or because the person who always dwells on the mount of God is called a mountaineer.

The stage at Selmona follows next (Num. 33:41; Zalmonah). Its meaning is "shadow of the portion." I think the shadow mentioned is the one about which the prophet said, "The breath of our countenance is Christ the Lord, to whom we said, 'In His shadow we shall live among the Gentiles' " (Lam. 4:20). Moreover, like this one is the shadow about which it is said, "The Spirit of the Lord will overshadow you" (cf. Lk. 1:35). Thus, the shadow of our portion, which gives us shade from all the heat of temptations, is Christ and the Holy Spirit.

Now from here they come to Phinon, which we think means "frugality of the mouth" (Num. 33:42; Punon). For the person who can contemplate the mystery of Christ and of the Holy Spirit, if he sees or hears what it is not right for men to speak (2 Cor. 12:4), will necessarily have frugality of mouth, since he will know to whom, when, and how he should speak of the divine mysteries.

Next they come to Oboth (Num. 33:43). Although we have not found an interpretation of this name, nonetheless we do not doubt that in this name as in all the others the logic of the progresses is preserved.

HOMILY XXVII ON NUMBERS

There follows next the stage that is called Gai, which means "chasm" (Num. 33:44; Iye-abarim or Iyim). For through these progresses one approaches the bosom of Abraham, who says to those in torments, "Between you and us a great chasm has been fixed" (Lk. 16:26). He comes so that he may also rest in his bosom, as blessed Lazarus did.

From there they come in turn to Dibongad, which bears the meaning "beehive of temptations" (Num. 33:45). How marvelous is the caution of divine providence! For look, this wanderer on his heavenly journey comes right up to the highest perfection by a succession of virtues; and nevertheless, temptations do not leave him, though I hear temptations of a new kind. It means "beehive of temptations." Scripture considers the bee a praiseworthy insect, and kings and commoners use what it produces for their health. This may rightly be taken of the words of the prophets and the apostles and all who wrote the sacred books. And I think this can be understood most appropriately as the beehive, that is the entire body of divine Scriptures. Thus, for those who strive for perfection, even in this beehive, that is in the prophetic and apostolic words, there is some temptation. Do you wish to see that the temptation in them is no small one? I find written in the beehive, "Beware lest . . . when you see the sun and the moon . . . you worship . . . things which the Lord your God has allotted to the Gentiles" (Deut. 4:19). Do you see what a temptation comes from that beehive? And again when it says, "You shall not revile God" (Ex. 22:28). And again in the beehive of the New Testament, where we read, "Why do you wish to kill me, a man who has told you the truth?" (Jn. 8:40). And again the Lord Himself says in another place, "This is why I speak to them in parables so that seeing they may not see and hearing they may not understand, lest they should turn and I heal them" (cf. Mt. 13:13, 15). Moreover, when the Apostle says, "In their case the god of this world has blinded the minds of the unbelievers" (2 Cor. 4:4). And you will find many temptations of this kind in this divine beehive. Each of the saints must come to them, so that also by them it may be known how perfect and religious his beliefs about God are.

Next, then, they come to Gelmon Deblathaim, which means "scorn of figs," that is, where earthly things are completely scorned and despised (Num. 33:46; Almon-diblathaim). For unless what seems to delight us on earth is rejected and scorned, we cannot pass through to heavenly things.

There follows next the stage at Abarim opposite Nabau, which is "passage" (Num. 33:47; Abarim, Nebo). But Nabau means "separation." For when the soul has made its journey through all these virtues and has climbed to the height of perfection, it then "passes" from the world and "separates" from it, as it is written of Enoch, "And he was not found, because God had taken him across" (Gen. 5:24). Someone like this, even if he seems to be still in the world and to dwell in flesh, nonetheless will not "be found." Where will he not be found? In no worldly deed, in no fleshly thing, in no vain conversation is he found. For God has taken him across from these pursuits and placed him in the realm of the virtues.

The last stage is east of Moab by the Jordan (Num. 33:48). For the whole journey takes place, the whole course is run for the purpose of arriving at the river of God, so that we may be made neighbors of the flowing Wisdom and may be watered by the waves of divine knowledge, and so that purified by them all we may be made worthy to enter the promised land. And so, this is what we have been able to touch upon in passing and to expound in public concerning the Israelites' stages according to one method of interpretation.

13. But lest an interpretation of this kind, which depends upon the Hebrews' language and the meaning of their words, should seem to those who do not know the conventions of that language contrived and forced, we shall give a comparison in our language by which the meaning of this logic may be clarified. In the literary game by which children receive elementary instruction, some children are called "abcd's"; others, "syllabarians"; others, "namers"; and others, "counters." And when we hear these names, we know from them how far the children have progressed. Likewise in the liberal arts, when we hear a passage recited or a consolation or an encomium or any other topics in order, we notice by the name of the topic how much progress the youth has made. Why, then, should we not believe that by these names of places as by the names of topics there can be indicated points of progress for those who are learning by divine instructions? In our analogy the students appear

to linger in each different topic for public speaking and to make, as it were, stages in them; and they set out from one to the next, and again from it to another. In the same way why should not the names of the stages and the setting out from one to the next and from it to another be believed to indicate the progress of the mind and to signify the acquisition of virtues?

But I leave the rest of the interpretation to be discussed and contemplated on this basis by any who are wise. For it is enough for the wise to give them the opportunity (cf. Prov. 9:9 LXX), because it does not help to let the understanding of the hearers remain completely idle and lazy. Therefore, on the basis of this discussion let him meditate upon the rest; indeed, let him contemplate something more perceptive and more divine. "For it is not by measure that God gives the Spirit" (Jn. 3:34). But because the Lord is Spirit (2 Cor. 3:17), He blows where He wills (cf. Jn. 3:8). And we pray that He may blow upon you, so that you may perceive better and higher things than these in the words of the Lord. May you make your journey through the places we have described in our weakness, so that in that better and higher life we may be able, as well, to walk with you. Our Lord Jesus Christ, who is the way and the truth and the life (Jn. 14:6), will lead us until we attain to the Father, when Christ hands over the kingdom to God the Father (cf. 1 Cor. 15:24) and subjects every principality and power to Him. To Him be glory and power forever and ever. Amen (cf. 1 Pet. 5:11).

INDEX TO PREFACE, FOREWORD AND INTRODUCTION

INDEX TO TEXTS

Body, contempt for, 43, 69, 107;
   corruptible, 42, 46, 76, 132, 216;
   death of, 65, 66; of death, 42,
   128; love of, 52; nature of, 211,
   212; properties of, 140–141;
   resurrected, 165; and sin, 133,
   149, 156, 157; and soul, 42, 65,
   76, 84, 99, 133, 152, 186, 214,
   216, 248, 264; sufferings of, 56,
   154.
Buthan, 258.
Butterworth, 195.
Caesarea, 143.
Cain, 79, 128, 161, 189, 195.
Calcol, 243.
Capernaum, 137.
Cataath, 264.
Chadwick, 44, 53.
Charadath, 264.
Christ, acceptance of, 77, 78; and
   angels, 102, 103; ascent of, 249;
   belief in, 96, 138, 174, 178, 209,
   226, 250, 259; blood of, 50, 79,
   139, 148, 241; body of, 167; as
   bread, 138, 139; as bridegroom,
   230; coming of, 175–179, 188,
   202; commands of, 66, 99, 118;
   confession of, 48, 65, 66, 124;
   cross of, 50, 67, 68; crucifixion
   of, 179, 202, 210, 228; denial of,
   48, 65–67, 71, 77, 154; descent
   of, 249, 250; disciples of, 49,
   68–70, 76, 85, 101, 105, 108,
   118, 135, 172, 174, 175; divinity
   of, 175, 207, 208; doctrines of,
   177–178; following of, 49–51,
   67, 256; friends of, 66; fullness
   of, 221; glory of, 124, 125, 139,
   166, 178, 209, 269; growth in,
   41; heirs of, 124; help of, 59, 68,
   107, 266; as High Priest, 50, 62,
   101, 114, 151, 242; humanity of,
   67, 125, 163, 208, 210; as image

of God, 204; as judge, 149;
   Kingdom of, 60, 117, 269; and
   love, 126, 226, 230; in man, 195,
   206, 207; mind of, 43, 145, 181;
   name of, 165; power of, 135, 166,
   167, 172, 173, 241, 249; praise
   of, 169, 170; and prayer, 85, 105,
   112–114, 118, 119; presence of,
   102, 103, 179; prophecies about,
   173–176, 178, 179, 184, 195,
   201, 202, 240; revelation of, 70,
   203; rule of, 133, 135, 136, 243;
   and salvation, 92; soul of,
   208–210; sufferings of, 72, 73;
   teaching of, 171–175; union
   with, 126, 132, 135, 136, 241,
   242; in us, 49; will of, 60; yoke
   of, 63.
Christianity, denial of, 45.
Christians, afflictions of, 41, 42, 57,
   66, 70, 71, 72, 73, 74, 77, 78,
   153, 162, 172, 229, 230; blessings
   of, 51, 76; born of God, 124, 125;
   comfort of, 72; in contest, 42, 43,
   51, 53, 57, 58, 62, 67, 152; and
   cross, 49, 67; divinized, 144;
   endurance of, 74; glory of, 41,
   42, 66, 70, 78, 124, 155, 184,
   209, 230; and image of God, 125;
   inheritance of, 124, 134, 137;
   Kingdom of God in, 131-132,
   134; perfection of, 216;
   persecutions of, 42, 43, 64, 77,
   78; rewards of, 43, 51, 74;
   simple, 222; testing of, 42, 45,
   48, 67, 70, 153, 161.
1 Chronicles, 16:8–9, 239; 16:22,
   239; 16:26, 63.
2 Chronicles, 32:25–26, 154.
Clement, 182, 183.
Clement of Alexandria, 83.
Church, 113, 114, 182, 240;
   allegorical, 128, 135, 195; as

and Son, 207; of soul, 50; visible, 187; and Word, 223.

Daniel, 63, 104, 106, 108, 115, 175.

Daniel, 3, 63; 6, 106; 6:13, 104; 7:9, 263; 9:24, 175.

Darda, 243.

David, 66, 81, 86, 92, 96, 99, 105, 114, 130, 143, 153, 169, 170, 174, 194, 207, 238, 249; Son of, 240–242.

Death, body of, 42; of Christ, 135, 262; for Christ, 64, 172; with Christ, 265; common, 61, 71, 197; destroyed, 133, 134, 241; and martyrdom, 49, 55, 56, 58, 61, 79; for religion, 44, 56; saved from, 56, 107, 163; threats of, 55.

Deborah, 238.

Deliverance, 42, 73, 132, 133; from devil, 162, 163; of Kingdom, 243; by Lord, 166, 238; from sin, 170, 249; from temptation, 152, 155, 169.

Demeter, 75.

Deuteronomy, cf. also Septuagint; 1:1, 201; 4:19, 46, 267; 4:20, 107; 5:1, 201; 6:5, 45; 6:13, 46; 8:2, 161; 8:3, 161; 8:15, 161; 9:9, 138; 9:18, 110; 10:20, 46; 10:22, 199; 13:3, 45; 14:5, 190; 15:1–3, 145; 15:9, 100; 16:9ff, 145; 16:16, 121, 146; 17:3, 46; 18:20, 22, 46; 23:1–2, 120; 23:3, 120; 23:7–8, 120; 23:14, 128; 25:4, 184; 29:18, 161; 30:14, 132; 31:19, 238; 32:1, 238; 32:2–3, 130, 238; 32:6, 123; 32:9, 43, 46, 53; 32:18, 123; 32:20, 123; 32:21, 174; 32:21–22, 47.

Devils, 48, 51, 53, 54, 60, 63, 68, 73, 77, 78, 83, 90, 104, 106, 107, 115, 125, 132, 133, 136, 143, 152, 154, 162, 163, 175, 189, 200, 221, 227, 230, 241, 249,

250, 256, 257, 258, 261, 262, 264, 269.

Dibongad, 267.

Dophkah, 261.

Dositheus, 191.

Ebionites, 195.

Ebrona, 265.

Ecclesiastes, and Church, 240; and natural philosophy, 231–232, 234; and Solomon, 240.

Ecclesiastes, 241, 242; cf. also Septuagint; 1:1, 240; 2:14, 221; 4:2, 55; 5:2, 128; 5:5, 89; 10:4, 265.

Eden, 128, 189.

Edomites, 120.

Egypt, 50, 53, 99, 107, 110, 120, 142, 158, 196–199, 237, 243, 248–252, 254–257, 259.

Eleazar, 56.

Election, call to, 91, 92; of foolish nation, 174; of Israel, 185, 194; and works, 91.

Eli, 53, 89, 148, 151.

Elijah, 54, 108.

Elim, 260.

Elizabeth, 110.

Elom, 111.

Enoch, 21:1, 213; 40:1, 213; 40:12, 213.

Ephesians, 1:3–5, 92; 1:18, 76, 203; 1:20, 200; 1:22, 200; 1:22–23, 208; 1:23, 126; 2:7, 146; 2:10, 147; 2:20–22, 72; 3:14–15, 165; 3:15, 51; 3:20, 95, 146; 4:10, 249; 4:13, 220, 221, 247; 4:27, 48, 265; 4:30, 148; 5:3, 154; 5:27, 120; 6:2–3, 193; 6:11–12, 162; 6:12, 77, 134, 135, 136, 152, 264; 6:14, 255; 6:16, 163, 200; 19:1, 132.

Ephesus, 72.

Ephraim, 178.

Esau, 86, 92, 161.

Esther, 105, 107, 110, 115.
Esther, 246; cf. also Septuagint;
   3:6, 7, 105; 4:16, 17, 105;
   9:26–28, 105.
Etham, 258.
Ethan, 243.
Ethiopia, 50, 143, 196.
Eucharist, 91.
Eusebius of Caesarea, 83, 205.
Eve, 127, 161, 195.
Evil, 45, 54, 58, 74, 75, 107, 108,
   139, 149, 150, 152, 154, 156,
   157, 159, 160, 168, 178, 179,
   209, 218.
Exodus, 1:5, 199; 1:14, 249; 2:1–2,
   145; 2:23, 249; 3:2ff, 267; 3:6,
   235; 3:14, 129; 3:15, 75; 6:6, 237;
   7:3, 160; 7:14–12:36, 199; 7:22,
   160; 8:8, 87; 8:9, 87; 8:19, 160;
   8:28, 87; 8:29, 87; 8:30, 87; 9:12,
   160; 9:27, 160; 9:27–28, 88; 9:33,
   88; 9:35, 160; 10:1, 160;
   10:17–18, 88; 10:20, 160; 10:27,
   160; 11:10, 160; 12:2, 145; 12:3,
   145; 12:6, 145; 12:8, 260; 12:12,
   256; 12:15, 145; 12:18, 145;
   12:29, 255; 14:29–31, 237; 14:22,
   259; 14:30, 259; 14:30f, 237;
   15:1, 237, 251, 259; 16:29, 190;
   19ff, 199; 19:6, 44; 20:3, 44; 20:4,
   44; 20:5, 47, 179; 20:7, 130;
   20:12, 193; 20:13–16, 193; 22:20,
   75; 22:28, 267; 23:13, 44; 23:26,
   223; 25ff, 199; 25:40, 184; 28,
   199; 32:8, 45; 30:17ff, 200; 30:29,
   236; 32:11, 110.
Ezekiel, 196.
Ezekiel, 23:4ff, 223; 26ff, 196;
   29:11–12, 196; 30:7, 196;
   30:10–12, 196; 32:5–6, 196;
   32:12–13, 196; 32:15, 196; 37:27,
   128; 48:15ff, 178.
Ezion-geber, 265.
Ezrahite, 243.

Faith, 44; ascent in, 250; Catholic,
   248; in Christ, 174, 180, 230,
   240; in God, 177; knowledge of,
   254; perfection of, 254; and
   prayer, 104; rule of, 180;
   suffering for, 54, 106; testing of,
   47, 70, 252; and unbelief, 72,
   179; and wisdom, 177, 200.
Father, cf. also Lord's Prayer;
   not circumscribed, 125–126;
   children of, 183; coming to, 248,
   249, 269; and confession, 65, 66,
   71, 72; denial of, 71; face of, 104;
   forgiveness of, 165; gifts of, 101,
   109, 113, 114; glory of, 49, 65,
   68, 105, 201; goodness of, 46; in
   heaven, 48, 65–67, 104, 111,
   123–128, 133, 148; knowledge
   of, 122, 123, 186, 216, 221, 230;
   of light, 253; and love, 70, 126,
   230, 231; and martyrs, 67; name
   of, 129; nature of, 205, 206, 213,
   215; perfection of, 216; praise of,
   85, 169, 170; and prayer, 86, 98,
   100, 112–114, 119, 121, 123,
   137, 140, 146, 156; and salvation,
   60, 92; sends Son, 139, 226; and
   Son, 112, 200, 205–206, 213,
   225, 230, 243; and Spirit, 64, 85,
   186; thanks to, 111; throne of,
   135; union with, 70, 121, 126,
   132, 226; will of, 60, 61, 103,
   112, 135, 136, 145, 160, 180; and
   Word, 207.
Fortune, 45, 46, 71.
Freedom, from evil, 159; of man,
   93–94; through martyrdom, 56;
   and prayer, 97, 103; and
   providence, 94, 96; of will, 136,
   157, 162.
Gabriel, 109, 207.
Gad, 249.
Gai, 267.
Galatians, 1:4, 132; 1:5, 170; 1:15,

91, 96; 2:19, 140; 2:20, 49, 206; 3:19, 236; 4:1–2, 123; 4:4, 66, 123; 4:6, 84; 4:10, 145; 4:19, 124; 4:21–24, 185; 4:26, 195, 241; 5:17, 152, 262; 5:18, 150; 5:22, 133; 6:8, 223; 6:14, 264.

inspiration, 117, 124, 178, 180, 185, 186, 188, 199, 205; knowledge of, 186, 213, 216; and love, 72, 223, 230, 231; nature of, 206, 213, 216; and praise, 169, 170; purpose of, 186–188, 192, 198; and Scripture, 244, 247; union with, 70, 116; will of, 240.

Hope, 41; in God, 43, 46, 54, 60, 153; of good things, 261; of heaven, 154, 184; in Lord, 59; as nourishing, 259; in resurrection, 58, 253; and sufferings, 72.

Hophni, 151.

Hor-haggidgad, 265.

Hosea, 3:4, 173; 7:6, 163; 14:9, 86, 145; 14:10, 255.

Idols, 44, 45, 47, 57, 63, 151, 172, 174, 201, 250, 256.

Ignatius, 121, 132, 228.

Immanuel, 174.

Incarnation, 263.

Iroth, 258, 259.

Isaac, 75, 86, 115, 153, 192, 195, 224, 225, 235.

Isaiah, 105, 239.

Isaiah, cf. also Septuagint; 1:2, 123, 140, 213; 1:12, 167; 1:15, 167; 1:18, 263; 4:4, 159, 160; 6:2–3, 203; 6:10, 43; 7:13–14, 174; 7:15, 179; 7:15–16, 209; 8:8–9, 175; 9:6, 248; 11:6–7, 179; 14:9–10, 54; 14:10, 54; 14:11, 54; 14:12, 54, 196; 20:2, 221; 23:4, 135; 25:8, 107; 27:12, 103; 28:1, 150; 29:13, 44; 34:5, 134; 38:1ff, 105; 40:6, 117; 40:10, 73; 43:3–4, 50; 43:20–21, 44; 45:2, 199; 45:2–3, 199; 45:7, 179; 49:2, 223; 49:8, 73; 49:22–23, 113; 51:7, 43; 55:12, 53; 58:9, 100; 58:10, 104; 61:1, 178; 61:2, 121; 62:11, 73; 65:11, 71; 65:11–15, 71; 66:1, 46, 127, 133, 135.

Iye-abarim, 267.

Iyim, 267.

Israel, 64; allegorical, 174, 185, 195, 196, 199, 200, 201, 235, 240; children of, 88, 103, 111, 158, 173, 237, 238, 242, 245, 248–251, 253, 256, 257, 261; God of, 63, 110; King of, 240, 241; meaning of, 195, 199; people of, 175, 185, 195, 197; tribes of, 51, 242.

Jacob, 75, 86, 88, 92, 115, 153, 161, 166, 173, 180, 192, 194, 195, 196, 224, 225, 230, 235.

James, 1:17, 253; 2:23, 145; 3:8, 104; 4:1, 152; 5:8, 143; 5:17–18, 108.

Jephthah, 90.

Jeremiah, 99, 102.

Jeremiah, 7:22–23, 99; 11:4, 107; 11:20, 98; 14:22, 63; 15:1, 105; 15:14, 179; 16:19, 63; 17:10, 98; 17:21, 191; 23:24, 100, 127; 50:1, 221.

Jericho, 226.

Jeroboam, 96, 194.

Jerome, 198, 200, 202, 213.

Jerusalem, 46, 85, 113, 168, 178, 179, 192, 194, 195, 196, 197, 223, 225, 226, 240, 241, 242.

Jews, 144, 153, 173, 179, 191, 194, 195, 244.

Job, 100, 108, 151, 162, 163, 175.

Job, cf. also Septuagint; 1:9–11, 163; 1:22, 100, 162; 2:10, 100, 162; 3:8, 108; 7:1, 155; 16:37, 140; 31:27–28, 63; 31:34, 140; 33:1, 140.

Joel, 2:32, 60.

John, 71, 103, 105, 205, 206, 228.

John, 1:1, 144, 186, 226; 1:1–2, 206; 1:3, 207, 209; 1:9, 252; 1:12, 124; 1:14, 139, 186, 250; 1:17, 201; 1:26, 100; 1:26–27, 208; 1:42, 129; 1:51, 103; 2:6, 183; 3:8, 269; 3:12, 83; 3:34, 269;

Law, 183; civil, 171, 172; deserted, 168; die for, 57; first, 201, 229; as foreshadowing, 145, 151, 184, 201; fulfillment of, 75, 99, 202; given, 256, 262; of God, 56, 57, 58, 59, 132, 145, 146, 147, 152, 155, 157, 220, 233, 248, 249, 252, 253, 257, 259; of Gospels, 61; of Holy Spirit, 253; and knowledge, 181, 182, 248, 254, 257; of Moses, 62, 144, 172, 175, 176, 190, 201, 237; obedience to, 58, 200; and prayer, 84; second, 201, 229; spiritual, 107, 136, 182; teaching of, 140, 155, 182, 184; understanding of, 185, 187, 188, 192, 229, 254.

Lazarus, 267.

Lebna, 263.

Levi, 194, 242, 251.

Leviticus, 246; cf. also Septuagint; 1:1, 201; 2:13, 263; 12–15, 200; 16:29ff, 145; 17:11, 152; 21:17–21, 62; 23:24, 145; 25:4–7, 145; 25:8ff, 145; 25:10–17, 145; 26:12, 128; 27–28, 145; 27:1–3, 88; 27:17ff, 145.

Libnah, 263.

Life, of body, 65; bread of, 138; with Christ, 265; Christian, 49, 107, 140; defiled, 44, 56; eternal, 51, 55, 57, 69, 120, 137–139, 142, 157, 226; evils of, 107; of Gentiles, 248, 252; light of, 72; love for, 52, 71, 76; pleasures of, 77, 78, 120; as prayer, 104; present, 55, 77, 120, 181, 250; renewed, 57, 64, 72, 73; righteous, 44, 253, 254; as temptation, 152, 155, 260; tree of, 67, 68, 142, 189; way of, 197, 254.

Lord, abomination to, 45; of all, 43, 44; awe of, 108; blessings of, 163, 261; boasting in, 77; commands of, 46, 76, 88, 252, 255; cup of, 71; Father of, 156–157; fear of, 52, 55, 56, 65, 123, 162, 166; following of, 256; forsaking of, 53, 71; friends of, 82; glory of, 99; hand of, 237; help of, 59, 60, 106, 111, 224, 238, 243; holiness of, 53; honoring of, 55; Incarnate, 125; mountain of, 71; name of, 130, 154, 238, 239, 261; power of, 167; praise of, 170, 237–239, 251, 259; presence of, 73; rejection of, 158; as Savior, 241; sins against, 148, 151; temple of, 89; tempting of, 45; union with, 100, 135; voice of, 111; will of, 81, 269; works of, 136, 239.

Lord's Prayer, contemplation of, 118; imperatives in, 130–131; versions of, 118, 123, 134, 137, 144, 147; Our Father in heaven, 123–128; Hallowed be your name, 129–131, 132, 133; Your Kingdom come, 131–134; Your will be done on earth as in heaven, 134–137; Give us today our daily bread, 137–147; And forgive us our sins, as we forgive our debtors, 147–152; And lead us not into temptation, but deliver us from the Evil One, 152–163.

Lot, 180.

Love, as affection, 224–232, 236; of Christ, 126, 226, 230; failure in, 155, 219, 223; for God, 42, 45, 52, 58, 59, 69, 72, 148, 162, 217, 226–229; of God, 84, 91, 92, 170, 226; of learning, 51; of life, 52, 71, 76; nature of, 219, 220, 228; of neighbor, 102, 147, 227,

providence, 65; rewards of, 51, 73; secret, 55; and testing, 52, 63, 71.

Mary, 210.

Matheca, 265.

Matter, 210–213.

Matthew, 118, 119, 123, 129, 134, 135, 140, 144, 150, 170, 249.

Matthew, 1:9–10, 105; 1:17, 249; 1:23, 174; 2:6, 175; 3:5–6, 85; 3:7, 143; 4:1–11, 163; 4:8, 189; 4:9, 63; 4:10, 46; 4:11, 103; 5:1–2, 118; 5:4, 72; 5:10–12, 43; 5:14, 199; 5:16, 54; 5:17, 140; 5:18, 265; 5:22, 193; 5:22–24, 83; 5:25–26, 159; 5:28, 191, 193; 5:29, 191; 5:34, 46, 127, 193; 5:35, 46; 5:39, 191; 5:45, 125; 5:48, 216; 6:2, 119, 120, 155; 6:5, 112, 119, 120; 6:5–9, 119; 6:6, 121; 6:7, 83, 97; 6:8, 91, 117, 122; 6:9–13, 118; 6:12, 98, 150; 6:19, 136; 6:20, 136; 7:2, 48; 7:7, 247; 7:7–8, 101; 7:11, 101; 7:12, 140; 7:13, 120; 7:13–14, 120, 7:14, 62, 73; 7:16, 150; 7:18, 156; 7:22, 173; 7:24, 77; 7:24–28, 76; 8:10, 121; 9:6, 112; 9:38, 83; 10:5, 64; 10:10, 191; 10:17–23, 64; 10:18, 172; 10:20, 70; 10:22, 70; 10:24, 243; 10:28, 65, 66; 10:29, 160; 10:29–33, 65; 10:30, 103, 201; 10:32, 48; 10:33, 66, 68; 10:34, 68, 69, 10:37, 54, 70; 10:39, 70; 11:9, 85; 11:23, 197; 11:27, 230; 11:30, 63; 12:36, 45, 46, 147; 12:42, 240; 13:3ff, 77; 13:12, 168; 13:13, 267; 13:15, 43, 267; 13:20–21, 78; 13:23, 78, 132; 13:47, 144; 13:44, 199; 15:8, 44; 15:24, 195; 16:24, 67, 257; 16:24–25, 49; 16:25, 70; 16:26–27, 49; 16:27, 201; 17:15, 112, 18:9, 191; 18:10, 104, 148; 18:13, 101; 18:33–34, 150; 18:35, 97, 150; 19:17, 46, 114; 19:18, 229; 19:21, 257; 19:27–29, 51, 52; 19:28, 134; 20:22, 60; 21:18–19, 168; 22:30, 52, 207; 22:32, 114; 22:35ff, 229; 22:37, 45, 148; 22:40, 140; 23:24, 265; 23:27, 263; 23:32, 48; 24:14, 172; 24:20, 83; 24:29, 150; 24:35, 198; 25:1ff, 183; 25:26, 150; 25:29, 168; 25:34, 134; 25:35–40, 102; 26:29, 71; 26:38, 208; 26:39, 60, 61; 26:41, 83, 156; 26:64, 133; 28:15, 144; 28:18, 135, 136.

Maximin, Emperor, 72.

Melchisedek, 113.

Mennas, 189, 202, 205, 208, 213, 214.

Mercy, 110, 112, 150, 216, 236.

Merit, 94, 95.

Mesopotamia, 86.

Mesoroth, 265.

Micah, 1:12, 179; 5:21, 175.

Michael, 207.

Migdol, 258.

Miracles, 175.

Misael, 63, 106.

Mithkah, 265.

Moab, 45, 268.

Moabites, 120, 144.

Mordecai, 63, 105, 107, 110, 115.

Moseroth, 265.

Moses, 62, 86, 87–88, 92, 105, 110, 138, 140, 144, 158, 171, 172, 175, 176, 184, 185, 190, 201, 211, 220, 237, 242, 248, 249, 252–254, 259, 261.

Motion, 93.

Mount Hor, 266.

Nabau, 268.

Nathan, 169.

Nebat, 194.

Nebo, 268.

Nebuchadnezzar, 63, 106, 115, 196.

New Testament, 244, 267.
Ninevites, 106, 108.
Noah, 161.
Nod, 128.
Numbers, cf. also Septuagint; 1:2, 200; 1:4, 200; 2:32f, 242; 3:5–6, 242; 4:47, 236; 6:1–3, 88; 6:13, 88; 6:20–21, 88; 11:4–6, 158; 11:10, 158; 11:18–20, 158; 21:16, 237; 25:1, 45; 25:2–3, 45; 30:1–4, 89; 33, 245; 33:1, 249, 253; 33:1–48, 253–268; 35:5, 191.
Nun, 194, 261.
Obedience, 46, 101, 108, 115, 132, 136, 140, 165.
Oboth, 266.
Ohalah, 223.
Ohalibah, 223.
Old Testament, 110, 123, 128, 185.
Origen, *Comm. in Joh.* II.10–11, 85; *Contra Celsum,* 44, 53, 75, 83, 105, 125, 131, 191; *In Eps. ad Rom. comm.* 10:23, 236; *Hom. Num,* 5:2, 236; 12:2, 237; 23, 24, 256; *Hom. Song of Songs,* 1:1, 239; *In Jer. hom.,* IX. 2, 107; *De principiis,* 49, 85.
Oulton, 153.
Paraclete, 231.
Paradise, 50, 67, 68, 78, 250.
Passover, 126, 255, 256.
Paul, cf. *passim.*
Pentecost, 255.
Perfection, of bride, 237, 242; on earth, 135; of faith, 254; of Father, 216; goal of, 201, 260, 267; and God's help, 130; and Gospel, 201; in heaven, 135; of knowledge, 133, 186, 254; of soul, 252, 258; of virtue, 102, 133, 216, 250, 252–254, 267, 268; way of, 133, 135; of wisdom, 133, 178; of Word, 126.

Peter, 51, 70, 104, 112, 129, 143, 144, 206, 209.
1 Peter, 1:6–7, 70; 1:19, 50, 79; 2:2, 218; 2:5, 72; 2:9, 44; 2:11, 152; 3:18, 148; 5:11, 269.
Pharam, 262.
Pharancades, 266.
Pharaoh, 87, 88, 160, 196, 249, 251, 259.
Philippians, 1:23, 76; 2:5, 43; 2:6–7, 210, 240; 2:7, 126, 186, 201; 2:8, 135; 2:9, 79; 2:10, 165; 2:15, 128; 3:13, 170; 3:14, 133, 204; 3:20, 125, 136; 3:21, 128; 4:7, 43, 68; 4:13, 59, 91.
Philistines, 111.
Philo, 183.
Philocalia, 171, 176, 187, 190–199.
Phinehas, 151.
Phinon, 266.
Pi-ha-hiroth, 258.
Plagues of Egypt, 87–88.
Platonists, 140.
Prayer, 45; cf. Lord's Prayer, Scripture; anticipated, 46; and Christ, 112–114; of confession, 169–170; constant, 101, 104, 105, 125, 133; content of, 82–85, 97, 104, 107, 109, 114, 117, 124, 133, 137, 169; disposition for, 83, 97–99, 119, 164; to Father, 112–114, 119, 121; heard, 95, 103, 105, 122, 153, 163, 167, 249; and hypocrisy, 119, 122; as intercession, 109, 111, 112, 114; life as, 104, 125; method of, 82–84, 97, 100; neglect of, 97; place for, 164, 166–168; posture of, 164, 165; and praise, 109, 110, 169, 170; preparation for, 99, 164; and repentance, 108; as request (supplication), 87, 95, 97, 101, 104, 105, 109–114, 123, 134, 139, 146, 163, 165, 169,

170; results of, 100, 105, 109, 115, 119, 146; to saints, 111–112; and Savior, 70, 112, 119, 136, 140, 152; and Son, 101, 112, 114; and Spirit, 69, 85, 86, 107, 120; spiritual, 86; superfluity of, 90–92; time of, 88, 104, 105, 125, 164; and vow, 87–90.

Predestination, 91, 92.

Prophecy, about Christ, 173–176, 178, 179, 184, 195, 201, 202, 240; faith of, 179; and inspiration, 175, 176; of nations, 197; and wisdom, 187.

Protoctetus, 41, 67, 69.

Proverbs, and ethics, 231, 232, 234, 235, 240.

Proverbs, cf. also Septuagint, 241, 242; 1:1, 240; 1:2ff, 233; 1:4, 233; 1:5, 233; 1:6, 233; 1:17, 160; 1:24, 234; 2:5, 216; 3:18, 142; 3:23, 221; 4:6, 225; 4:8, 225; 4:23, 154; 7:14, 89; 8:22, 205; 9:2, 71; 10:19, 122; 10:31, 155; 14:29, 73; 15:17, 140; 15:26, 45; 15:32, 150; 17:3, 57; 20:1, 150; 20:5, 266; 20:25, 89; 22:28, 244; 30:9, 154.

Providence, of angels, 167; dissatisfaction with, 100; and freedom, 94, 96; of God, 43, 91, 129, 175, 176, 177, 186, 199, 267; and martyrdom, 65.

Psalms, cf. also Septuagint; 1:2, 155, 233, 253; 3:7, 222; 4:1, 162; 4:6, 99; 5:3, 105; 5:9, 221; 7:9, 98; 8:3, 104; 10:12, 256; 10:15, 222; 17:30, 152; 19:8, 76; 20:7, 106; 22:22, 114; 22:27, 215; 25:1, 99; 26:2, 153; 26:4–5, 168; 27:1–3, 60; 27:3, 60; 30:1, 130; 31:18, 131; 33:6, 207; 33:17, 106; 34:3, 130; 34:7, 166; 34:19, 73,

153, 162; 37:14, 154; 37:30, 233; 38:4, 70; 38:5–6, 170; 38:13–14, 47; 39:7, 73; 39:8, 170; 40:6, 151; 41:5, 239; 42:1–2, 42; 42:2–4, 43; 42:4, 250; 42:5, 11, 43; 42:11, 43; 43:19, 55; 43:20, 55; 44:14, 202; 44:13–16, 55; 44:17–18, 55; 44:20–21, 55; 44:21–22, 55; 44:25, 84; 45:1–2, 174; 45:7, 209; 45:17, 130; 46:4, 178; 51:7, 263; 55:9, 222; 57:5, 122; 58:3, 91; 58:6–7, 107; 62:12, 73; 66:11, 160; 67:12, 220; 68:14, 263; 68:15, 266; 72:7–8, 174; 73:2, 221; 73:8, 149; 73:13, 143; 73:19, 107; 74:13–14, 143; 78:14, 252; 78:25, 142; 82:1, 227; 82:7, 120; 84:1–2, 250; 84:7, 252, 254; 86:13, 197; 90:1–2, 92; 90:4, 144; 91:13, 107; 92:13, 62; 95:7–8, 144; 96:1, 239; 96:5, 63, 227, 256; 96:11, 104; 96:13, 239; 98:8, 53; 99:6, 105; 101:5, 257; 103:1–4, 261; 103:3, 247; 104:1–7, 169; 104:4, 50; 104:15, 143; 104:24, 81; 105:37, 253; 107:20, 138; 109:1, 96; 109:7, 92; 109:7–8, 92; 109:11–12, 131; 110:4, 113; 116:7, 251; 116:12, 59; 116:13, 60, 61; 116:15, 61; 118:14, 59; 119:6, 250; 119:62, 105; 120–124, 239; 123:1, 99, 128; 128:2, 262; 138:16, 212; 141:2, 105, 164; 148:3, 96.

Punon, 266.

Purification, and prayer, 97, 100; and scripture, 183.

Rachel, 224, 225, 230.

Rameses, 255.

Ramesse, 255, 256, 257, 258.

Raphaca, 261, 262.

Raphael, 101, 102, 167.

Raphidin, 262.

Rathma, 262.

Samson, 111.
Samuel, 105, 108, 115.
1 Samuel, 1:9ff, 105; 1:9–11, 89;
    1:10–11, 110; 1:11–13, 86;
    1:12–13, 86; 1:19–20, 115; 2:5,
    222; 2:25, 53, 148, 151;
    12:16–18, 108; 15:1, 179; 18:10,
    179; 25:29, 46.
2 Samuel, cf. also Septuagint; 13:1,
    224; 13:2, 224; 13:14–15, 224;
    22:1–2, 238.
Sanctification, 215; and Christ, 81;
    of name of God, 134; and Word,
    206.
Sarah, 82, 101, 167.
Satan, cf. Devils.
Savior, authority of, 136, 166, 209;
    coming of, 181, 201;
    commandment of, 99, 148, 152,
    153, 229; divinity of, 136;
    heresies of, 179; imitation of,
    135; obedience to, 140; and
    prayer, 70, 112, 119, 136, 140,
    152; and proverbs, 232;
    resurrection of, 260; and
    righteousness, 226; and
    temptation, 155, 163; and truth,
    182; and understanding of, 196.
Saul, 179, 238.
Saul (Paul), 129.
Scriptures, 41, 52, 56, 59, 77, 78,
    91, 138, 142, 144, 215, 220, 221,
    222, 224, 228, 230, 249, 260, 267;
    allegories in, 185, 193, 195;
    canon of, 110, 244; and
    inspiration, 171, 175, 177, 178,
    180, 188; interpretation of, 127,
    155, 156, 189, 193, 196, 202,
    218, 223, 247, 248, 252, 253,
    262, 268, 269; literal expressions
    of, 126, 180, 182, 190, 192, 199,
    202, 225; mysteries of, 180, 181,
    189, 195, 198, 201, 234, 257;
    mystical sense of, 126, 194, 218;
    narrative meaning of, 179, 182,

184, 187, 188, 189, 190, 192,
    193, 198; nourishment of, 247;
    and prayer, 86–89, 98, 101, 102,
    105, 114, 123, 169; spiritual
    meaning of, 126, 128, 178, 180,
    182, 183, 184, 187, 188, 190,
    192, 193, 194, 199, 219, 225,
    234, 235, 237, 248.
Scythians, 197.
Selmona, 266.
Sephar, 264.
Septuagint, 255.
Septuagint, Deuteronomy, 32:43,
    113; 8:2–3, 251; Ecclesiastes,
    7:24–25, 203; Esther, 110, 4:17,
    63; Genesis, 1:1, 211; 17:14, 190;
    49:10, 173; Habakkuk, 3:1–2,
    110; Isaiah, 10:17, 211; 26:18,
    221; 28:9–11, 41; 38:19, 105;
    41:22–23, 203; 43:10, 66; Job,
    1:5, 152; 2:9, 163; 2:10, 163; 3:8,
    175; 7:1, 152; 14:4–5, 209; 40:8,
    161; 40:19, 136; Judges, 5:12,
    238; Leviticus, 11:3, 190;
    Numbers, 6:11–12, 88;
    21:17–18, 237; Proverbs, 7:1, 55;
    9:9, 269; 13:8, 154; 19:13, 89;
    22:20–21, 182; 22:26–27, 149;
    23:5, 52; 24:32, 154; 30:9, 154;
    58:4, 122; Psalms, 18:30, 152;
    39:16, 212; 42:4, 239; 44:18, 55;
    44:19, 55; 45:13, 202; 68:11, 220;
    74:13–14, 143; 74:19, 107; 78:11,
    69; 85:13, 197; 120:6, 250;
    139:16, 212; 2 Samuel, 7:18–22,
    170.
Shechem, 192.
Sheper, 264.
Siddim, 258.
Sidon, 196, 197.
Silas, 105.
Simon, 129.
Sin, against God, 53, 100, 124, 128,
    146, 148, 149, 151, 154, 165;
    against man, 53, 112; burden of,

216; perfection of, 133, 178; and prayer, 98; preaching of, 178; and scripture, 199; Spirit of, 78, 147; visions of, 133; and Word, 206, 207, 233; of world, 178.

Wisdom, 246; 3:6, 57, 67; 7:23, 78; 7:25, 128; 7:26, 66; 8:2, 225; 9:13–16, 81; 9:15, 42, 46, 76; 11:17, 211; 11:24, 91; 13:2, 128; 15:10, 63; 16:28, 164.

Word, 43, 52, 257; ascent of, 126; as bridegroom, 116, 217, 223, 224, 230, 234; commands of, 46, 253; contemplation of, 76; and enlightenment, 135, 186; Firstborn, 86; generation of, 205; glory of, 223; is God, 144, 186, 206; help of, 124, 128, 162; and immortality, 117, 142; Incarnation of, 263; and love, 223, 230, 236; made flesh, 186, 250; makes man divine, 58, 144; nature of, 205–207, 209; as nourishment, 138–142, 245, 246; Only Begotten, 124, 125, 186; place of, 126; and prayer, 100, 132; receiving of, 159; sent by God, 138; serving of, 124; suffering for, 74; sword of, 68, 69; teaching of, 86, 102, 140, 264; union with, 123, 125, 131–132, 217, 221.

World, and Christians, 70; cleansed, 62; contempt of, 43, 55, 72, 73, 234; creation of, 94, 96, 218, 220; error of, 249; gaining of, 50; light of, 199; love for, 70, 77; lower, 198; Kingdom of, 189, 190; new, 51; vanities of, 252; wisdom of, 178.

Worship, of Christ, 113, 172; of Father, 156; of Gentiles, 267; of God, 46, 177, 179, 215, 246, 257; of other gods, 75; of idols, 44, 45, 63, 172, 201, 250, 256; of Lord, 52, 53, 256; of Son, 156.

Zalmonah, 266.

Zechariah, 109–110.

Zechariah, 7:10, 99; 9:10, 178.

Zerod, 237.

Zeus, 75.

Zin, 266.

Zion, 159, 195.